ES

W9-BFV-427

TOLSTOY

TOLSTOY

The Making of a Novelist

EDWARD CRANKSHAW

A Studio Book

The Viking Press · New York

Acknowledgments

Moura Budberg: From *Fragments from My Diary* by Maxim Gorki, translated by Moura Budberg.

Doubleday & Company, Inc.: From *Tolstoy* by Henri Troyat, translated by Nancy Amphoux. Translation Copyright © 1967 by Doubleday & Co., Inc. Reprinted by permission of the publisher.

Oxford University Press: From *Nine Stories, War and Peace, A Confession, Recollections, Hadji Murad* by Leo Tolstoy, translated by Louise and Aylmer Maude. From *Life of Tolstoy*, Volume One, by Aylmer Maude, published by Oxford University Press.

Penguin Books Ltd.: From *Childhood, Boyhood, Youth* by Leo Tolstoy, translated by Rosemary Edmonds (Penguin Classics 1964), Copyright © Rosemary Edmonds, 1965. From *The Cossacks* by Leo Tolstoy, translated by Rosemary Edmonds (Penguin Classics 1960), Copyright © Rosemary Edmonds, 1960.

Illustration credits appear on page 276.

Copyright © 1974 by Edward Crankshaw

All rights reserved

First published in 1974 by The Viking Press, Inc.
625 Madison Avenue, New York, N.Y. 10022

Published simultaneously in Canada by
The Macmillan Company of Canada Limited

SBN 670-71861-0

Library of Congress catalog card number: 73-6078

Printed in U.S.A.

CONTENTS

Leo Nikolayevich Tolstoy in 1868, when he was working on *War and Peace*.

INTRODUCTION

Leo Nikolayevich Tolstoy was not content with being the greatest novelist in the world; he wanted much more to be a great philosopher and teacher. This was a peculiar ambition in a man of powerful intellect who for most of his life was so frightened of death that he could not think straight; who was, at the same time, so unrestrained in his pretensions that he angrily rejected the terms of life, which must end in death, and refused to submit to the framework that contains all philosophy and all human greatness of spirit. He was Lucifer in the magnitude of his presumption, pathetic in the twists and turns to which he was reduced in his vain flight from reality.

When he had recovered from the suicidal depression induced largely by the strain of producing his masterpieces, *War and Peace* and *Anna Karenina*, and, at fifty-one, composed the celebrated *Confession*, he presented himself as a changed man. In the course of that essay, describing the great change that had come over him, he said: "My mental condition presented itself to me in this way: my life is a stupid and malicious joke which someone has played on me. Although I did not acknowledge a 'someone' who had created me, that formulation—that someone had played an evil and stupid joke on me by placing me in the world—was the form of expression that came most naturally to me."

It was characteristic of him that this very usual and unoriginal sense of the futility of life had to be dramatized as a sudden revelation, although it had haunted him since adolescence. On another level, it was also characteristic that he should see the stupid joke as being perpetrated at his, Leo Tolstoy's, personal expense. A little later, he went on to reflect that we are all in the same boat, invoking in witness Solomon ("or whoever wrote the works attributed to him"), Schopenhauer, Socrates, and Buddha; but the first formulation of the idea that obsessed him for the rest of his long life—and I think it may justly be said, the formulation that "came most naturally" to him—expressed an immediate sense of personal outrage.

It was also characteristic of the impact of Tolstoy's personality, backed by his authority as a novelist of immeasurable stature, that when in middle age he started preaching, when he button-holed the world, fixing it with the eye of an angry and contemptuous ancient mariner, so many ran to proclaim him as a great and revolutionary teacher. They did this although the best of his teaching, which he presented with the air of an Old Testament prophet, consisted largely of various elementary truths and half-truths believed in *and lived* by many of the finest spirits, including countless nameless ones, for two and a half millennia—and although he proved himself incapable of living his own ideas until his superb vitality had burned itself out and he was fit for nothing but to run away from everything and die at a wayside station on the Moscow-Kharkov railway.

His greatness lay elsewhere. Everybody knows about it. It blazes across a century of human suffering: a signal of hope, a fixed point of orientation, a monument to a man who refused to take any stock in what seems hope to most of us, a celebration of life by a man who turned his back on it. All done by art, that art which he said he despised. The man who bore the burden of this achievement was, as a human being, a failure, impossible to live with, horrible in many ways, absurd in others, magnificent in some. The radiance of his marvellous genius was the reflection of a light that was too strong for his own eyes to bear. He bellowed his pain aloud and tried to drag into it all who would listen, pointing away from his triumphs and into the pit.

Tolstoy was not a great man in the fullest, the roundest sense of the term; nobody will find comfort, encouragement, example, in his life seen as a whole. But he was a giant. Everything about him was excessive, his virtues no less than his failings. There can be no question of debunking Tolstoy: except as a thinker, he debunked himself. And side by side with so much nonsense written about his thinking, there has been a steady process of clarification, beginning with the Russians, Leo Shestov and Konstantin Leontiev, moving on through Maxim Gorky and B. Eykhenbaum,

8

to the recent work of John Bayley and Elizabeth Gunn. But it seems to me that even these and other acute and perceptive critics (with the possible exception of cool, unblinking Shestov) have on occasion been half-hypnotized by the sheer size of the man and by the implacable resonance of that tremendous voice into accepting too much at its face value, perhaps into beginning at the wrong end. How remarkable, they say in effect, that so great a man should have had such failings. The attitude is beautifully expressed in Isaiah Berlin's Oedipus image, the closing words of *The Hedgehog and the Fox*: "At once insanely proud and filled with self-hatred, omniscient and doubting everything, cold and violently passionate, contemptuous and self-abasing, tormented and detached, surrounded by an adoring family, by devoted followers, by the admiration of the entire civilised world, and yet wholly isolated, he is the most tragic of great writers, a desperate old man, beyond human aid, wandering self-blinded at Colonus."

But Tolstoy was not always an old man. He started *War and Peace* at thirty-five and finished it at forty. And although *Anna Karenina* still lay before him and he had another ten years to go before he achieved the final, painful, never complete transformation from artist into prophet, he had fulfilled his genius and deployed all those elements which went into the making of the bearded patriarch of the Tolstoy legend. It may help us, therefore, to a fuller understanding of his towering genius and the limitations that went with it if we tear our eyes away from the terrible gaze of the tortured and cruel old man whose story has been told so many times and try to see him as he was before he became a world figure: Count Leo Nikolayevich Tolstoy, born August 28, 1828, the fourth son of Count and Countess Tolstoy of Yasnaya Polyana in the district of Tula.

A Note on Translations

I have used Louise and Aylmer Maude's translation for *War and Peace*; Aylmer Maude's for *Confession, Recollections*, and *Hadji Murad*; Rosemary Edmonds' new translations for *Childhood* and *The Cossacks*. All other quotations from the Russian, including passages from *Anna Karenina* and extracts from Tolstoy's diary and letters, are in my own translation unless otherwise indicated in footnotes.

1

FAMILY HAPPINESS

The Russia into which Tolstoy was born in 1828 was very much the Russia he was to evoke nearly forty years later in *War and Peace*. Alexander I, the conqueror of Napoleon, had died less than three years before, and many of the men who had stood close to him now surrounded his younger brother, the new Emperor, Nicholas I. Thus, for example, when Tolstoy came to describe the would-be reforming minister, Mikhail Speransky, at the height of his early fame, he was writing about a man who was still alive and politically active in his own lifetime. Pushkin was twenty-nine, still unmarried, with nine more years to live; *Eugene Onegin* was published in its entirety when Tolstoy was three years old.

Such is the distancing quality of Tolstoy's art, so far is 1812 from us, that it is hard to realize that *War and Peace,* though by all means a historical novel, dealt with history so recent that for many of its readers, as the first volumes came out in 1865, it was part of their own childhood memories. Some, indeed, had themselves fought at Borodino or lived through the burning of Moscow. Tolstoy's own father had been taken prisoner by the French.

The nature of Russian society and the Russian land remained virtually unchanged from the Napoleonic era until the great reforms, especially the abolition of serfdom in 1861, when Tolstoy was thirty-three. Here the continuity was absolute, and Tolstoy in childhood, youth, and early manhood was part of it. The peasants he wrote of in *War and Peace* were the peasants on his own estate at Yasnaya Polyana; the high society of St. Petersburg in 1812 was the high society he encountered, half attracted, half repelled, as an awkward and hard-up young aristocrat with his own way to find. It was a country of landowners and peasants, run by a highly centralized bureaucracy which, in theory, was unquestioningly obedient to the Autocrat, the Emperor. The thinking intelligentsia was only beginning to emerge. The peasants were slaves. Very often they were well-treated slaves, idle and comfortably looked after, sometimes even pampered. But their masters could do what they liked with them—beat them, lock them up, banish them to Siberia, sell them away from their families (a good dog would cost more), detail them for military service (twenty-five years was the term: in effect, a life-sentence), marry them against their will, or forbid them to marry.

Not all serfs were peasants tied to the soil; far from it. Even on the smaller estates, house-serfs could attain positions of trust and influence as stewards, major-domos, housekeepers, children's nurses—family confidants of the kind immortalized by Pushkin. It was the practice on larger estates to form companies of serf-actors and orchestras of serf-musicians. On the estates of the very great magnates, such as the Sheremeteyevs, who possessed 200,000 serfs at the time of the Emancipation, talented serfs were educated at great expense as singers, instrumentalists, actors, and architects, achieving wide fame in their careers. But all remained serfs entirely at their masters' disposal and could be sent back to menial tasks at their masters' whim. The exceptions were those who could buy their freedom. These, as a rule, were serfs who, having shown a talent for trading or managing factories and mills (worked by serf labour) on their masters' account, sometimes did so well that they became rich enough to buy their freedom at a price their owners found impossible to resist. When Tolstoy was born, these were already the making of a new mercantile and bourgeois class, above all in Moscow and the provinces, far less in St. Petersburg. But the young Tolstoy knew little of this urban sub-culture, which he regarded with distaste: he belonged to the old paternalistic world of ancient aristocratic families and their peasant slaves.

His development and thinking were conditioned by this background. He was always the aristocrat, but an aristocrat who, as time went on, sought to identify himself with the only other class he knew, the peasants who

11

A Russian village. This drawing by J. A. Atkinson was made in 1804, but the villages did not change much throughout the nineteenth century.

Interior of a Russian peasant house.

were the heart and soul of the land, who, as Tolstoy saw it, in accepting their destiny with uncomplaining and enduring patience achieved a grandeur and a dignity lacking in the glittering society that they sustained. All this was as true, or untrue, of Tolstoy's Russia as it had been of the Russia of *War and Peace*. In *War and Peace* he chose to idealize the Russian peasant and to oppose the sound, instinctive, faith-borne heart of Russia to the nonsensical attitudinizing of the great men who thought they were purposefully in charge. He ignored the kindness and public spirit that were to be found in many individuals in high places no less than the moral squalor, the corruption, the brutality that ran through the whole of Russian society; the vicious aspects of serfdom; and the far from uncomplaining selfishness and roughness of a peasantry which was forever breaking out into mindless acts of violence. For a considerable part of his own lifetime he also chose to ignore these things and, except superficially and obliquely, the great changes brought about by the halting but very real development of industry and the more rapid growth of a radical intelligentsia.

Thus for Maxim Gorky, the gifted young seeker from the lower depths, Tolstoy in old age, the apostle of brotherly love and Christian humility, the bearded prophet already poised for flight into the anonymous desert of physical and spiritual abasement, appeared always as the *barin*, the master, who, disguise himself as he might as a preacher or a ragged peasant, expected instant obedience and submission—and would usually obtain it.

To the inherited authority of the *barin* was added the acquired authority of the genius. But the genius was profoundly conscious of the antiquity of his line, which on his mother's side was extreme. It has always to be borne in mind that Tolstoy was related to or connected with a great part of the highest Russian nobility. His mother's family belonged to that inner circle of the ancient aristocracy whose lustre survived the levelling reforms of Peter the Great. She was a Volkonsky, and the Volkonskys claimed direct descent from Rurik, the Viking adventurer who, in the ninth century, was invited by the Slavs of the Dnieper basin to rule over them and bring order to their land. As Grand Princes of Kievan Russia, his successors brought Christianity and the culture of Byzantium. For centuries, Volkonskys served as generals, administrators, courtiers. They were the equals of the Romanovs when Michael Romanov was chosen Tsar to start a new dynasty in 1613, and they continued in the service of the new Tsar. Tolstoy's maternal grandfather, Prince Nikolai Sergeyevich Volkonsky, had

Russian landowners gambling away their serfs. Print by Gustave Doré, 1854.

A view of the Nevsky Prospekt in St. Petersburg.

been Catherine the Great's Commander-in-Chief until he offended the reigning favourite, Potemkin, by contemptuously refusing to marry that potentate's niece and mistress. Instead, he married a girl from a family as old as his own, Princess Marya Trubetskoy, who died comparatively young. After a spell as Governor of Archangel under the Emperor Paul, the widower retired to one of his estates at Yasnaya Polyana, where he conducted himself as a model landlord, treating his peasant serfs with stern but kindly paternalism and taking great pains with their welfare and with the practical management and improvement of house and land. His sole companion was his daughter, Marya Nikolayevna, whom he educated as though she were a boy. This was Tolstoy's mother, through whom he inherited Yasnaya Polyana, which was to be his home and refuge for all but a few years of his young life. Old Prince Volkonsky and his daughter were the models for Prince Bolkonsky and Princess Marya in *War and Peace*.

The Tolstoy line was less ancient and less grand. Its most celebrated luminary, who brought wealth and title to the family, then lost both, was also the most unpleasant. Peter Andreyevich Tolstoy was first favoured by Peter the Great, who sent him as Ambassador to Turkey, because of his intelligence, shrewdness, and interest in modern ideas. But soon he had become an indispensable aide in some of the Tsar's most cruel and violent enterprises. It was he, with false promises, who lured Peter's wretched son from sanctuary at the court of Charles VI in Vienna back to Moscow to be murdered, and it was widely believed that he personally helped to hold the Tsarevich down while he was being suffocated with a pillow. Certainly he assisted in other murderous episodes. Peter the Great, who despised and distrusted him but valued his talent, rewarded him with his title and with vast estates—all of which were taken from him when Peter died and the new Count Tolstoy gambled and lost in a court intrigue over the succession. He was imprisoned in the dreaded Solovetsky Monastery, the arctic prison on an island in the White Sea, where he died. His son, who went to prison with him, survived. His grandson made good under the Empress Elizabeth and won back his title and some of the forfeited lands. This was Tolstoy's great-grandfather, who had twenty-three children, all by one wife. One of these children, Tolstoy's grandfather, was to become the model for the old Count Ilya Rostov in *War and Peace*. He was amiable, easy-going, pleasure-loving, and extravagant beyond all reason. He married into a family grander and richer than his own, his wife being a Princess Gorchakov, a name celebrated in the military and diplomatic annals of Im-

Prince Nikolai Sergeyevich Volkonsky, Tolstoy's maternal grandfather, owner of Yasnaya Polyana. The original portrait hangs at Yasnaya Polyana.

Count Ilya Andreyevich Tolstoy,
Tolstoy's paternal grandfather.

perial Russia. Count Ilya Tolstoy managed in no time at all to get through his wife's fortune as well as his own, largely at cards, but also because he gave balls, theatrical entertainments, and parties on a scale wildly beyond his means. In the end, driven to seek a job to save himself from ruin, he was appointed Governor of Kazan. All his attempts to economize came to nothing; he was soon in very deep water indeed, and forced to resign. The shock of reality killed him. His affairs were in such disorder that Nikolai, his son, saw himself faced with immediate bankruptcy and refused to accept what was left of his father's estate and the crippling obligations that went with it.

This Nikolai, Tolstoy's father-to-be, was a pleasant, engaging, highly personable, neither-here-nor-there young man, fairly typical of a soft generation of spoiled, well-mannered, well-meaning nobility. He despised the time-servers who took their cue from the Tsar, but he lacked the drive, the recklessness, or the conviction to associate himself with the political movement among his contemporaries that culminated in the Decembrist revolt of 1825. He had fought in the 1812 campaign, stayed on in the peacetime army after his release from French captivity when his countrymen entered Paris in 1814, retired as a lieutenant-colonel five years later, and drifted into government service under his father's wing. When the old man died in 1820, there was only one thing for Nikolai to do if he desired, as he did most earnestly, to maintain himself in anything like the style to which he was accustomed: make a good marriage. This was expeditiously arranged.

The old Prince Volkonsky was dead. His daughter, though highly intelligent, well-read in several languages, and a good pianist into the bargain, was plainness itself. She was also thirty-three. As a young girl she had been engaged to a Prince Golitsyn—curiously, the son of that questionable niece and mistress of Potemkin whom her own father had refused to marry. But the young man had died of consumption before the marriage could take place, and Princess Marya seems to have laid up her romance in lavender and resigned herself to spinsterhood, without visible repining; she looked after her father, cultivated the arts, and, at the same time, learned how to manage a not inconsiderable estate with eight hundred serfs. Her inheritance, which included several other properties, was just the right size to allow a penurious young man, fallen on bad times, to re-establish himself as a country gentleman and hunt and shoot as much as he liked. Count Nikolai Tolstoy and Princess Marya Volkonsky, six years older, were brought together by friends and married with open eyes, each seeking the

20

Count Nikolai Ilyich Tolstoy, Tolstoy's father.

The only existing portrait of Countess
Marya Nikolayevna Tolstoy, Tolstoy's mother.

fulfilment and security that the other could provide. The old maid was transformed by motherhood. There were three children before Leo was born, all boys; after him came one girl. A few months later, when Leo was two years old, his mother died.

On the face of it, Tolstoy's early childhood was idyllic. Until he was nine years old he never moved more than a few miles outside the Yasnaya Polyana estate, which was a universe in itself, paradisial for children. The house was a large, white-painted, wooden mansion, serenely classical in its proportions, refashioned in the Catherine manner by his Volkonsky grand-father. It had thirty-four rooms and was approached by a long avenue of birches. The estate was several miles in circumference: open, pleasantly undulating farmland, broken by little woods, led down to the Voronka river with a bathing place and then lost itself in the fringes of an immense Crown forest, Zasyeka forest, which seemed to go on forever and harboured wolves. The entrance to the birch avenue was flanked by small twin towers of whitewashed brick, originally designed as guard-houses, a little comical in appearance, but imposing enough to keep the outer world at bay.

The house stood in some of the most pleasant country of central Russia, undemanding and endlessly fluid in the manner of the southern fringes of the central forest zone where the great horizons are still marked, but not closed, by the dark blue smudges of distant woods. It was close to Tula, the provincial capital, long famous for the manufacture of sporting-guns and samovars. The estate was skirted on one side by the main highway from Moscow to Kiev, and in due course the new railway from Moscow to Kursk was to come very close. In the same sort of country, but sixty miles to the south, near Orel, was the much larger estate of Spasskoye, just outside Mtsensk, where Ivan Turgenev was brought up by his violently capricious widowed mother, absolute mistress of five thousand serfs. The Tolstoy country might have been the country of *A Sportsman's Sketches,* and the nightingales of Tula and Orel sing to this day. Mtsensk itself, it may be recalled, was the scene of Nikolai Leskov's violent and bloody village trag-edy which was later made into an opera by Shostakovich: *Lady Macbeth of Mtsensk,* now renamed *Katerina Ismailova.*

The Tolstoy home was far from luxurious, and much of the furniture consisted of pieces made on the estate. Volkonsky ancestors looked down from their clumsy portraits on the walls. There was all the room in the world for the five children and their friends to play the most boisterous games. Outside in the yards and stables there were horses and dogs—Rus-

Yasnaya Polyana, where Tolstoy was born and spent most of his life.

Yasnaya Polyana, from a recent photograph by Inge Morath.

The Imperial Theater in St. Petersburg. Print by B. Patterson, 1806.

St. Petersburg. Print by B. Patterson, 1806.

sian wolfhounds, or borzois, a pack of harriers—pony traps, sledges, the great travelling carriage. Besides the river, there were ponds to fish in. There were coachmen, grooms, and keepers to talk to and learn from, peasant serfs to watch at work in the fields. Year after year the children's lives were dominated by the slow, strong, seasonal rhythm of the great landlocked plain: the short, searing summers, periods of almost violent activity in the fields, alternating with the longer, dark, and snow-bound winters when no field work could be done at all; in between, the autumn rains and the torrential spring thaws which made the roads impassable for weeks on end. Tolstoy in his strictly autobiographical writings left surprisingly little record of the dark, house-bound winter days, even of the exhilaration of sledding at a gallop over frozen snow, the horses' hooves kicking back a hail of icy chips, the deep snow gleaming, with its blue and rose shadings and reflections under a powder-blue sky. He wrote little too of the marvellous breath of spring, where one chaffinch starting to sing, one blade of grass piercing the compacted snow, bear the promise—more than the promise, the declaration—of tempestuous rebirth, and almost at once the whole land is alive with the sound of moving waters, first invisible beneath the crusted snow, then seeping, swelling, gushing out to sweep the snow away. Tolstoy wrote more frequently of the summer memories of his childhood:

"The chatter of the peasants, the tramp of the horses and the creaking of the carts, the cheerful whistle of the quail, the hum of insects hovering in the air in motionless swarms, the smell of wormwood, straw and horses' sweat, the thousand different lights and shadows with which the burning sun flooded the light yellow stubble, the dark blue of the distant forest and the pale lilac of the clouds, the white gossamer threads that floated in the air or lay stretched across the stubble—all these things I saw, heard and felt."

In a boy who spent so much of his time so close to nature and whose powers of observation can never have been surpassed—who later was to fix a landscape indelibly with perfect economy of words, to establish a character with a glancing reference to a single physical trait—it is interesting, I think important too, to note the striking lack of curiosity about the natural world about him. He knew a snipe or a woodcock when he saw one; he could delight in a butterfly's wings; he responded to the call of the quail. But to all appearances he moved through the magical world of nature, which he loved, without in the least wanting to know about the names and singularities of the birds, insects, flowers, grasses, trees, or the earth which supported them all. The appeal was to his senses, not his mind.

A view of the Yasnaya Polyana estate.

Opposite: The Voronka river, near Yasnaya Polyana, where Tolstoy liked to walk.

His childhood was, to say the least, a privileged one. But there was no mother. In years to come Tolstoy was to make a cult of the mother he never knew. She was to embody in their chemically purest form, so to say, the ideals of generalized human love, chastity, sainthood indeed, which (he had to tell himself) lay within man's grasp if only he knew how to reach for it. Part of the impulse behind the fabrication of this legend was of the same kind as the impulse which, later, in *War and Peace,* was to compel him to present the peasant Platon Karateyev as the embodiment of goodness and wisdom unattainable by anyone not privileged to be born a peasant, and to transform the real Marshal M. I. Kutuzov, the hero of 1812, idle, lecherous, and venal, into an embodiment of the deep Russian native virtues—because, to the great military captain Napoleon, deluding himself into believing that he was a free agent in command of his own destiny and imposing his will on the course of history, Tolstoy needed to oppose a wise old man who knew that all such pretensions were vain.

This is not to say that Tolstoy's mother was neither good nor loving: quite clearly she was both. But she was also a woman of affairs, used to managing her own small empire, and by no means the saint of his private cult. Had she lived longer, the boy would have found himself in conflict with her. Intelligent and kind, her plainness relieved by those immensely large and beautiful eyes which in so many Russian women appear to mirror, perhaps indeed do mirror, an openness of understanding and a steadfastness of acceptance frequently out of all proportion to their cerebral equipment, she was not by nature easy-going and had very strict views about the upbringing of her children. She believed in being cruel in order to be kind. She believed also that small boys must school themselves to behave like men. When her eldest, Nikolai, burst into tears at the sight of a dog with a broken leg being hanged to put it out of its misery, his mother, who idolized him, was shocked and ashamed into scolding him: boys do not and must not cry. Tolstoy himself was nicknamed the Howler by his brothers and his aunts because, living always on the edge of emotional upheaval, he burst into tears a dozen times a day. His mother would have found it hard, if not impossible, to put up with this, and Tolstoy knew this when he came to write of her—as he knew everything. He was too honest not to record it. But, at the same time, he had also to present her as a figure of unalloyed tenderness and gentleness, a concept rather than a person. Thus the figure of the mother in *Childhood, Boyhood and Youth* is always shadowy. Surrounded by a gallery of individuals sharply drawn from life, the imaginary mother quite lacks definition and is never brought into focus.

His effective mother from infancy was his Aunt Tatiana—Tatiana Andreyevna Ergolskaya, the strongest force for goodness in his life, who was able to retain his affection and stand for sense and decency in his difficult early manhood in a way that his real mother, had she lived, could hardly have hoped to do. Certainly Aunt Tatiana had the makings of a saint, a very cheerful and down-to-earth one. Gay, small, black-haired, black-eyed, with quick, brown hands, she led a life of unobtrusive and efficient service to those close to her. She was not a real aunt. She was Tolstoy's father's second cousin who, orphaned and penniless, had been taken into the family as a child by Tolstoy's grandparents. In due course she had fallen in love with the son of the house, Nikolai, as Sonya in *War and Peace,* also an orphaned cousin, fell in love with Nikolai Rostov. Like Sonya, who was modelled on her, Aunt Tatiana gave up her Nikolai, but more cheerfully, knowing that he had no choice but to marry well. Later, when Nikolai was widowed and the children came under the official guardianship of their old grandmother, he did indeed ask her to marry him and devote her life to his children. Marriage she refused, but she would look after the children joyfully so long as they needed her. And so she did.

Much later, in old age, Tolstoy was to write that above all she had taught him "the spiritual delight of love. She did not teach me that by words, but by her whole being she filled me with love. I saw and felt how she enjoyed loving, and I understood the joy of love." Aunt Tatiana would have had a short, sharp word for that had she allowed it to pass her lips, or even to dwell in her mind. The real lesson she taught in all her actions was never learned by the boy, the youth, the man, who aspired to universal love but could never truly love those closest to him. The sort of love she gave was of a finer and higher quality altogether than the mindlessly beaming kindergarten benevolence of the old man's retrospect, and Tolstoy knew it. Aunt Tatiana understood very well the path she had chosen, as she understood what she was doing when, without revealing her feelings, she first surrendered her claim to Nikolai, then later refused to marry him. She loved those nearest to her for what they were, and what they were was often painful. She went on loving the young Tolstoy, always there when he needed her, never reproaching him; but goodness knows what perturbations troubled her heart when he developed into an insufferable and sometimes revolting young man, and went to her, hot with guilt, from uneasy nights with prostitutes and peasant girls to wash himself clean at her cool, unfailing spring—knowing that she knew all about it, knowing that she must be hurt by it, knowing also that no matter what he did he was always her Lvyochka who must and would, as far as she was concerned, be allowed to find his own way.

All this Tolstoy himself could record with that faithfulness to the truth which was, all other things notwithstanding, his true way—even as he could also, and almost simultaneously, diminish the courageous reality of her love by transferring to her his own life-long hankering after the womb—or at least the nursery. Aunt Tatiana was not a born nanny: she was a keen-eyed adult of quite remarkable character, who was also good. She was no puritan. Indeed, it was she who urged him, in vain, to have an affair with a married woman, as the best way to learn civilized behaviour. It may well be that the young Tolstoy felt the need of a mother who would be less perceptive and understanding than Aunt Tatiana and at the same time more demanding and severe, and that this lack was behind the mother fixation that throughout his life was to interact with his overbearing masculinity, helping to ruin his marriage and revealing itself in extreme old age in a desolate cry for help.

It was a lively and cluttered household in those childhood days. Grandmother Tolstoy, born Princess Pelageya Gorchakov, was the matriarch. Very much a great lady of the old school, she features strongly first in *Childhood* as the awe-inspiring but usually kindly mistress of the house at Yasnaya Polyana, spending most of the time in her own sanctum. There the children took it in turns to spend the night with her, listening with her, as she prepared for bed, to the interminable tales of the old serf storyteller, who sat on a stool in a dark corner, quite blind and thus no offence to the old lady's modesty. In *Boyhood* she is shown in her element in her Moscow drawing-room, receiving the compliments of the great world on her name-day, in a scene that might have been the detailed sketch for Madame Scherer's reception in the opening pages of *War and Peace*.

Also part of the household was Tolstoy's real aunt, his father's sister, Alexandra, who was a little soft in the head—as well she might be, having survived two painful and all-but-successful attempts on her life by a husband who went out of his mind in the early days of their marriage. She had been pregnant at the time and her child was stillborn. To protect her from further shock, which might have been fatal, the infant daughter of one of the family serfs was substituted, and this adopted child came also, in due course, to be brought up at Yasnaya Polyana. It was Aunt Alexandra who, with her gentle religious mania, attracted to the house an endless succession of those ragged pilgrims and wandering holy fools who swarmed over the landscape of nineteenth-century Russia, battening, bullying, cajoling, exercising a sort of moral blackmail over characters stronger than Aunt Alexandra. The slightly sinister Grisha in *Childhood*, now bullying, now cringing, was a good example of the type.

But it was Aunt Tatiana who ran the house in detail and who had complete charge of the children in their nursery days. The first crisis for the child Tolstoy was when, at five, he was removed from the nursery, the company of the little girls, and the enveloping protection of Aunt Tatiana, and brought down to the schoolroom to work and play with his three older brothers, Nikolai, Sergei, and Dmitri, in the charge of the kindly, absurd German tutor, Fyodor Ivanovich Rossel. (This tutor was the original of Karl Ivanich in *Boyhood*, with his nose forever in one of his three most precious books: a treatise on hydrostatics, an odd volume of a set on the Seven Years' War, and a monograph on the cultivation of the cabbage.) The transition from the nursery to the school-room is a climacteric in the life of any small boy: the stomach heaves, the nerves tingle with apprehension, the tiny mind quails before its dark imaginings. But this was not enough for Tolstoy. This superb and compulsive dramatist who chose to disguise himself as a flat, matter-of-fact chronicler of events, this master of the overstatement slyly disguised as understatement, had in retrospect to heighten the drama of his infant debut: "For the first time," he wrote, "I realized that life was a serious matter." This is not at all the thinking of a child—not even the child Tolstoy. There will be opportunity later to examine the virtuosity with which he used this particular trick (exaggeration masquerading as meiosis) to make people believe anything he wanted them to believe, or to distort a character by referring casually and in passing to some damaging physical detail, unerringly selected, and presented in that deceptively off-hand, unaccented diction. But it is here, as the man looks back on the child emerging from the nursery, that we encounter it for the first time. It is not a case of an old man fondly looking back to far-away days. *Childhood* was the first published work of a young man of twenty-four.

There is not a great deal that needs to be spelled out in detail about the next decade. If little Leo was suddenly seized with the seriousness of life on that exciting day in 1833, he quickly forgot all about it, and for the next four years he lived a life indistinguishable from the lives of countless other small boys brought up in the easy, ramshackle freedom of a Russian country house bursting at the seams with servants, relatives, and hangers-on. The boys were a very close group. Nikolai, who was ten when Tolstoy was five, was the natural master and contriver of all their games: he was a boy of outstanding natural gifts, a lively and warm imagination, a born mystifier, and an irrepressible weaver of tales. It was he who invented the legend of the green stick, buried in a forest glade, on which was carved the secret of life: one day it would be found and thereafter all mankind would live in perfect happiness and concord: no more strife. But although Nikolai was the leader, the individualist was the younger Sergei, who was closer in years to Leo and was idolized by him: it was on Sergei—with his total lack of self-consciousness, his talent for doing precisely what he wanted to do without caring what others thought, his talent, also, for knowing just what he could do and could not do and for accepting his own limitations—that the infinitely self-conscious, infinitely complex, infinitely confused, infinitely demanding and self-demanding younger brother sought to model himself.

Leo's special characteristics, as they emerged, were an extreme sensitivity to pain coupled with an almost overpowering capacity for joy. Joy came flooding out of him: when life was good he himself and the whole world around him were transfigured. It was this quality of joy, the immediacy of his delight in the physical aspects of a magical universe shining with the enamelled colours, transfixed with the sense of space and solemn stillness of certain Flemish masters, which was to find expression in the great work of his maturity. A child is lifted up to look down for the first time into a thrush's nest: as the young Mozart was affected almost unbearably by the clear, plangent tones of the trumpet sounding alone, so the child is transported with wonder and joy to the point of faintness by the unimagined blue of those five so common eggs, lustrous, secret, and yet alive and warm with their speckles of dark brown. And the vision is heightened and sharpened by the complex of warm smells: the smell of dusty bark, the acrid-sweet smell of fresh green leaves, the musty smell of the dead grasses in the nest, the sickly smell of the mud and dung that make the smooth lining of the nest, the faintly choking smell of bird and bird's feathers. In that moment of revelation, which can never be recaptured in precisely that form—though there may be many other similar revelations before the senses are finally subdued and organized to respond in an orderly manner and to subsume what was once revelation into conventional pat-

Russian peasants. Illustration from M. A. Davidoff's *Voyage dans la Russie*, 1843.

terns—the child is back in the first week of the creation of the world. Tolstoy was to retain the child's vulnerability, shared in some degree by all artists of all kinds, all his life. He was isolated in his experience by the overpowering, the almost monstrous directness of the impact of every aspect of the world around him on the senses of the child, then the man, whose nerve endings were excruciatingly exposed.

Verses of congratulation written by Tolstoy when he was twelve years old to his Aunt Tatiana on her nameday.

2

BOYHOOD AND YOUTH

The first major change in his life occurred in his ninth year, when the whole family uprooted itself and moved to Moscow. Nikolai was ready for the university. And it was this move that for the first time made Leo Tolstoy aware of the existence of a world outside Yasnaya Polyana—or, to be more exact, an apparently limitless series of separate but partly overlapping worlds with an individual family or soul at the heart of every one of them. The Tolstoys carried their own world with them when they travelled in an imposing procession of carriages and sledges moving down the desolate winter roads, refreshed with scalding hot tea at the posting stations every seven miles or so, putting up for the night in primitive, bug-ridden, overpoweringly hot and fuggy inns. There was Grandmother Tolstoy, the two aunts, six children, and no less than thirty serfs, all organized, their transport detailed as in a military movement-order by Count Nikolai, who was in his element. First, as the procession bumbled along, the child was struck by the mystery of fellow travellers on the road whom they passed, isolated in their separate worlds. Looming close, for a moment they stared into each other's eyes, and then were gone forever. Who were they, these people who were wholly strange? What were they doing, thinking, dreaming? Once in the great city, this new consciousness of strange and unknown worlds was magnified a thousand times. Until now the whole world had revolved round the Tolstoy household: the peasants bowed deeply, the local officials swept off their hats, neighbours saluted and smiled. Now, suddenly, they were nobodys in a great city, anonymous individuals in a nameless throng of others all intent on their own business, all living their own lives, all the centres of their own private universes, all totally incurious about the new strangers in their midst. But the nine-year-old boy was far from incurious. In one breath he was chilled and chagrined at being no longer the centre of attention; in the next he was straining himself to imagine, to discover for himself, the secrets of the countless lives hidden behind the unresponsive countenances of the city crowd. It was the birth of a curiosity that was never to leave him, that was to gather the power of a driving force until it came to dominate a large part of his existence, insatiably greedy as he was for understanding and experience.

For a few months the excitement of the new city life, enjoyed against the stable background of the familiar household transported bodily from Yasnaya Polyana, was happiness enough. Then calamity struck twice. First the children lost their father, who dropped dead in what was called a fit of apoplexy in Tula, where he had gone to sort out a legal muddle over the Volkonsky properties. Then came the death of the old grandmother, whose mind had been partly unhinged by the loss of her son. The legal guardianship of the children now fell upon Aunt Alexandra, a move had to be made from the very grand Moscow house to a much more modest apartment, and almost at once it was decided that poor old Fyodor Ivanovich, whom the boy had come to love and trust, had served his purpose: it was time for a more knowledgeable tutor.

The new teacher was a Frenchman, able, ambitious, snobbish, and a bit of a dandy and a coxcomb. Fyodor Ivanovich told him that the nine-year-old Leo was a dreamer, but capable of learning. He could not be driven, however; he would respond only to kindness and love. M. Saint-Thomas thought otherwise: a little sharp discipline and a touch of the cane was his immediate prescription. And this led to the situation dramatized in the famous scene in *Boyhood* in which the hero (Leo), though threatened and locked in an empty room, defies a whipping, refuses to apologize, and stands alone against the united forces of the adult world. Saint-Thomas did not make that mistake again. He was sensible enough to realize that he must win the boy's confidence, and he succeeded quite well.

Tolstoy in his old age reverted to this moment and concluded that what had happened then "was perhaps one reason for that horror and aver-

40

sion for every kind of violence which I have felt throughout my whole life." This speculation would carry more weight had Tolstoy abjured violent behaviour as well as condemning it. But violence was very much a part of his own nature. The significant thing about this childish episode was that the nine-year-old Tolstoy got his way after colliding head-on with his tutor, who never again tried to coerce him. This little drama, indeed, was the first demonstration of a major element in Tolstoy's character which was to be developed in manhood and carried through into old age with frequently disastrous consequences: an absolute rejection of any kind of criticism, a stubborn and, indeed, violent refusal to be crossed.

It is important to fix this element as firmly as may be. Soon Tolstoy himself will largely take over this book, as in life he took over everything he touched. His diary, his autobiographical writings and confessions, expose to the world, often with searing honesty, an array of weaknesses and faults which, at first sight, seems the ultimate in self-revelation. In the diary, especially, the breast-beatings, the expressions of self-loathing, the processional admissions of abject failure to live up to self-imposed ideals, are such that the reader may well feel that here as nowhere else, even in Rousseau, is the complex image of the whole man. But it was evidently one thing for Tolstoy to confess that with all his strivings after chastity he was an inveterate womanizer, to set down in cold blood all his silly vanities and boastings, to record how night after night, in spite of repeated resolutions never to play cards again, he steadily gambled his inheritance away; it was evidently quite another to confess to that element of violence and devilish pride which first showed itself in conflict with Saint-Thomas and was to recur again and again, causing more destruction than all his other faults put together. This he was never fully able to bring himself to do.

There was another aspect of that school-room crisis in which the child showed himself as the father of the man. While the boy crouched in the darkness of the punishment room, almost ill with fury, humiliation, and self-pity, he was seized by fantasies of revenge. Now he was at the wars, astounding everyone by his sacrificial courage, covered with wounds, promoted to be general, meeting his Emperor and granted as a boon permission to destroy his enemy, Saint-Thomas; now he was dead, a pathetic, ill-used child, surrounded by his nearest and dearest who understood, too late, the terrible consequences of their neglect and turned on Saint-Thomas and drove him from their midst in spite of his entreaties for forgiveness.

Moscow, Red Square, 1840. This is how the
center of the city looked in Tolstoy's childhood.

There was nothing out of the way about the nature of such fantasies in a child. What was unusual was their intensity—and the reaction when the euphoria wore off and, still in the dark, he had to admit that, dream as he might, he remained a small boy at the mercy of his tutor. How could God be just if Saint-Thomas went unpunished, as he clearly would do? Why go on living in a world where such iniquity could be? How much better to die, so that his soul could take wings and fly up and away into the blessed purity of infinity! The dream of flying obsessed him. It stayed with him when the punishment was over. Surely all he needed to fly was faith: to crouch down and hug his knees and let go. And this, in a strange kind of delirium, he did, falling heavily from a third-floor window, to be found unconscious by the cook. No bones were broken—all he suffered was a sharp concussion—and when he came to, after eighteen hours, it was as though nothing had happened.

It is impossible to get at the exact truth of this incident. Tolstoy was later to say that he had jumped not because he really thought he could fly, but to impress others. Of course he wanted to impress others. He was about to enter on a long period of his life, marked by pathological self-consciousness, in which pretty well everything he did, good or bad, was done to impress others. But it is hard to believe that he was not at least half-convinced that he would in fact be able to fly, or at least to fall gently in defiance of the laws of nature. This was not a passing, childish conceit. Soon he was to give expression in a variety of ways to a profound conviction that he was not as other men are, that he was set apart, chosen indeed, to transcend the limitations of common humanity. This proved to be the truth, though not in the way he understood it. There were to be countless false starts—diplomacy, the law, popular education, agrarian reform, music, soldiering, the foundation of a new and universal religion. Time and time again he was to launch himself into a new field almost wholly oblivious of all that had been done before in that field, convinced that he was divinely endowed with knowledge and understanding denied all others. No sooner did he decide to take up music and practise the piano than he embarked upon a teaching manual to end all teaching manuals. No sooner did he decide to apply himself to farming than he was laying down the law about agricultural practice as though he were the first person who had ever ploughed a field.

We are a long way from the nine-year-old boy throwing himself out of the window of a Moscow apartment house, but he was to plunge himself

44

into all these activities, and many more besides, in much the same spirit. And after a short time, sometimes a ludicrously short time, he would abandon the latest enthusiasm and carry on as though it had never been, very much as he awoke from that childhood concussion. Tolstoy was indeed a genius, and one of the elect, but when at last that genius manifested itself in its supreme blaze of glory he was unable to recognize it for what it was, the unique and unparalleled gift that justified his whole existence. After *Anna Karenina*, at fifty, he turned his back on his gift and contemptuously dismissed it. Of course he was the greatest novelist in the world! That went without saying; he was the greatest man in the world. It had been a waste of time trying to teach peasant boys to read; it had been a waste of time trying to teach adult peasants to respect themselves and learn to use their brains; it had been a waste of time writing novels—worse, like all artistic endeavour, it was frivolous to a degree: his task was by precept and example to teach men how to live. He and he alone knew the secret of the good life, and even when example faltered, he remained incomparably strong on precept.

The dichotomy between theory and practice that marked all his activity except his art began to show even before adolescence, together with his profound conviction that for him to will was to be. The will was far from negligible. It was a powerful force. When it was a simple question of steeling himself to bear pain and to vanquish fear, to learn to ride brilliantly when he was terrified of riding, to develop a naturally formidable physique (of course with the aim of being the strongest man in the world) by straining his muscles to the point of agony, to force himself to go to grand parties although he was racked by shyness and could only make a clumsy exhibition of himself, his will achieved wonders. Later on, at Sevastopol, he was to show great courage under fire, and later still he was to persist in the dangerous sport of bear-hunting although, on his first hunt, he was badly mauled, lucky not to have been killed by a bear: with a characteristic mixture of carelessness, arrogance, and vanity, he had omitted to tread down the deep snow round his station, so that when the great beast came at him and he missed with his first shot, he could not move out of its path.

It was soon after the Saint-Thomas episode that the Tolstoy grandmother died, leaving the children now under the formal guardianship of Aunt Alexandra, to face yet another change of life. It was decided that Aunt Alexandra should keep on the new Moscow apartment to look after

View of Moscow from the Sparrow Hills, 1825.

the two older boys, Nikolai and Sergei, still under Saint-Thomas as they prepared for university, while Aunt Tatiana should take Dmitri and Leo and the two little girls back to Yasnaya Polyana. For the next three years Leo thus spent the best months of the year in the familiar country surroundings, supervised once again by the old German tutor, Fyodor Ivanovich, who was taken back into service, and coming up to Moscow for the winters. Nikolai and Sergei moved out into the world and made new friends of their own age; Dmitri in his early teens already showed every sign of contracting out of the everyday world of his social class and exhibiting that *nostalgie de boue* which was to lead him to marriage with a prostitute before his early death of consumption. And it was now that the young Leo began to exhibit the potential of a powerful, original, and deeply penetrating mind.

It was a horse he had no idea how to ride. It ran away with him. And he gloried in the headlong motion. Not for him the discipline of the schoolroom. Like so many others destined to achieve great things, he refused to apply himself to subjects that did not stir his imagination, but unlike most of these, he drove his brains to their limit and beyond with precocious speculation about the nature of reality, of life and death, of God and the universe. By the time he was twelve he was developing theories about reincarnation derived from what he took to be the laws of symmetry; at the same time, unaided by any philosophical reading, he hit on an approach to something like the Berkeleyian position about appearance and reality: "I imagined that there was nothing and nobody in the universe except myself, that objects were not objects at all but only appearances, visible only when I paid attention to them and vanishing the moment I stopped thinking about them." It is clear enough that these ideas and many more of a like nature were developed less in the disinterested search for truth than as a direct consequence of an insuperable egotism which insisted that he was indeed the centre of the universe, a creature apart. It was in this spirit that he would challenge God to prove his existence by performing a miracle—and when no miracle immediately transpired, proclaim that there was no God and that thenceforth he would be an atheist. His brain at times seemed to boil with the intensity of its effort, consumed in a quite unmanageable welter of childish desperation and premature cerebration. Later he was to attribute to these early exercises his habit of endless dissection and analysis, destroying spontaneity of teaching and clarity of reason. In fact they were the first manifestations of an almost brutal scepticism, which he was never

48

to lose. At the time, he wrote in *Boyhood,* "My vanity was immensely flat-tered by my philosophical discoveries: I often imagined myself as a great man discovering new truths for the benefit of mankind, and I contemplated other mortals with a proud awareness of my own worth. But the strange thing was that the moment I encountered those same mortals I lost all my confidence before the lowliest among them; and the higher I held myself in my own esteem the less capable I was, not only of imposing my own sense of worth upon them, but even of teaching myself not to blush for my simplest remark or most ordinary action."

It was at this time, too, that he began to write. Encouraged by the reception accorded to a set of fairly inept verses he composed for Aunt Tatiana's name day in 1840, he threw a large part of that tremendous, manic vitality into literary compositions, tackling the grandest historical subjects and epic conflicts as though no one had ever written about them before, dreaming of winning fame and honour as a poet. But it was the fame and honour that counted: if not a poet he would be a great soldier and the saviour of his country: if not a soldier, then a great philosopher and teacher; if not a philosopher, then anything, anything at all that would establish him firmly in the eyes of all mankind as what he was, the chosen one.

This was his mood when the death of Aunt Alexandra brought yet another change in the family's circumstances. Aunt Alexandra had a sister, Pelageya Yushkov, who lived in Kazan, married to a retired army officer. She was the perfect mirror of provincial smartness, shallowness, and vanity. It was Nikolai, now eighteen, who wrote to her begging her to assume legal guardianship. "Do not abandon us, dear Aunt, you are all we have left in the world." The complication here was that Aunt Pelageya's hus-band had once been deeply in love with Aunt Tatiana. She had rejected him, having sworn eternal devotion to Nikolai Tolstoy. Aunt Pelageya had never forgiven Aunt Tatiana for having been her husband's first choice, and now she had her revenge. Of course she would assume guardianship of the dear children, but they must come and live with her at Kazan. Know-ing that Aunt Tatiana was bound to refuse, she kindly offered her house-room too. It was the cruellest manoeuvre. All that was required of Aunt Pelageya was that she should assume legal responsibility while leaving the children in Aunt Tatiana's daily care. But Aunt Pelageya herself had no intention at all of putting herself out for the children, and they were absorbed into yet another of those portmanteau Russian households, smartened up a little, and left to themselves—while Aunt Tatiana ate her heart out alone in Moscow. Thus it was that when the time came for university, Leo, transported with the whole household from Yasnaya Polyana to the old Tatar city on the middle Volga, went to Kazan instead of Moscow.

He and his brothers were much bigger fish in Kazan than they could ever have been in Moscow. Grandchildren of the ex-Governor, living in the house of the Governor's daughter, they were at the very centre of Kazan society. The university itself was one of the three best and most famous in Imperial Russia, scarcely inferior to the universities of St. Petersburg and Moscow. It was no disgrace for Nikolai to transfer to Kazan from Moscow, and Leo asked nothing better. While he waited for his time to come he found himself caught up and quite carried away on a new and heady current of enthusiasm. Philosophy, the mysteries of the universe, even worldly ambition on a major scale were forgotten. He was seized now, with the old familiar intensity, with the passion to shine in the *beau monde*. The only thing that mattered was to be what he called *comme il faut!* "My way of being *comme il faut* consisted first in perfect mastery of French and, in particular, the correct accent. A man who spoke French badly filled me with contempt. . . . The second condition for being *comme il faut* was to have fingernails that were long, well-shaped, and clean; the third was to be able to bow, dance, and converse; the fourth, and a very important one, was to appear indifferent, to assume an air of refined and disdainful *ennui* at all times."

The trouble was that he was awkward, clumsy, tongue-tied, and, he thought, hopelessly ugly. Even as a child he had been distressed by his ugliness. Now, looking at himself in the mirror, he saw "only the most ordinary, coarse, and ugly features. . . . My small grey eyes looked more stupid than intelligent. . . . My face was the face of a peasant, and so were my large feet and hands." He envied his brothers Nikolai and Sergei as never before: Nikolai with his easy and amiable brilliance, honesty, and charm; Sergei who seemed to be the model of self-contained, self-assured elegance. It was Sergei he was trying to copy; Nikolai was too remote. But the more he contemplated Sergei, the more he felt himself to be the ugly duckling.

He could still dream, however. He was sixteen now. Encouraged by Aunt Pelageya, he had suddenly decided to make a splendid career for himself in, of all things, the diplomatic service. This would go very well with the ideal of being *comme il faut*. It also called for study. He began to work

50

quite hard to pass into the faculty of Oriental Languages, the examinations for which called for all the ordinary subjects as well as Latin, French, German, English, and elementary Arabic and Turko-Tatar. He possessed, as he was to show again and again, extraordinarily swift assimilative powers. And the mental effort seems to have induced in him a state of exaltation. Partly because of this, partly because he alone among the brothers seemed to be drifting rudderless with no sense of direction ("Why is everything so beautiful and clear inside, and so formless on paper and in my life in general?" he despairingly demanded), he was seized with the determination to make a pattern of his life, to create his own form. It was not enough to live for oneself; one must live for others. After taking much thought, he surfaced with the first of those remarkable documents wherein the broadest aspirations towards nobility and altruism were inconsequently jumbled with particular prescriptions detailed to the point of absurdity. He would read the Gospels for precisely one hour each day; he would give precisely two and a half roubles a month to the poor (but only he would know); he would do his own domestic chores to avoid being waited on by others; if, as he expected, his family gave him his own carriage when he attended the university, he would sell it at once and give the money to the poor. But even in this mood he still had to show off. He would dazzle and confound his university professors, win two gold medals, and emerge as one of the greatest teachers and scholars in the land. In due course he would be rich, honoured, the talk and admiration of the world, and his happiness would be crowned by domestic bliss, when the perfect, the ideal woman entered his life to share his glory.

He failed his first examination. That is to say, he did very well indeed in the new and difficult subjects he had been tackling seriously for the first time, but forgot that for many years he had idled his time away over history, geography, Latin. A sympathetic examiner tried to save him by putting an elementary question: "Name the sea-ports of France." He could not think of one; Brest, Cherbourg, Bordeaux, Toulon, and Marseilles were all blacked out in his mind. . . . It was a blow. The more so because at first, well-tubbed and dressed to the nines, driven to the university by Saint-Thomas in the smartest possible turn-out, a gleaming phaeton drawn by a spirited trotter, he had felt ashamed and uneasy rubbing shoulders with the student hoi polloi. Then, he had reacted sharply: very well, he was in fact a superior being, why pretend otherwise? Now, the superior being had to change out of his fine linen and go back to his books. He worked all through the summer vacation, and this time passed.

There was no question now of selling all he had and giving it to the poor. He positively strutted in his student's uniform: cocked hat, dark blue tunic with gleaming brass buttons, overalls strapped round patent leather boots, sword in its scabbard at his side. He had his own carriage and enjoyed it. It was 1844, but the world of Aunt Pelageya still belonged to the eighteenth century. She insisted that each of the student brothers must have his personal servant, a young serf to wait on him everywhere. And it was she who had urged Leo to enter the diplomatic service when he rejected her first recommendation: at all costs to so contrive things, using his exalted connections, to become one of the Emperor's aides-de-camp.

He was still in a muddle, as he was to remain for years to come—perhaps indeed all his life, beneath the willed pattern which, in due course, he was strong enough to impose on the world around him and to which he himself fell captive. His university career was undistinguished and curtailed. Repelled at first by the coarse and loose familiarities of student life, he was soon half-fascinated by them, joining in noisy and self-conscious carousals, afterwards despising himself for it and, characteristically, convincing himself that everybody present had only pretended to enjoy themselves. He religiously attended the innumerable parties and routs open to a young Count Tolstoy, desperately wanting to dance, to flirt, but paralyzed by awkwardness and shyness, spending his time with folded arms, glaring at the company with angry little eyes under the heavy barrier of those exaggerated eyebrows that he deplored. He forced himself to indulge in amateur theatricals, setting his teeth to overcome his horror of making a fool of himself. He dreamed of girls, as he always had done, now actively lusting after them, but not daring to lay hands even on one of his aunt's serf-girls in case she should laugh in his face. He allowed himself to be dragged to a brothel and afterwards was overcome with disgust at the idea of sex without love. It was all very ordinary, if, as always, exaggerated in its intensity. So was the new joy he found in friendship with a philosophically minded but worldly student five years his senior: he was never again to submit himself to a friend or a mistress or a wife as he submitted himself to Mitya Dyakov, the only father confessor in his life; henceforth he was to confess only to himself—though others, for their own good, might be forced to listen.

52

Leo Tolstoy as a student, around 1840.

His first-term results were so poor that he was forbidden to sit for the end-of-year examination. In one of his rages, this time not confined by his tutor, but shutting himself up for three days and nights on end, weeping and moaning and cursing, he blamed his humiliation not on himself but on his history professor and, dreaming as he had done in his conflict with Saint-Thomas seven years earlier of dying a hero's death, seriously considered going off to fight in the Caucasus with brother Nikolai, who had just been commissioned as a gunner cadet. But perhaps it would be better to kill himself? In this mood he turned up his old Rules of Life, was smitten with remorse, decided formally to revise them, and went off to Yasnaya Polyana. There he fell once more beneath the soothing spell of darling Aunt Tatiana, and was moved to tears by the beauty and purity of nature, so long betrayed by his shoddy way of life.

He began to read again. The two poles of his mind were reactivated, first by Descartes, then by Rousseau. Descartes was all very well, but he had got his formulation wrong. Leo Tolstoy would put him right. "I think, therefore I am" must be changed to read: "I want, therefore I am." He was stunned by the brilliance of this discovery, quite blind to the self-revelation: he had stumbled on one of the keys to his own development. Here also was the contemptuous, rejecting mind at work, seeking originality at all costs—an aspect of himself that he was to fix in the fragment of an autobiographical novel, *A Landlord's Morning*. Criticizing his theorizing in a void about social reform, the hero's aunt writes in a letter: "You always wished to appear original, but your originality is really nothing but excessive self-esteem." As usual in Tolstoy's self-criticism, direct or indirect, there is truth in this verdict—which, however, overlooks one not unimportant point. Tolstoy was eaten up with self-esteem, and he pandered to it, but behind all striving for effect he was an original because he was in fact original and could not help himself.

The other pole was shown in his reaction to Rousseau. Just as the young Tolstoy could be carried away and swept up into the Empyrean by the splendour of his own ideas, so he could prostrate himself before the ideas of others when, all too rarely, they touched a responsive chord. He did not in the least mind making a fool of himself when a big issue was at stake. For years to come, with a dour and dogged persistence, he was to make a fool of himself with his rules and resolutions for attaining perfection of conduct—resolutions not confined to his diary, but trumpeted forth again and again to all who would listen. Now he was to make a fool of

Russian officers. Illustration from M. A. Davidoff's *Voyage dans la Russie*, 1843.

himself over Rousseau, who affected him profoundly both with the revelation that he, Leo Tolstoy, was not the only man in the world who masturbated and was filled with impure desires, and with the sympathetic appeal for man to return to the primitive life. He solemnly devised, cut out, and sewed with his own fingers an extraordinary linen garment, a sort of dressing gown by day which, with an ingenious arrangement of flaps and folds, turned into a sleeping bag at night. Here was life reduced to the barest simplicities, leaving room for the spirit to wander free. Even Aunt Tatiana found her fathomless patience tried when the young Count appeared among her visitors dressed in this shapeless poncho with his not very beautiful legs and feet naked to the world.

But life was a good deal less simple. His readings in philosophy he alternated with a positive orgy of the fashionable French writers—Paul de Kock, Alexandre Dumas, and Eugène Sue. Swallowing them whole, enthralled, the sceptic in him was overcome by the highly coloured life unfolded: "Not only did I never dare suspect the author of lying, but the author himself did not exist for me: real and living characters and real events sprang up before my eyes out of the printed page. . . . I discovered in myself all the passions described in every novel, as well as a likeness to all the characters—both heroes and villains—just as a hypochondriac discovers every symptom of every conceivable disease in himself when he reads a treatise on medicine."

Back at the university he decided to switch from studying for diplomacy to reading law. It was so much easier. It was the late summer of 1845. He still did next to no settled work, but now his brain was beginning to show signs of taking an edge. His friendship with Dyakov developed into positive love. Later he was to declare that this love had a strong element of the physical in it, though he had no idea that he had been approaching pederastic practice when he gave way to his desire to embrace and to kiss. It was to be an enduring affection. Dyakov remained one of the very few real friends he ever had. In those early days they discussed everything together, life and sex and philosophy and religion, in a kind of golden glow. And it should be recorded that Tolstoy, who was to reject and repel all criticism and to frighten off so many who would have been his friend, nevertheless remained faithful to the one man who knew all about him and had piloted him through his first explorations of "Gogol, Rousseau, Pushkin, Goethe's *Faust*, Hegel."

Tolstoy worked hard and with serious application at things that in-

Pushkin. Portrait by O. Kiprensky.

terested him, notably a comparison between Catherine the Great's *Directives* (*Nakaz*) and *L'Esprit des lois* of Montesquieu, which had inspired them. He discovered for himself that "the *Directives* brought more glory to Catherine than benefit to Russia." But with all this he still found time to burn up boisterous nights with fellow students—afterwards recoiling, to try once again, and yet again, to compose new series of Rules which, unbreakable, would change his life and forever abide. Thus, in January 1847, he recorded his determination: "1) To get up at five, go to bed at nine or ten, and perhaps sleep for two hours during the day; 2) To eat in moderation, nothing sweet; 3) To walk for an hour; 4) To fulfil all my written injunctions; 5) To[have] one woman only, and then only once or twice a month; 6) To do as much as possible for myself." But less than three months later, on March 17, 1847, he started to keep a diary in which he recorded that he was under treatment in a Kazan clinic. The opening sentence ran: "It is six days since I entered the clinic. . . . I have had gonorrhoea, obtained from the customary source."

A month later, in spite of the stimulus and helpfulness of one or two of his tutors, he decided finally that the university was not for him. He was a young man in a hurry. "The university," he wrote much later, "with all its rules and regulations not only did not help me to study but actually prevented me from doing so." If he was to be a great thinker he must learn to think for himself, withdrawn from the importunities of the vulgar world and the pedantries of dons. At the shortest possible notice the Rector let him go, and within a fortnight, leaving Sergei and Dmitri to carry on with their studies in Kazan, he was packed up and on his way home to Yasnaya Polyana. He knew just what he was going to do. As an *aide memoire*, he committed to his diary before setting out from Kazan a detailed programme:

"Now I ask myself the aims of my life in the country for the next two years? 1) Study the whole course of jurisprudence, necessary for the university finals. 2) Study practical medicine and a degree of theory. 3) Study languages: French, Russian, German, English, Italian, and Latin. 4) Study agriculture, both theoretical and practical. 5) Study history, geography, and *statistics*. 6) Study mathematics, the high-school course. 7) Write a dissertation. 8) Achieve an average degree of perfection in music and painting. 9) Write down rules. 10) Acquire some knowledge of the natural sciences. 11) Compose essays on all the subjects studied." Nobody can have felt less like a drop-out than the nineteen-year-old

Kazan University, where
Tolstoy studied in 1844–47.

Right: The Yushkov house
in Kazan where Tolstoy lived
with his Aunt Pelageya.

Tolstoy. On the contrary, he was removing himself from the university in order to work the harder, to devote himself to a far wider range of studies than was possible at Kazan, and, into the bargain, to complete the law course on the side, ready to take his final examinations and obtain a useful diploma without benefit of dons.

But he did not last out his two years. Again and again he gave himself a detailed daily programme of work. Again and again he had to write against the programme the two words "nothing done." He was wrestling hard now with his lust. The sight of peasant girls moving about their business or working in the fields distracted him past bearing. When his adoptive sister, newly married, arrived at Yasnaya Polyana with her husband on a short visit, the thought of the couple in bed together under the same roof inflamed his imagination to such a degree that he was stimulated to utter the first of those dreary and violently morbid outbursts against women which, recurring into extreme old age, reflected more clearly than anything else that warped and almost absolute egotism that destroyed his personal relationships, but also fuelled his genius: "Now I shall set myself the following rule: Regard the company of women as an unavoidable social evil and keep away from them as much as possible. Who, indeed, is the cause of sensuality, indolence, frivolity, and all sorts of other vices in us, if not women? Who is to blame for the loss of our natural qualities of courage, steadfastness, reasonableness, fairness, etc., if not women?"

That was on June 16, 1847.

Yasnaya Polyana was now his own property. His mother's considerable estates had now been formally and amicably divided up among the brothers and their sister, Marya. All thus came into comfortable properties within a day's ride of each other. Yasnaya Polyana was the least imposing, the least profitable too, with about 330 serfs occupying 4000 acres of land. But Tolstoy was well pleased with it and was happier to be there than anywhere else. And in the intervals of serious reading, idling, and wrestling with sex, the young barin took his new status with proper seriousness. For the first time now he came up not only against his own limitations as a practical agricultural reformer (his proud introduction of an expensive steam threshing machine, naturally designed by the man who understood such things better than anyone else, Count Leo Nikolayevich Tolstoy, ended in a fiasco), but also against the incurable inertia

Peasant Girl with Calf. Painting by A. G. Venetsianov, c. 1829.

and mocking sycophancy of his peasants, degraded by centuries of slavery. Tolstoy was not politically minded in the least. At Kazan University he never showed the least sign of awareness of, let alone interest in, the ferment of political consciousness that was building up among the new intelligentsia who were beating against the iron front of the autocracy with their bare hands. He had read Gogol as a novelist. There was no indication that he had ever heard of the great pioneering critic V. G. Belinsky or of Peter Chaadeyev, who had lately been disgraced and declared insane as a result of his celebrated *Philosophical Letters*, with its violent denunciation of Russia's moral and administrative failures. Now, responsible for the lives and well-being of his own serfs, he was impatient to improve their conditions, but that sceptical mind that had already seen through the reforming pretensions of Catherine the Great seems to have accepted without question the fact of serfdom as part of the natural order of things. "The idea that the serfs should be liberated was quite unheard of in our circle in the forties," he was to write years later in his *Recollections*. "The hereditary ownership of serfs seemed an indispensable fact of life." This is a very remarkable statement, referring as it does to a period when for at least thirty years serfdom had been recognized as an evil by two successive Emperors, both defeated by vested interests in their attempts to achieve its abolition, and when some of the best brains in the land were working away, sometimes systematically, towards the act of abolition that was to be promulgated by a third Emperor only fourteen years after the young Tolstoy first recoiled in despair from the problem of amelioration: if the serfs wanted to live like pigs, he had decided, they had better be allowed to get on with it; or, as he was to declare through the mouth of his hero, Nekhlyudov in *A Landlord's Morning*, "Ah, if only I had seen my plans succeeding, or met with any gratitude . . . but no, I see nothing but wrong-headed routine, vice, suspicion, helplessness. I am wasting the best years of my life."

Tolstoy did not waste very long on those first abortive efforts to be a good landlord. After eighteen months at Yasnaya Polyana he could stand the solitary life no longer and once more bolted from a self-appointed routine—and himself: first to Moscow, where he had an abundance of relatives and connections; then to St. Petersburg, which was initially a disappointment, with its vast, imperial, and empty impersonality, but soon a revelation.

In Moscow he stayed long enough to develop a new vice, which in

62

Leo Tolstoy as a student in 1849.

St. Petersburg. View of the Palace Quay from the Peter
and Paul Fortress. Painting by F. U. Alexeyev, 1794.

due course was to lead him into serious trouble: cards. He also fell in with a number of disreputable companions and went with them to St. Petersburg, where he fell in with more. But not before he had been seized with a new enthusiasm for work and sobriety, induced by the purposeful career atmosphere of life in the capital. He too would be purposeful and make a career. He would take his law examinations at St. Petersburg University and work his way up in government service from the lowest class. "I know you won't believe that I have changed," he wrote to his brother Sergei. "You'll say, 'That makes it the twentieth time already; but nothing comes of you—the emptiest of fellows. . . .' No, this time the change is completely different from previous changes; up to now I've said to myself: 'Just watch me change!' But now I can see that I have changed and say, 'I have changed.' " To Aunt Tatiana he wrote: "I like life in St. Petersburg. Here everyone has his job, everyone works and minds his own business and pays no attention to anyone else; even though the atmosphere is cold and selfish, it is essential for young people like us, who are inexperienced and lack *savoir faire;* it will teach me to be orderly and keep myself occupied, the two indispensable qualities in life, of which I am totally devoid. . . ."

Less than three months later, on May 1, 1849, he was writing in desperation to Sergei, begging him to read the letter alone: "God knows what I have done! I came to St. Petersburg for no good reason, I've done nothing worth-while here—simply run through a lot of money and fallen into debt. Stupid! Insufferably stupid! You can't imagine how it torments me." The debts that worried him most were his gambling debts, his debts of honour. Sergei must act quickly, say nothing to anyone, and sell off one of the villages on the Yasnaya Polyana estate—the resident serfs, of course, going with it. "While I am waiting for the money to come through, I must absolutely have 3500 roubles [about £3000] right away. I know you will groan aloud, but what else can be done? You can only commit this kind of idiocy once in a lifetime. I have had to pay for my freedom (there was no one to thrash me; that was my chief misfortune) and for philosophizing, and now I have paid."

He was wrong about the unrepeatable nature of the mistake. Indeed, Tolstoy did not stop gambling disastrously until, years later, he had gambled away the main part of the old manor house itself.

And so on.

He had gone quite wild. All that fantastic vitality was running loose, almost amok. The wonder is that it did not lead him into disaster. He had not a thought in the world beyond the intoxication of the moment and the subsequent remorse. One idea for escape from reality tumbled after another. Once again he saw himself as a soldier. He would enter the Horse Guards. The Emperor Nicholas was about to make history by sending an army to Hungary to subdue, on behalf of the young Austrian Emperor Franz Joseph, the nationalist revolution of 1848. It was this action, performed at a moment when the whole of Europe seemed to be going up in flames, that earned for Nicholas, who had his own empire well in hand, the title "Gendarme of Europe." Tolstoy, at twenty, far from condemning the massive intervention of the Russian Autocrat to crush in the name of the monarchical principle the desperate and heroic rebels of a distant land, saw in it a chance to distinguish himself. That he did not in fact then join the Horse Guards as a noncommissioned officer and serve under Prince I. F. Paskevich in Hungary was the result not of moral revulsion but of yet one more change of mind. Perhaps, after all, it would be more sensible to stick to his plans and apply himself to his law studies in St. Petersburg. No sooner said than not done: now he was writing secretly to Aunt Tatiana to send him just enough money to get back to Yasnaya Polyana. He would never leave his dearest aunt again; instead he would work hard for the civil service exams and take a government post in Tula. It was spring. The countryside called. St. Petersburg was getting too hot to hold him. He fled, owing money to unfortunate shopkeepers as well as to friends who had been too easy with their trust.

It was April 1849. Tolstoy was coming up to twenty-one The next two years were chaotic. All his conflicting influences were meeting head-on, as he oscillated between town and country, never able to settle for more than a few months. He was more self-assured now, no longer shy of women and driven to furtive visits to brothels. He played cards as hard as ever, and gave himself some severe frights. He developed a devouring passion for the gypsies, whose wild abandoned music, to say nothing of their wild abandoned women, subjugated him entirely. At Yasnaya Polyana itself he did his best to limit his seductions of serf girls and even managed to develop a romantic attachment to one of them. In old age, passing by their meeting place, he was to write: "I remembered the nights I spent there, and Dunyasha's beauty and youth (I did not have a real affair with her), her strong womanly body. Where is it? Long since,

Russian Guards leaving for Hungary. Painting by Yebens, 1849.

Opposite: Tsar Nicholas I.

nothing but bones." * But there was no romance about other episodes in the life of a young landlord. "Could hold out no longer," he wrote in his diary for April 18, 1851. "I beckoned to something pink which seemed to me very attractive from a distance, and I opened the back door— She came in. Now I can't bear to look at her—repulsive, vile, hateful, for causing me to break my rules."

But above all his diary is filled with self-accusations of every conceivable sin of commission and omission, with day after day, "nothing done." Almost the only thing he had to show on the surface for these two years was a certain facility in piano playing; he had taken a drunken German musician back with him to Yasnaya Polyana from St. Petersburg and had dreams of becoming a composer. When the German had to be sent away for getting the serf girls into trouble, Aunt Tatiana brushed up her old skill to play four-handed with her nephew. Her idea was to keep him out of mischief as much as she could; his was to become a virtuoso. Already he was writing a monograph entitled, *Foundations of Music and Rules for its Study*. But soon he was thinking of new rules for a treatise on card-playing. And at the end of 1850 he solemnly decided that he must stop dreaming and building castles in the air, stop aspiring towards higher things that he could not achieve, forget his idealistic rules of conduct, and apply himself seriously to recognizing his own limitations and working within them. "Up to now everything ordinary has seemed unworthy of me; from now on, however, I shall not respect as good or true any conviction I cannot test in action and apply in practice." The first fruits of this new mood were strictly utilitarian. Quite a new set of rules had to be drawn up: "1) Join a circle of card-players, and play when I have money. 2) Get into the highest society and, under certain conditions, marry. 3) Find a good position."

This general design called for practical elaboration: "Try to dominate the conversation at all times; speak loudly, calmly, and distinctly; try to initiate and conclude the conversation. —Seek out the society of people more highly placed than I. . . . At dances, invite the most important ladies. —When rebuffed do not be discouraged, but persist. Be as cold as possible and let no feeling show."

But one other thing had happened. He had begun to write—not much, it is true, and nothing considerable. But at least he was beginning to see how to use the experience of the wasted years. It was the first glimpse of

* Quoted in Henri Troyat, *Tolstoy,* trans. Nancy Amphoux (New York, 1967), p. 63.

71

Opposite: The onion domes of a church near Tula.
Yasnaya Polyana lay in the province of Tula.

reality, his own reality, looming faintly and indistinctly through the choking mists of confusion. There were the first signs that he was ready for a decisive break. He could not escape from himself, but he could perhaps escape from the environment that was stifling his development. The opportunity quite suddenly came. His brother Nikolai was home on leave and had soon to return to his regiment, which was engaged in sporadic fighting to subdue the tribesmen of the Caucasus. Come with me, he said, in effect. Get away from your Moscow third-raters and your mooning about with aunts and peasant girls at home. Get out into the hills with me, enjoy mountain air, live free among free people, Cossack settlers, in the most romantic and spectacular scenery in the world, live dangerously under constant threat from still unsubdued tribesmen swooping down from their mountain strongholds. It was a heaven-sent chance, considerably more promising than Tolstoy's latest idea, which was to apply for the postmastership of Tula. At twenty-two he could rule a double line, boycott an unsatisfactory past, write off his embarrassments and problems, and start a new life, a new man.

None of this, of course, happened. Like everybody else seeking to escape from himself by travel, he remained unchanged. But if he did not purge himself, he added greatly to his stature and tempered his character during his Caucasian interlude and his subsequent service in the Imperial Army. He was to go on womanizing and recklessly gambling; he was to catch gonorrhoea again; he was to despair of ever correcting his weaknesses; he was to show himself as incapable as ever of spontaneous, open-hearted love or self-denying attachment. But he was to prove not only his physical but also his moral courage when a profound conviction was at stake. More than this, he was to reveal himself to be a writer of formidable talents and, in the process, to exhibit an unsuspected capacity for gruelling self-discipline and for sticking at a self-appointed task (once he found one that engaged his whole being) in adverse circumstances with invincible persistence. He went off to the Caucasus a tiresome, spoiled, rudderless young man of twenty-two. He returned from the Crimea nearly five years later recognized by some of the great figures of the Russian literary world, including, above all, Turgenev, as a writer of mature achievement, unlimited potential, and, probably, genius.

Having decided to put his old life behind him and go south, Tolstoy took his time about it. Instead of following the direct route via the Don, he and Nikolai decided to make a broad eastward detour through Moscow and Kazan, and thence by boat down the Volga to Astrakhan. His plan gave him the chance to revert for a short spell to the city life he was so eager to leave behind him. In Moscow he called on all his old friends, gambled through the night (winning for a change), and paid a last visit to the gypsies—triumphantly and somewhat facetiously reporting to his aunt that he had successfully resisted the temptation to sleep with any of the girls. In Kazan the mood was different. For a week he imagined himself to be in love with a girl who was clearly quite ready to fall in love with him, if she did not in fact do so. Zinaida Molostvov had attracted him in his student days. Now she was five years older, not a beauty, but full of character, charm, and humour. He spent all the time he could with her and said later that he had been on the edge of declaring his love. Instead, he ran away, as he was for so long to run away from any dawning emotion which might undermine his single-minded contemplation of himself. He was later to rationalize the episode by explaining, apparently in good faith, that to declare himself would have been to degrade "this pure yearning of two souls for one another." In fact he had got enough out of Zinaida to give him something to dream and write bad poetry about, and a valuable insight, so necessary for the writer-to-be, into what it felt like to be in love. It gave him something to think about in the Caucasus. Was he in love with her at all? Did he really understand "what men call love"? On the whole he thought not. He did not like to think of Zinaida married to anyone else. He could still write in his diary that he did not rule out the thought of returning to marry her himself. But he made no move, wrote her no letter—limiting himself to sending her a decorous message of remembrance, enough to keep her wondering, through a mutual friend. A year later he received the news that she had stopped wondering and engaged herself to another man. By that time he had entertained with momentary enthusiasm the idea of marrying a Cossack girl and living with her in a hut. He found himself only mildly jealous: "The fact vexes me," he wrote, "the more so because I have felt so little distressed." It was an affair for a novel. But he never forgot Zinaida, and much later, in his seventies, when she had long been dead, he was visited by her nephew and questioned him, minutely and eagerly, about the way she had lived and died.

The hero of *The Cossacks,* Olenin, is not Tolstoy: nondescript, characterless to the point of vacuity, there is no suggestion in him of Tolstoy's own dark pride and unmanageable vitality. But what the character of Olenin does do rather well is to display in his person the outer garments of his creator's personality.

"Olenin was a young man who had left university before completing his course, who had never worked (he held only a nominal post in some government office or other), who had squandered half his fortune and reached the age of twenty-four without doing anything or even choosing a career. He was what in Moscow society is called *un jeune homme*.

"Since his eighteenth year he had been free as only a wealthy young Russian in the 'forties, who had lost his parents at an early age, could be. Neither physical nor moral fetters of any kind existed for him; he could do as he pleased, lacking nothing and bound by nothing. He had no family, no country, no religion, no wants. He believed in nothing and accepted nothing. But though he acknowledged no belief he was not a morose, blasé, argumentative youth; on the contrary, he continually allowed himself to be carried away. He had decided there was no such thing as love, yet his heart missed a beat whenever he found himself in the presence of a young and attractive woman. He had long regarded honours and rank as mere dross, yet he could not help feeling gratified if at a ball Prince Sergei came up and spoke to him affably. . . . He had toyed with a society life, the Civil Service, farming, music—to which at one time he had thought of devoting himself—and with love, in which he did not believe. He meditated on the use to which he should put all the energy of youth which comes to a man only once in life. Should he devote this power, which is not the strength of intellect or heart or education, but an urge which once spent can never return, the power given to a man once only to make himself, or even—so it seems to him at the time—the universe into anything he wishes . . . ? Up to this time he had loved only himself, and could not help it, for he expected nothing but good of himself and had not yet had time for disillusion. He was leaving Moscow in that happy youthful state of mind in which a young man, while recognizing mistakes, suddenly confesses to himself that he has not been on the right track but that all that has gone before was accidental and unimportant. Till then he had not really tried to live *properly* but now, with his departure from Moscow, a new life was beginning, in which there would be no more mistakes, no more remorse and, of course, nothing but happiness."

I have quoted the passage at length because nothing, it seems to me, could show up in sharper relief the absolute difference *in kind* between

74

Leo and his brother Nikolai Tolstoy,
before leaving for the Caucasus, 1851.

the young Tolstoy, as we have watched him developing, of whom everything in that passage except for one thing is true, and the young Olenin, about whom it is the whole truth. The exception to the partial truth about Tolstoy is in the sentence: "Neither physical nor moral fetters of any kind existed for him." Tolstoy dragged his moral fetters with him like a heavy ball and chain. Thus there was nothing in the least unusual about his behaviour as a young aristocrat of his day (always apart from the intensity of degree), as a womanizer, gambler, and idler. What was unusual was his overpowering sense of guilt. It is perhaps not too much to say that his tremendous strength of character derived above all from the unceasing effort to resolve the conflict between his natural instincts and his moral sense. The moral sense, of course, arose from an inescapable vision of what may be called the good life. This sort of conflict and this sort of vision are not rare, though always mysterious. Olenin lacked both.

There are moments throughout the story when Tolstoy endows his commonplace, amiable, and characterless hero with insights and qualities that no Olenin could aspire to: "He sat on the floor of the sledge, his coat unfastened, and the three shaggy post-horses dragged themselves out of one dark street into another, past houses he had never seen before. It seemed to Olenin that only travellers bound on a long journey ever went through such streets as these."

Again, as they move at last to meet the mountains: " 'So now we've come to it!' thought Olenin, and kept looking for the snow-clad mountains of which he had heard so often. Once, towards evening, the Nogai driver pointed with his whip to peaks behind the clouds. Olenin looked eagerly but the sky was overcast and the mountains were almost hidden by the clouds. All he could make out was something grey and white and fleecy: try as he would, he could discover nothing beautiful about these mountains of which he had read and heard so much. Mountains and clouds appeared alike to him, and he began to suspect that the special beauty of peaks, of which he had so often been told, was as much a figment of the imagination as the music of Bach, or love, in neither of which did he believe."

This is pure Tolstoy, the Tolstoy of *War and Peace* as he contemplates the legend of great men and purposeful activity, already revealing itself in his middle twenties—which was when he began *The Cossacks*. It has nothing to do with Olenin. Nor has the marvellous passage that immediately follows, when he at last does see the mountains for the first time and is overcome. "From that moment whatever he saw, whatever he thought, whatever he felt, acquired a new character, sternly majestic, like the mountains. All his recollections of Moscow, his shame and repentance, all his trivial fantasies about the Caucasus—vanished never to return. A solemn voice seemed to say, 'It has begun.'"

Nothing to do with Olenin, everything to do with Tolstoy.

Travel in Russia.

3

A WRITER AT WAR

Tolstoy was in his twenty-third year. Apart from a month's leave on the eve of Russia's declaration of war on Turkey, he was to spend the next five years, from April 1851 to November 1855, with the Imperial Army in the Caucasus and the Crimea. For the first nine months he was a civilian camp-follower, after that a soldier. At the beginning of this period the sort of impression he made was still the impression he had made on the student, Nazarev, at Kazan, who had found himself repelled by "his assumption of coldness, his bristly hair, and the piercing expression of his half-closed eyes," who had never met a young man "with such a strange, and to me incomprehensible, air of importance and self-satisfaction." * At the end of it he had something to be satisfied about. His assurance had a firm basis now, and he had learned how to behave in society. He was also well turned out and his hair no longer bristled:

"I see him quite clearly at the time of his return from Sevastopol in 1855 as a young artillery officer and remember what a pleasant impression he made on us all [wrote his beloved cousin Countess Alexandra Tolstoy, who was a lady-in-waiting at Court]. . . . He was himself simple, extraordinarily modest, and so playful that his presence enlivened us all. He very seldom spoke of himself, but observed every new face with particular

* Quoted in Aylmer Maude, *The Life of Tolstoy* (London, 1929), p. 37.

78

attention, and afterwards amusingly gave us his impressions, which were nearly always rather extreme. . . . He was not good-looking, but his clever, kind, and expressive eyes made up for what he lacked in elegance and, one may say, was better than beauty."

But he could still use those eyes as a weapon, and was to do so unscrupulously for the rest of his life. Acquaintance after acquaintance, friend after friend, recorded the way in which that penetrating gaze pierced to the very soul. But until the advent of the young Gorky nearly fifty years later, the student Nazarev seems to have been the last person to whom it occurred that a gaze of that sort is at least a breach of good manners, at worst insufferable, and who objected to this kind of public undressing of the soul. All his contemporaries, even those with whom he quarrelled violently, like Turgenev, seem to have taken it quite for granted that they must put up with it, such was the overwhelming power of his personality —such, too, by the time he came back from the Crimea, his manifest achievement.

And it is quite clear that Tolstoy only half realized the effect his eyes produced. Certainly he knew that he could outstare anybody in the world, certainly on occasion he took a sadistic enjoyment in putting on the kind of stare normally cultivated by seekers of worldly power. But at the same time he was also searching. He was searching for a man who was as morally good as himself—by which he meant a man who believed as passionately as he believed in the desirability of moral goodness. What he was never to understand was that in comparing himself with others he was measuring their conduct not against his own conduct but against his aspirations. For him those aspirations were reality; in others it was conduct alone that counted. In spite of his own self-knowledge, he was as incapable as any peasant of believing in what he called the "sincerity" of others, including his close friends, if their conduct fell short of the aspirations, which, of course, it invariably did. He quite simply did not believe in the existence in others of aspirations as worthy as his own. It was a lifelong blindness—a blindness that made it possible, as he wrestled unavailingly with his own freely admitted shortcomings, to write (as he did on November 3, 1853, when he was twenty-five): "Almost every time when meeting a new man I experience an oppressive feeling of disappointment. I picture him as being like myself, and study him, weighing him by that standard. Once for all I must accustom myself to the thought that I am an exception, that either I am ahead of my age, or—that I am one of those incongruous, unadaptable natures that will never be satisfied. I must adopt a different standard (lower than my own) and measure people by that. I shall rarely make a mistake— For long, I deceived myself by imagining that I had friends, people who understood me. Rubbish! I have not yet met a single man who was morally as good as I, or who would believe that I myself cannot remember a single instance in my life when I was not attracted by the good and was not ready to sacrifice everything to it." To "everything" add "everybody."

It is very much a feature of the Russian cast of mind, this confusion of the intention with the deed, of the dream with reality, but in the extent and intensity of its application Tolstoy was unique. His own lack of humility was absolute. And the passage I have just quoted seems to me a key passage for an understanding of the man. Nobody was more acutely aware of his own failings or castigated himself more severely for them. But in the final accounting these counted for nothing; they were unfortunate lapses from total holiness. He was his own confessor, wiping the slate clean every day and granting himself absolution because the intention was good. And nobody was more aware of the failings of others: his own conduct supplied him with a complete lexicon of sin, and he had that deadly eye which told him at a glance the hidden failings of everyone he met. What he did not have was fellow feeling. This may seem a peculiar thing to say about a man who, in his novels, showed an unsurpassed ability to identify himself with his main characters. But real life is not a novel, and the ability to put himself inside the skins of his fictional characters was bound up with that cold detachment which made him such uneasy company. In fact there are important reservations and qualifications to be made about his seeming identification with all but a few of his characters, which will be examined later in the context of his masterpieces. For the time being we are concerned with a young man of twenty-three who had achieved nothing, showed no specific promise of achieving anything, was in the process, to all appearances, of making a mess of his life, put on superior airs which had no visible correspondence with any special gift, and yet possessed a special quality which impressed even those who most resented his manner.

With his Caucasian adventure Tolstoy, quite unwittingly, was involving himself in a major process of Russian imperialism. His long stay in the south fell into two parts. From the spring of 1851 to the new year of 1854, he was caught up in a frontier war against primitive mountain tribes. From March 1854 to November 1855, he served as a junior officer in the campaign against Turkey, which quickly developed into the Crimean War, ending with the defeat of Russia by England and France. Tolstoy himself was in Sevastopol when it fell. Thus an interlude that had started as a light-hearted adventure ended in some of the most desperate and bloody fighting of the century.

Russian operations in the Caucasus formed a part of the long south-ward drive that was then reaching its culmination. Over the centuries the Tatars and Kalmucks of the southern steppe-lands had been pushed back until the Imperial power commanded the northern shores of the Black Sea and virtually the whole of the Caspian. The Crimea had been taken from Turkey in the last decade of the eighteenth century, and, soon after, the mountain kingdom of Christian Georgia, far to the south, had made sub-mission, so that the Russian Empire now marched with Persia. Pushkin and Lermontev had celebrated the Russian discovery of this magical south-ern landscape; and the legend of the so recent glories of Georgian princes and Tatar khans, the beauty of Circassian women, the splendour of snow-clad peaks and dizzy precipices, the exoticism of sub-tropical vegetation and boiling thermal springs held a magnetic attraction for the more ad-venturous spirits of the slow-moving Russian plains. The army in the Caucasus was also a refuge for officers who in one way or another had failed, or blotted their copybooks, and sought to recover their fortunes or rehabilitate their reputations—or simply escape.

But the western flank of the new Russian Imperium was still threat-ened by the mountain peoples of the high Caucasus, above all by the fierce and warlike Chechens, a Moslem people led by a notable ruler, Shamyl, whose continued independence St. Petersburg was determined to destroy. All along the river Terek a highly individual Cossack clan, the Grebensky Cossacks, had been encouraged to establish themselves in a string of loosely knit settlements, or frontier stations. They were technically Old Believers, descendants of men and women of passionate conservative faith who had taken to the wilds rather than submit to the liturgical reforms of the Patriarch Nikon in the seventeenth century. But they had intermar-ried with Tatars, Circassians, and Chechens, and were now more pagan than Christian, living the lives of frontier raiders, hunters, horse-thieves. The women, strong and handsome, did all the work in the fields and the homes, but were allowed remarkable sexual freedom. The men proved themselves to the women by their horsemanship, their bravery, their marksmanship, and their drinking capacity. Both men and women regarded themselves as responsible to nobody but the clan and considered all outsiders, especially the Russian soldiery, to be inferior beings.

It was among these people that Nikolai's unit was now established, with its headquarters at Starogladovsk. Nikolai was an able, conscientious, and well-loved officer, though already drinking far too much. Tolstoy, as an unattached camp-follower, could move as he liked between regimental headquarters and the Cossack settlements; and this he did. He chased the Cossack girls, gambled and caroused with the officers, revelled in the marvellous hunting and shooting offered by an untamed land which teemed with game of every kind. If he had hoped, as he did, to get away from the temptations of women and cards, he had come to the wrong place.

The experience was to give him a number of stories, most notably *The Raid,* the much longer tale *The Cossacks,* and *The Woodfelling* and his marvellous swan song of old age, *Hadji Murad,* which derived from major actions against Shamyl. It also showed him that the primitive life was not for him. At first he simply drifted, powerfully attracted by the call of the free, instinctive, mindless life of riding, gambling, hunting, and sex. He was in full reaction against the scented artificialities of urban society. Here, in the Caucasus, was real life: men were born, learned to ride and shoot, lusted, fornicated, fought, drank themselves silly, married, reproduced themselves, and died in an endlessly repetitive cycle, as the grass grows with the warmth of the spring and withers under the frosts of autumn. He dreamed for a moment of setting up house with a Cossack girl and spending the rest of his life on the banks of the Terek River. Even when he realized the idiocy of this idea, he still clung to his new friends, above all a renegade Chechen called Sado, who became his blood-brother and devoted familiar, and a dreadful old man who was to be the model of the giant, freebooting, half-domesticated bandit Yershov in *The Cossacks*—horse-thief, braggart, lecher, and inspired hunter, whose life was as simple and direct as the lives of the animals he lived to kill, but much noisier and dirtier.

But it would not do. It was not merely that a Count Tolstoy could have no part in the simple certitudes of these handsome and infinitely boring children of nature. Even at the time when he sought to immerse himself in the simple life, the simple life was not enough: he needed the conversation of Russian officers, however irritating and banal; he needed

Shamil, leader of the Chechens. This newspaper illustration derived from a sketch
made in 1855 by a Russian princess imprisoned by the Chechens. For many years
the legendary Shamil defied the might of the Russian army.

the hectic stimulus, or anodyne, of all-night card sessions; he needed to get away from his new companions. And the entries in his diary continued as before: a record of constant lapses into all his favourite sins and transgressions, and consequent waves of remorse and furious self-condemnation —these interspersed, more frequently now, with speculations about the mysteries of life and religion and references to brief, quasi-mystical moments of revelation. He brooded on the riddle of prayer. He decided that the reason why he could not settle down to connubial bliss by the Terek was his inborn need to serve others; all he needed was the opportunity. How to find it?

In July of that first year he leaped at the chance to take part in a raid across the river and into the mountains, a punitive expedition against a Chechen village. He behaved so well under fire (though he thought he had done badly) that the commanding general urged him to apply for a cadetship in the army. After three months of indeterminate time-wasting he decided to take the plunge. He seems to have felt quite strongly, as he himself wrote, that unless he submitted himself to some external discipline he would never make anything of his life. He was, indeed, already trying to discipline himself—not simply in the old, familiar routine of self-flagellation after sin (this continued unabated for years to come); not simply in the hopeless and unconvincing quest for self-perfection; but, more practically, in his determination to apply himself to a set task and stick to it. He had begun quite seriously to write. The book he was working on was *Childhood,* which he had conceived even before he left for the Caucasus, and now saw as the first part of a major novel in four volumes. But he was making heavy weather. A week after celebrating his twenty-third birthday, in August, with a new programme of "Rules," he was crying out again: "Unhappily I remain always the same: in the last few days I have done all the things I disapprove of. It is impossible to make a sudden change. I had a woman, showed myself weak on a number of occasions—in simple relations with people, in situations of danger, at cards, and I am still held back by false shame. I have lied a great deal. . . . I have idled; and now I *cannot collect my thoughts and write,* indeed I don't want to write."

But writing he was. And from that time on he was to show that no matter how much he idled away his days and nights in debauchery and dissipation, somehow he had discovered how to discipline and canalize enough of that colossal vitality to keep him more or less steadily writing, not at first for cash, but for glory, and because, as he was so fond of saying

A skirmish between Cossacks in the Russian army
and a mountain tribe. Lithograph by Mitreuter.

A typical scene of Caucasian warfare as Tolstoy described it in *The Cossacks*, *The Raid*, and *Hadji Murad*. Lithograph by Prince G. G. Gagarin.

when deploring his transgressions (but rarely, if ever, when recording his virtues), he could not help himself.

In the autumn he went off to Tiflis, where he had to take an examination, a formality required before he could be gazetted. With him he took the opening pages of *Childhood*. But first he had to wait before certain papers came through, and the first thing that happened was that he suffered yet another attack of gonorrhoea, which pulled him down very sharply. "The venereal sickness is cured," he wrote to his brother Nikolai, "but the after-effects of the mercury have caused me untold suffering." They also gave him a long period of convalescence, two months out of the world, in which he could write. And in spite of the excruciating pains arising from the mercury treatment, he wrote hard. It was a characteristic irony, which was to dog his whole life, and which this supreme ironist was never able to perceive, that the quiet time that he so badly needed to make real headway with this gravely beautiful evocation of the days of innocence was the outcome of this by no means innocent disease.

In January 1852 he passed his examination and was posted to his brother's regiment at Starogladovsk. And it was on the journey from Tiflis to join his unit that he sat down to write a long and remarkable letter to Aunt Tatiana confiding his dream of the future:

"After an indefinite number of years, neither young nor old, I am at Yasnaya—my affairs are in order, I have no anxieties or worries; you are living at Yasnaya too. You have grown a little older but you are still active and well. We live the life we used to lead, I work in the morning but we see each other almost all day long. We dine together. In the evening I read aloud something which does not weary you, and then we walk. I tell you of my life in the Caucasus, you tell me your recollections of my father and mother; and you tell me the 'terrible tales' we used to listen to with frightened eyes and open mouths. We remind each other of those who were dear to us and are now no more; you will weep, I shall do the same, but these tears will be sweet; we shall talk about my brothers, who will come to see us from time to time; of dear Marya, who with all her children will also spend some months of the year at Yasnaya which she loves so much. We shall have no acquaintances—no one will come to weary us and tell tales. It is a beautiful dream, but it is not all that I let myself dream— I am married. My wife is a gentle creature, kind and affectionate; she has the same love for you that I have. We have children who call you Grand-

Georgian woman in Tiflis. Lithograph by Prince G. G. Gagarin.

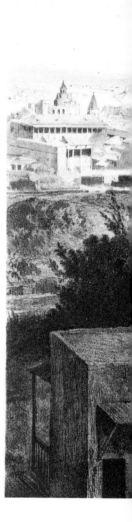

The rooftops and terraces of Tiflis. Lithograph by Prince G. G. Gagarin.

mama; you live upstairs in the big house, in what used to be Grandmama's room. The whole house is as it was in Papa's time, and we recommence the same life, only changing our roles. You take the role of Grandmama, but you are still better; I take Papa's place, though I despair of ever deserving it; my wife, that of Mama; the children take ours; Marya that of the two aunts (but not their misfortunes) . . . but someone will be lacking to take the part you played in our family—never will anyone be found with a soul so beautiful, so loving, as yours."

And so on. The letter concludes: "If they made me Emperor of Russia or gave me Peru: in a word, if a fairy came with her wand asking me what I would wish for—my hand on my conscience, I should reply that I only wish that this dream may become a reality." *

This dream, this idyll, was more than a passing fantasy induced by homesickness and by the return to his own remote past demanded by the writing of *Childhood*. What, in any case, was the nature of the urge that drove him, an active and turbulent young man of twenty-three, dreaming of glory, to fix on his own infancy as the subject of his first book?

The spirit of that letter to his beloved aunt was central to his nature and was never to leave him. To attribute a fear of life to a man bursting with vitality and driven by a positive hurricane of vital impulses, physical and mental—and in his writing so manifestly rejoicing in the surface aspects of life in all their colour and teeming multiplicity—may seem absurd. But it existed. This is a paradox that will dominate Tolstoy's story from now on. Much earlier in these pages, when referring to his cult of the mother he never knew, I spoke of his life-long hankering after the womb —or at least the nursery. It is all in those words to Aunt Tatiana, spelling out a dream in which life is held at arm's length, in which nothing ever changes, in which grown-ups play at being fathers and mothers, into which no outsiders may intrude, in which death itself occurs, as it were, off-stage, and is not real. The spirit of that letter was to manifest itself in Tolstoy's own approach to marriage in years to come and to triumph when at last he did in fact marry and carry off a child-bride to retirement at Yasnaya, cut off from all the world. But what happened then at Yasnaya was not at all like the dream, and he was driven once more to escape into the dream by recreating it in fiction, in the enclosed household of the Rostov family in *War and Peace*, where nobody is quite grown up and where the pressures and complications of adult life are alien and intrusive.

* Quoted in Maude, *Life of Tolstoy*, pp. 73–74.

For the time being he had to turn his back on dreams. He was now a soldier under discipline, a man of the world as well. He carried back with him a considerable part of *Childhood* and arrived just in time to share in a sharp and furious campaign designed, unsuccessfully, to smash Chechen resistance forever. Once again, now as an ensign in charge of a small mountain gun, he did well under fire and was, indeed, extraordinarily lucky not to be killed when an enemy shell hit the wheel of the gun he was laying. Back again at Starogladovsk, recommended for the St. George's Cross for gallantry, he picked up *Childhood* as though he had never had to lay it down; in spite of all distractions, he plugged away at it, rising early to get some writing done before he was caught up in the routine of a soldier's day, sitting up into the small hours after bouts of cards and heavy drinking. Four months later it was finished—not merely finished, but rewritten and recopied three times with that obsessional care for exactitude of expression that he was to bring later to the back-breaking revision of his great novels.

Both physically and mentally it was a very remarkable achievement. And it was no flash in the pan. *Childhood* was sent off to the distinguished poet and editor of *The Contemporary*, N. A. Nekrasov, in July 1852, accepted immediately, and published and widely acclaimed in September. In the next three years of active and sometimes strenuous and dangerous soldiering, with plenty of dissipation thrown in, Tolstoy managed to produce *Boyhood* and part of *Youth*, *The Raid*, *The Woodfelling*, and part of *The Cossacks* (which he was not to finish for another ten years), *Notes of a Billiard Marker*, and the three inspired Sevastopol sketches, written during the siege. In addition he produced a large part of *A Landlord's Morning* and the greater part of a story called *Christmas Eve*, which he never finished. All these works were very largely autobiographical. Tolstoy had the gift, rare among creative writers, of transmuting immediate experience into art. He had no need for a long gestatory period while the things he had seen, heard, and done arranged themselves in the unconscious into some sort of perspective. The perspective was there, ready-made. And his detachment was such that he could write about his own most intimate thoughts and feelings, his own idiocies and failings, only perfunctorily disguised as fiction.

But perhaps detachment here is not the right word. Heaven knows, he was deeply enough involved in his unending spiritual drama, which he contemplated with a compulsive honesty that had a strong element of

Marya Nikolayevna Tolstoy, Tolstoy's sister, described in
the character of Lyubochka in *Childhood* and *Boyhood*.

narcissism. Because, too, he was the absolute egotist, he sought to involve others in this drama. I have said that he was his own confessor. But even in his early days this was not enough. One of his fellow officers at Sevastopol recorded how Tolstoy, normally such good company in mess, the very soul of gaiety indeed, would suddenly vanish for a day, for two days, for three, "trotting off to Simferopol" and leaving the mess feeling very flat without him: "At last he would return—the very picture of a prodigal son. . . . Then he would take me aside, quite apart, and begin his confessions. He would tell me all: how he had caroused and gambled, and where he had spent his days and nights; and all the time, if you will believe me, he would condemn himself and suffer as though he were a real criminal. He was so distressed that it was pitiful to see him. That's the sort of man he was. In a word, a queer fellow, and to tell the truth one I could not quite understand. He was, however, a rare comrade, a most honourable fellow, and a man one can never forget." *

Eight years later this same queer fellow, on the eve of his wedding, gave his diary into the hands of his eighteen-year-old fiancée and insisted on her reading it through. After two more decades, with the publication of his *Confession,* he was to embroil the whole world in his personal drama, insisting with that strange hectoring, bullying violence that now that he had achieved sainthood, everybody, man and woman, old and young, must stop what they were doing and follow his instructions or consider themselves to be forever damned.

What struck the first readers of *Childhood* were the wonderful freshness and exactness of these scenes of innocence, qualities of radiance and joy which sprang not from loose rhapsodizing but from a precise, matter-of-fact presentation of the physical aspects of the familiar world as though created for the first time; a sharp and delicate response to the finest details of texture, colour, odour, gesture, sound, and form; an astonishing insight, based on something like total recall, into the delights and miseries of the awakening mind. There had been nothing like it before. Pushkin had fixed aspects of the Russian landscape, of the natural and domestic world indelibly in his poetry, so that for generations to come his readers, without knowing it, saw that world through Pushkin's eyes. He had done this in language as simple, as matter-of-fact, as direct, as Tolstoy's, and far more elegant. But Pushkin was a poet, recreating the world, as Chaucer and

* Quoted in Maude, *Life of Tolstoy,* p. 129.

93

A page from Tolstoy's first-draft manuscript of *Youth*, written while he was in the Caucasus. The drawings are Tolstoy's.

Opposite: A modern illustration for the scene in *Childhood* of the tutor waking the young boy, by K. A. Klementieva, 1949.

Shakespeare recreated the world, through poetic imagination. It was Pushkin's snowstorm, Pushkin's troika ride, Pushkin's Bronze Horseman, Pushkin's Tatiana. Nobody was less a poet than Tolstoy, whose fanatically literal mind had not a breath of poetry in it. And yet the poetry was in his work, intermittent but strong and clear. It was the work of a man with the eye of a great portrait painter—and with all his senses as highly developed as the eye. He recorded. What he recorded was life itself. To each reader Tolstoy lends his eye, his ear, his nose, his sense of touch—and also his joy in the use of these senses; and with these uniquely heightened perceptions the individual reader, looking at life through Tolstoy's eyes, becomes his own poet, in his own way.

This was not, could not, have been clear to the literary world of St. Petersburg and Moscow when the publication of *Childhood* in 1852 announced the rise of a new star. Nobody then could have had any idea of the magnitude of that star. Nobody knew at first its name: *Childhood* had been published over Tolstoy's bare initials. But a star was very much needed. The first great flowering of Russian literature was over. Pushkin, Gogol, Lermontev were dead. The death of the passionately engaged critic Belinsky in 1848 had removed the cutting edge from intellectual discontent, but in the 1850s the major preoccupation of the new generation of writers was still with social reform; with Russia's backwardness and the problem of shaking off the terrible legacy of the past, above all the institution of serfdom; with the corruption, moral squalor, and heartlessness of the bureaucracy, the irresponsibility of the landlords, the philistinism of the new mercantile classes; with the animal degradation of the peasantry; with the frivolity and extravagance of the courtiers; with the reactionary absolutism of a Tsar who excluded the eager and gifted from participation in politics. Together with this went a restless, probing search for the causes of the disease so that a cure might be devised. And it was here that the sharp division between the Westernizers and the Slavophiles arose. In very crude terms, the Westernizers were atheists and agnostics who took their convictions from liberal Western philosophers and revolutionary thinkers, whether Hegel or Saint-Simon, and believed that Russia could be saved only by the injection of Western ideas—and institutions, too, up to a point—to let in light and air. The Slavophiles were Christian aristocrats, who were sustained by the belief that although Russia was sunk deep in obscurantism, corruption, and sloth, her regeneration must come from within by self-purification and the development of traditional Russian attitudes and institutions, above all the village commune. It would be tragic, it seemed to them, for Russia, after all she had suffered, to abandon her unique virtues and simply repeat the terrible mistakes of the West. There was no sharp dividing line between the two groups, represented on the one side by the revolutionary Alexander Herzen, the historian T. N. Granovsky, and the novelist Turgenev, on the other above all by the poet Alexsei Khomyakov, the publicist Ivan Kireyevsky, and the much younger Aksakov brothers. But the general sense of their opposition was clear enough; it was a polarization that persisted through the century and, with variations of emphasis, through the Revolution and to the present day. Both groups were agreed on one thing: namely that Russia, dwelling in darkness for so long, had nurtured a profound and hidden spring of simple virtue, holding close to her bosom a spiritual integrity long lost to the West in its restless, heedless quest for material wealth; and that one day she, Russia, would break out in all her untested strength, astonish the world, and redeem it.

It was against this intellectual and spiritual background, and deeply engaged at the same time in problems of immediate social reform, that the young Tolstoy's seniors and contemporaries in the world of the arts had their being. For the poet Nekrasov, the main task was to keep his *Contemporary* going in the teeth of the censorship and government distrust, as a vehicle for the best reforming spirits of the day. Turgenev himself, the supreme stylist, who was temperamentally as far removed as anyone could be from political strivings, had won fame with his *Sportsman's Sketches* not through their poetry alone, although this was saluted and cherished, but more particularly because of his unforgettable presentation of the degradation of the peasantry. Alexander Ostrovsky in his plays was depicting the wretchedness of spirit among the lower bureaucracy and the trades-people. Saltykov-Shchedrin, a highly placed civil servant, was beginning his career as a satirist of the most savage kind while actually presiding, as Vice-Governor of Ryazan, then Tver, over the sort of society he was holding up to contempt. Fyodor Dostoevsky, six years older than Tolstoy, had published *Poor Folk* before his sentencing to death and reprieve on the scaffold as a member of the Petrashevsky Circle, had served his time in the mines, and was now eating his heart out as a conscript in a Siberian infantry regiment.

Into this self-enclosed, desperately questioning, furiously rejecting world, obsessed with the great problems of the hour, interminably discussing, bickering, intriguing, united only in impotent rejection of the status quo, the voice of Tolstoy—contemplating his own childhood with absorbed, almost hypnotized concentration as though it were the most important thing in the world, indeed, the only thing that mattered, accepting the social structure of that world without the shadow of a question—now sounded with all the impact of a voice from another planet. As indeed it was. It was real, it was marvellously real, and yet it was utterly remote. It must also have brought with it a sense of release. Vanished, when it sounded, were the urgent questionings, the obligatory strivings, the endless, hopeless arguments as to ways and means of transforming Russia into a country fit for Russians to live in. Here was a man who could rise above the struggle and take time off to remind his readers of the eternal truths of human existence. Nekrasov himself, Turgenev, who recognized genius when he saw it, and many others too all metaphorically fell on Tolstoy's neck. He was in the army. Very well, there was nothing strange about that. The army was one of the very few careers open to a gentleman. The heroes of the Decembrist insurrection at the beginning of the reign had almost all been army officers; Lermontev had been a soldier. Soon an officer of the Imperial Guard, Modest Mussorgsky, an army doctor, Alexander Borodin, and a naval cadet, N. A. Rimsky-Korsakov, were to embody in their work the first great flowering of the Russian musical genius. There was nothing strange about Tolstoy being a soldier. What his admirers had no idea of was what a peculiar soldier he was, still less that in *Childhood* he showed himself, already at twenty-three, in flight from the world, seeking, as he was to seek forever, escape from the terrible terms of life, and that necessity of choice between evils which is the condition of maturity, by recovering the innocence of childhood and condemning all adult activity impartially as evil.

They could not see this. Who could possibly have guessed it? And when *Childhood* was followed by the superb, unromanticized reportage of *The Raid*, followed by *Boyhood*, followed by the exact observation of the gambler's temperament in the *Notes of a Billiard Marker*, what struck them was, above all, the controlled realism, unstrident, dismissive, low-keyed— a realism that, when applied to the great problems of the hour, as they thought it inevitably must be, would open the eyes of the world as nothing else could do. And when this was followed by the *Sevastopol Sketches*, particularly the second, with its polemical rejection of all the pretensions of the governmental and military establishments, they must have been convinced that here, at last, was a new and most powerful ally in the fight for

Seeing off recruits. Painting by I. E. Repin.

secular reform. They were wrong. What they were witnessing in the *Sevastopol Sketches* was simply one aspect of the writer's rejection of established order, of any pretensions on the part of anyone at all, good or bad, reactionary or liberal, to lay down the law.

Tolstoy's objection to war was not at that time, or indeed for long afterwards, a conscientious objection to violence as such, but, rather, to the organization of violence. Much later on, in *War and Peace*, he was to justify to himself the heroic aspects of a great patriotic war by glorifying the peasant soldier and (since even Tolstoy had to admit that soldiers in battle have to be led, even if the progress of the battle cannot be controlled) by attributing to Marshal Kutuzov all the imaginary qualities of wisdom and nobility of spirit which, on occasion, he convinced himself he saw in the Russian peasant.

In fact, before Sevastopol, Tolstoy was inclined to respect and admire the better sort of senior officer. He was impressed by General Baratynsky, his commander in the Caucasus. He might soon start to kick against the mechanics of soldiering and those restraints on his freedom that he had at first welcomed as a means of escape from the necessity of choice. He might chafe at the slowness of promotion. But he continued to do well in action. Three times he was recommended for the St. George's Cross, which he coveted but never received. The circumstances are not entirely clear. He told his Aunt Tatiana that he could not be formally awarded the decoration because he was still waiting for his personal papers, without which he was officially deemed non-existent. Certainly there was some truth in this; but it is unlikely that it was the whole truth. For the fact was that, although brave in action, Tolstoy played fast and loose with the regulations and could not be relied upon. It was not simply an absence of what is called team spirit. There have been plenty of officers in all countries who would have held team spirit in contempt, but did their duty by their colleagues, and more. Tolstoy did his duty when he felt like it; that is to say, he had no sense of duty. Towards his senior officers he behaved as he had behaved towards his fellow students at Kazan and as he was soon to start behaving towards his distinguished contemporaries in the literary world. With the Cossacks, with the simple soldiers under his command, he could get on very well: they had something to teach him, he was sure, and he wanted to find out what it was. With them he was absolutely and unassailably the barin: he did not have to assert himself to demonstrate his superiority, which was taken for granted, and he could afford to relax in their company and allow all the warmth in his nature to shine through, as it was later to shine through in his relations with small children. But with the officers he was awkward, stiff, contrary, as though determined to demonstrate his superiority and hold any challenge to it at a distance. It was only when in action, above all in the shared suffering and danger in the Crimea, that he could unbend among his colleagues. Even then, even when he had played his part in the defence of the notorious 4th Bastion at Sevastopol, he seems never to have been quite *there*. We have seen through the eyes of a brother officer how he would suddenly absent himself from duty and ride off to Simferopol for a good, refreshing bout of drinking, gambling, and womanizing—and return overcome with remorse. Here is another glimpse, this time through the eyes of a regular colonel, of the sort of behaviour that, one feels, may have contributed to his failure to win the St. George's Cross:

"Count Tolstoy, as sub-lieutenant of artillery, is in command of two mountain batteries, but he himself roams anywhere he pleases. On 4 August [the date of the battle of Chernaya; August 6 New Style] he attached himself to me, but I could not make use of his pop-guns in the affair, as I was holding the position with the battery guns; on 27 August [when the French captured the Malakov redoubt and resistance collapsed] he again applied to me, but this time without his guns, so, owing to the shortage of officers, I was able to entrust to him the command of five battery guns. This at any rate shows that Tolstoy is eager to smell powder, but only fitfully, as an irregular, avoiding the difficulties and hardships incidental to war. He travels about to different places like a tourist, but as soon as he hears firing he at once appears on the field of battle. When it is over, he is off again at his own discretion wherever fancy takes him. Not everyone is able to make war in so agreeable a manner." *

And Tolstoy himself gives us an insight into his general attitude when he writes: "Now you have seen the defenders of Sevastopol. . . . The principal joyous thought you have brought away is a conviction of the strength of the Russian people; and this conviction you gained, not by looking at all these traverses, breastworks, cunningly interlaced trenches, mines, and cannon, one on top of another, of which you could make nothing; but from the eyes, words and actions—in short, from seeing what is called the 'spirit' of the defenders of Sevastopol." †

* Quoted in Maude, *Life of Tolstoy*, p. 126.
† Ibid., p. 120.

The fortifications, referred to so impatiently and dismissively, had in fact been laid out and raised in a superhuman effort against time (after the disastrous battle of Alma) by, precisely, the defenders of Sevastopol, organized, driven, and inspired by a military engineer of genius, General Todleben. Without them not all the spirit in the world could have held the fortress for more than a few days. Tolstoy would have nothing of them. To have acknowledged the brilliance and necessity of Todleben would have been to acknowledge the validity and necessity of any sort of hierarchical order—perhaps even, later, the genius of Napoleon.

Tolstoy's mass of inconsistencies would have been endearing if only he could have been a little less self-righteous about them. Despising the high command, he himself moved heaven and earth on more than one occasion to get a staff appointment—just as on others he demanded to be transferred to the firing line. In the Crimea he was, in fact, under very high protection, and everyone knew it.

After two years with the army in the Caucasus he was sent on leave and, at the same time, received his promotion to sub-lieutenant. By that time (October 1853) Nicholas had declared war on Turkey, having failed to secure the cooperation of England and France in what was ostensibly a crusade to come to the relief of the Christian peoples of the Balkans who for centuries had been part of the Ottoman Empire, now believed to be in an advanced state of decay. The Western powers saw in the Russian determination to dismember the "sick man of Europe" not a profound concern for the well-being of fellow Christians but an unfolding of a long-term plan to dominate Constantinople and the Straits and emerge as a Mediterranean power.

The newly promoted sub-lieutenant, Count L. N. Tolstoy, was ordered to report not to the Caucasus, but to Bucharest, to the headquarters of Prince Gorchakov's army, which had occupied the Principalities (Moldavia and Wallachia) with the aim of crossing the Danube and moving down the Black Sea coast towards Constantinople. Gorchakov was, of course, a kinsman of the Tolstoys, and the family pulled strings to get Tolstoy appointed as aide-de-camp to the theatre commander. But although the distinguished soldier went out of his way to be pleasant, that particular dream came to nothing. After frittering away some time among the urban delights of Bucharest, Tolstoy was posted to a divisional staff just behind the front, and it was now that he started to experience the realities of major warfare at first hand. At first, without a qualm, he was able to watch from a distance and on high, as it were (from the vantage point of the hill-top garden of the late Turkish Governor) the ritual but quite bloody skirmishing, and the violent cannonading, which accompanied the investment of the elaborate fortifications of Silistria on the river plain. He learned what a battle, with all its inconsequence and frenzied rushing about, looked like from a bird's-eye view. Then, sent down with messages to the fighting troops, he was suddenly brought face to face with blood and smashed bodies on a scale quite different from anything he had known in the Caucasian campaign. He was very deeply shocked and only wanted to get away. But he soon recovered and became deeply interested in the preparations for the impending great assault. While recording with perfect detachment and that eye for caricature disguised as neutral realism the absurdity of Gorchakov's appearance and manner (he gobbled like a turkey-cock), he came to see and admire his remarkable qualities as a patient, careful, resolute commander of men who managed somehow, in spite of his aristocratic assumptions, to identify himself with the trials of the common soldier. And he shared the bitterness and chagrin of his fellow officers when the assault had to be called off in the very moment of its launching, because the Austrians, technically neutral, had built up a great army in Galicia, ready to fall on Gorchakov's rear and cut all his forces off from Russia, or drive them into the sea, unless Nicholas responded to their demands and withdrew from the Principalities.

It was not a smooth withdrawal. The Russians were a long way from home; they were suffering from hunger and disease, and the first part of that long march was embarrassed by hosts of Bulgarian refugees fearing massacre at the hands of the returning Turks. Scenes for *War and Peace*, images of suffering, bloodshed, and chaos, were already registering in Tolstoy's mind. And in the calmness of Gorchakov, who did not repine when the prospect of a major victory was snatched from him, but who seemed, rather, to be pleased that he was not after all required to drive his men on to be slaughtered, there is a foretaste of the idealized Kutuzov.

Meanwhile he went on being Tolstoy. On the day after the raising of the siege of Silistria he declared once again in his diary that he was firmly resolved to devote his life to serving his fellow men. "For the last time I tell myself, 'If I have done nothing for someone else within three days, I shall kill myself.'" He did nothing of the kind. Instead, he went on losing at cards and desperately trying to borrow money. Day after day on the long march back to Russia he went on recording his failures—and doing next to nothing about them. But all the time he was becoming more and more convinced that the thing to do was to cling to his writing. *Boyhood* was finished and about to be published: so was *Notes of a Billiard Marker*. "There is one thing I love more than goodness: fame," he wrote in the course of that long journey home. "I am so ambitious, and this craving in me has had so little satisfaction, that if I had to choose between fame and virtue, I am afraid I would very often choose the former. . . ."

He was still unthinkingly accepting the Russian system as a whole, regretting only that he had not been born into a more exalted position; there is no sign that it ever crossed his mind that he was far more fortunately placed than all but a handful of his fellow countrymen. He could record in his diary: "I spent the whole evening talking to Shubin about our Russian slavery. It is true that slavery is an evil, but an extremely pleasant evil." He was still in the mood he had expressed in an adolescent letter to his brother Sergei when he had first joined the army: "With all my strength I shall help with my guns in the destruction of the predatory and turbulent Asiatics." * Settled now in the garrison town of Kishinev, he was seized with the idea of starting an army periodical called *The Military Gazette*, which was to be a morale-raising exercise supplementing the dry official despatches with real-life tales of heroism on the part of the common soldier, eyewitness accounts of battles, instructive essays on tactics, weapons, and military engineering. He was ready, if necessary, to write the whole thing himself. Prince Gorchakov was impressed by the idea and forwarded a specimen issue to St. Petersburg. But where was the money to come from? Tolstoy himself was deeply in debt. There was only one thing to do: sell off the main house at Yasnaya Polyana.

And so began the farcical episode that expresses the wild, uncentred chaos of Tolstoy's life at this time better than any other single episode. The central block of Yasnaya Polyana was sold for 5000 roubles, taken down, timber by timber, by the new owner, and re-erected some miles away: only the two wings were left. The money arrived almost simultaneously with the Emperor's refusal to countenance a magazine that would not only reflect personal initiative but also introduce the dangerous principle of treating soldiers like human beings. What to do with the money? The obvious thing to do was gamble with it. He gambled and, as usual, lost.

Before this happened he was approaching a major test. In September

* Quoted in Maude, *Life of Tolstoy*, p. 69.

104

1854 the Anglo-French army had landed in the Crimea and things were beginning to go very badly for the Russians. While Tolstoy gambled away his days at Kishinev, the Russians suffered their first major reverses, at Alma and Inkerman, and among the killed was the fellow officer designated as editor of the abortive *Gazette*. Suddenly Tolstoy could no longer bear his spoiled and sheltered existence at Kishinev, where the officers and their wives and mistresses lived in a gay whirl of balls and routs and dinner parties without a thought for their fellow countrymen fighting for their lives from one disaster to another. He applied for a transfer to the front, and early in November found himself in Sevastopol, which had been under siege for some months and was to hold out until September of the following year.

The young gunner officer now found himself involved for the first time in full-scale warfare; in a defensive battle, moreover, in which officers and peasant conscripts were sustained by a passion of patriotism of a kind that had not been experienced in Russia since 1812. Hitherto his military experience had been of the sort to which it was fairly easy to bring the detachment he had so far shown in his attitude to all people and all things: limited actions against Caucasian tribesmen, copy-book manoeuvres and skirmishing in preparation for the grand assault on Silistria. Now he was to live under heavy fire and suffer shoulder to shoulder with his fellow human beings in a desperate, losing battle with an insolent invader. It was to be the most intense and immediate experience of the realities of life and death, of human courage, self-sacrifice, and failure that his life was to offer. If the warring elements in his make-up were ever to be fused together into a coherent whole, it should surely have been under the quite exceptional pressures of the Sevastopol experience. But it did not happen. There was a moment when it looked as though shared fear, shared hardship, shared horror, shared exaltation in comradely endurance, might crack the so far impenetrable shell of self-regard. But it was only a moment.

All through that Crimean year Tolstoy oscillated as wildly as before: the only constant elements against the habitual background of debauchery and gambling were his writing, which he stubbornly pursued in the most trying circumstances, his never-ending, cool-eyed observation of the external world in all its aspects, and his obsessed concern with himself. Even in his approach to his own part in the war, his moods fluctuated without cease. Thus, when he arrived in Sevastopol in November he was at first

Officers in the Caucasus.

irritated to find himself posted not to the fortifications where the action lay, but to the city itself, where the highly coloured civilian life continued amid the swarming military. But he was soon quite happy to be sent off to Simferopol, where he could enjoy the social delights of a city that was also a base, and grumbled angrily when he was taken away from these urban comforts to serve with his battery of light mountain guns at Belbek, an outlying post some miles from Sevastopol, cut off from all life, where he held most of his fellow officers in contempt. It was at Belbek that he gambled away the money received from the sale of the main house at Yasnaya Polyana; and it was from Belbek that from time to time he trotted off to enjoy the night-life at Simferopol. He seemed to have quite forgotten his impulse to take part in the fighting and after some months of idleness at Belbek applied for a staff appointment. He was not at all pleased when he found himself instead posted to the thick of the battle—to the notorious 4th Bastion at Sevastopol, known to the allies as the Flagstaff Bastion, which was under continuous and murderous bombardment from the French at point-blank range. Now, on April 11, 1855, running a cold with a touch of fever, immured in an embattled casemate in daily peril of his life, he wrote: "It makes me furious—especially now that I am ill—to think that nobody can get it into his head that I might be good for something other than cannon-fodder of the most useless kind." But he was brave enough, soon got over his bad temper, and made the most of the next six weeks of intensive siege warfare. Even in the cramped squalor of this troglodyte existence he managed to go on writing, carrying on with *Youth* and his *Sevastopol Sketches*.

"My little soldiers are very nice, I feel quite gay with them," he recorded immediately after his attack of self-pity. And the next day: "The continual attraction of danger, and being able to watch the soldiers I live with, and the sailors, and the ways of making war, is so pleasing that I don't want to leave this place, especially as I should like to be here when the assault comes, if it does."

The fascination of observing—this, it was becoming clearer every day, was now his driving force. Observing and recording. He watched everyone and everything about him with a cool, uncorruptible gaze. One day, many years later, he was to say of the young Maxim Gorky: "Gorky is an unkind man. . . . He has the soul of a spy, he has come into the land of Canaan, where he feels himself a stranger, watches everything that goes

107

Interior of the 4th Bastion at Sevastapol. Lithograph by M. Berg.

Russian artillery in the defense of Sevastapol.

Artillery battery in the Crimea, 1855.

on around him, notices everybody and reports to a god of his own. And his god is a monster. . . ." Tolstoy might have been describing himself.

For a short time in the Crimea it looked as though he was ceasing to be a stranger. He seemed to be aligning himself with common humanity, at least with the peasant soldiers, in travail beneath the many tribulations inflicted upon him by the terms of a hostile universe in general and a harsh governmental system in particular. More than this, he seemed also to be on the side of everything that was decent and considerate in the men who were born to run that system and yet sought to improve it and soften its effects. He showed an eagerness to sort out the good from the bad and to take what action he could—through his writing, that is—to encourage and support the good. Already on the journey from Kishinev to Sevastopol he had been deeply shocked and affronted, as a patriotic Russian, by what he saw of the imbecilities of the higher command, the corruption and muddle of the supply services. His admiration for the patient endurance of the Russian conscript peasant on the one hand and the humanity of a senior commander like Gorchakov on the other had for once given him a focus outside himself. He had seen in Odessa a group of British and French prisoners and had been startled and impressed by their superior physique and pride of bearing: "The air and manner of these men gives me, why I don't know, a sinking certainty that they are far superior to our soldiers," he had written as early as October.[*] And after he had arrived at Sevastopol, having learned in the course of his journey of the scale of the catastrophe at Inkerman, he saw and talked with more prisoners—prisoners from those armies whose equipment, medical services, and flamboyantly incompetent leadership were soon, in England at least, to become a national scandal and shame: "During this trip I became more than ever convinced that Russia must either fall or be completely transformed. . . . The Cossacks want only to plunder, but not to fight, the hussars and lancers demonstrate their military prowess in drunkenness and debauchery, the infantry in thievery and greed. A hideous situation—like army, like government. I spent two hours talking to some English and French wounded. Every soldier among them prides himself on his position and is self-respecting; he feels he is a positive asset to his army. He has good weapons and is skilled in their use, he is young, he has ideas about politics and art, and this gives him a consciousness of his own dignity. On our side: senseless training . . . useless

[*] Quoted in Troyat, *Tolstoy*, p. 118.

111

weapons, floggings, decrepitude, ignorance, and bad equipment and food—dull the last spark of pride in a man. . . ." He was particularly scathing about the beating of the conscripts by their officers and the drunkenness of those same officers. And yet he himself, before long, recorded more than once that he had struck his own men in a sudden burst of fury. And he drank with the best of his colleagues.

Nevertheless, in March 1855, just before going to serve his term in the 4th Bastion, he had been sufficiently moved by the urgent need for a drastic spring-cleaning to see himself in quite a new role: he would compose an elaborate *Plan for the Reform of the Army,* and he actually began to write it: "We have no army, we have a horde of slaves, cowed by discipline, ordered about by thieves and slave traders. . . ." * But after the initial diatribe, and before starting on constructive suggestions, he abandoned what turned out to be his first and last attempt to improve the workings of the Imperial governmental system from, as it were, the inside. This was not his line of country. Indeed, it is easy to see that this sudden enthusiasm for reforming a system on the part of a man who was to reject all systems was only one more manifestation of that limitless personal ambition that had sent him off on so many false starts in the past. Almost at once he was seized with a much bigger and better idea. Instead of reforming the army he would found a new religion.

"Yesterday [he wrote in his diary for March] a conversation about divinity and faith suggested to me a great and tremendous idea, to the realization of which I feel capable of dedicating my whole life.—This is the idea—the founding of a new religion corresponding to the development of mankind: the religion of Christ, but purged of faith and mystery, a practical religion, not promising future bliss but realizing bliss on earth. —I understand that to bring this idea to fulfilment the conscientious labour of generations towards this end will be necessary. One generation will bequeath the idea to the next, and some day fanaticism or reason will achieve it. *Consciously* to contribute to the union of men and religion is the basic idea which I hope will dominate me."

Not even Leo Tolstoy could aim higher than this. Dreams of being a great secular philosopher, a scholar to dazzle all scholars, a great historian, a great agricultural reformer, only yesterday a great military reformer, were, as the saying goes, chicken-feed. He was to be the new Jesus Christ—once he had overcome the little matter of his penchant for cards, drink, and

* Quoted in Troyat, *Tolstoy,* p. 118.

112

whores, outdoing St. Augustine. There was to be no nonsense about humility. He was to hand down the tablets of revealed truth from a great height and harness mankind to the cause of his own self-improvement. He was in corrigible.

But he was indomitable too. Twenty-five years later the author of *War and Peace* and *Anna Karenina* was to take up this "stupendous idea" that had come to him when he had been a subaltern in the Crimea, insisting in effect that since, after much dusty trial and error he, Leo Tolstoy, could not trust himself to improve himself except by denying life (in this way also cheating death), all the world must follow his example.

But for the time being the stupendous idea had to wait while Tolstoy the novelist made ready for his appointment with destiny. Besides working hard at *Youth,* he had written the greater part of the first of his *Sevastopol Sketches,* "Sevastopol in December," using some of the material intended for the abortive *Military Gazette.* When it was published by Nekrasov, its impact on St. Petersburg and Moscow was tremendous. For the first time stay-at-home civilians were given a picture of the realities of war and could identify themselves with the suffering and heroism of the ordinary soldier. The new Emperor read it and was deeply moved, and a legend quickly arose (it was only a legend) that Alexander himself had commanded that this young genius must no longer be exposed to the risk of death in battle. Tolstoy was, indeed, taken out of the Bastion and sent back with his battery to the Belbek River before May was out. But not before he had gathered the material for his second instalment, "Sevastopol in May," which was to be very different in tone, and, because of its strictures on the conduct of the war, was to run into serious trouble with the censor, so that the first published version, to Nekrasov's despair and Tolstoy's fury, was badly mangled.

But what these *Sevastopol Sketches,* including the third instalment, "Sevastopol in August," achieved was to prove once and for all, if proof were needed, that Tolstoy was a born writer whose eyesight, to quote George Moore, "exceeds all eyesight before or since." He had published nothing yet to show that he could write a great novel; but the reportage of the *Sevastopol Sketches,* taken together with his earlier autobiographical work, was enough to show that he was equipped, as far as surface vision and the power to communicate that vision were concerned, as no novelist had ever been equipped. I have recorded his own comment: "The interest with which I observe the soldiers around me, and the sailors, and the ways

Leo Tolstoy in 1855.

Sergei, Nikolai, Dmitri, and Leo Tolstoy. "I was friends with Mitya and respected Nikolenka, but I admired Serezha; I loved him and wished I were he." (*Childhood,* Chapter IX.)

of making war, is so rewarding." It was indeed. That cool, dispassionate eye went on seeing and recording amid scenes of carnage and destruction, even in crises of personal peril, with the same atomizing and clinical precision with which the boy had regarded the mourners, including himself, at his grandmother's funeral; the students, including himself, at Kazan university; the Cossacks, as well as himself, in his Caucasian outpost; the gamblers, including himself, at the pool-room in Tiflis. He watched everyone and everything around him—their behaviour under fire, the faces of the dying, the desperate, untiring work of the surgeons in the dressing-station, the moans and shrieks and agonized heroism of men held down while their limbs were cut off without an anaesthetic.

He was glad, indeed, to have gone through all that. Without it much of *War and Peace* could never have been written. The scene in which Prince Andrew, mortally wounded at Borodino, watches through his own daze of pain the surgeons removing Anatole Kuragin's leg, that "plump white leg," and holding it up, still in its boot, for poor Anatole to see, was a memory from Sevastopol.

The tour of duty in the 4th Bastion lasted only six weeks, but those six weeks had served their purpose. Towards the end he experienced the bloody consequences of a major sortie in which the Russians, suffering extremely heavy casualties, tried to drive the French from the trenches which had been pushed up to within eighty yards of the Bastion itself. Then he was sent off once again to a quiet outpost on the Belbek River, missing the long series of bitter assaults and counter-attacks that continued through the summer. This was the period when he seems to have led a remarkably detached existence, behaving more like a roving war correspondent than a soldier under discipline. But he turned up, as we have seen, in the middle of the battle of Chernaya, which was the last vain attempt to relieve Sevastopol, and he was actually in the city, a few days later, on August 27, when the French stormed the Malakov Redoubt and ran up the Tricolor over the fortifications that had defied them for so long. This was the end.

It was the end, too, of Tolstoy's involvement with the army. He had to stay in uniform for another year (soon promoted to full lieutenant for bravery under fire). But he contrived to get himself sent back as a courier to St. Petersburg, celebrating his farewell by losing a frightening sum at cards on his last night; and there, while the defeated and shattered army straggled back to regroup, while the new Emperor, Alexander, sued for peace, obtained for himself a sinecure post as inspector of a factory manufacturing military rockets. He had been very deeply moved by the spectacle of a defeated army, retreating in confusion, embittered and shamed. He had formed a part of that army. For a moment he had identified himself with his "nice little soldiers." But it was all over now; and although in St. Petersburg he wrote the last of his *Sevastopol Sketches,* the mood, the whole attitude was different: his experience was no longer actual and personally overwhelming. It had become material for a would-be novelist.

Would-be, because by no stretch of imagination could anything that Tolstoy had yet done be called a novel. He was still writing what amounted to inspired reportage: scenes from the life of Leo Tolstoy, sometimes straight autobiographical reporting, sometimes with the attributes of one character transferred to another (as when, in *Boyhood,* he substituted for his own father the father of one of his childhood friends), sometimes with a contrived fictional gloss. But although he had created what was virtually a new genre in Russia (deeply influenced for a time by Laurence Sterne, Stendhal, and others), he had not shown any gift at all for taking the essence of an experience, shaping it, buttressing it with the faithful rendering of things seen, which in itself was his supreme gift, and manipulating the whole to convey a poetic vision, a coherent philosophy of life, or even a social purpose. All he knew now was that he wanted to write. "My career is literature!" he exclaimed in his diary immediately after the fall of Sevastopol. "Write! Write! Beginning tomorrow I shall work at it all my life, or abandon everything, rules, religion, decency—everything!"

For the moment it did not matter that his writing appeared to be unrelated to any central core: his gifts were so manifest and abounding that his contemporaries could only stand in awe of them. Soon it would begin to matter a great deal.

Deputies of the Caucasian tribes to the coronation of Tsar Alexander II in 1856.

Opposite: Soldiers of the Imperial Guard.

Coronation procession of Tsar Alexander II, August
1856. It was for the coronation that Valerya Arsenev
went to Moscow, outraging Tolstoy with her frivolity.

Opposite: The coronation of Tsar Alexander II.

Gala performance at the newly rebuilt Bolshoi Theater, part of the celebrations for the coronation of the new Tsar.

N. A. Nekrasov, editor of *The Contemporary*, 1861.

4

"MY CAREER IS LITERATURE"

From the moment of his arrival in St. Petersburg, Tolstoy entered a new dimension. Hitherto he has been visible to us almost exclusively from the inside. Scattered brief references from fellow students and fellow officers have enabled us to glimpse his outward appearance and manner. We know what he looked like, or thought he looked like, in the mirror. But almost everything we have so far seen of his development has been supplied by his autobiographical writings in conjunction with the diary. Now, suddenly, he emerges into the world, and for the rest of his life will be under constant scrutiny from the most articulate of his contemporaries.

No young writer of genius ever received more encouragement from his seniors and contemporaries. At first he made an exciting, if somewhat barbaric, impression among the intellectuals of St. Petersburg grouped round Nekrasov. Most of these were a few years older. All were city dwellers, physically soft, revolving in small, overlapping circles, knowing each other's strengths and weaknesses inside out, sometimes sleeping with each other's wives, speaking the same language, absorbed in the tricks of the same trade, endlessly discussing without issue. They shared the characteristics of literary coteries everywhere in the world, but were even more introverted than is usual in the West because they were confined, as it were, to a fortress under constant siege from the big guns of the autocracy—and, at the same time, more politically minded in the sense that all were in revolt against the manifest social evils of the day. Tolstoy the aristocrat, the soldier straight from the battlefield, the self-taught writer of magnificent gifts, was more than ignorant (oblivious, in fact) not merely of the problems that exercised all minds, but also of the very circumstances that governed the lives of his new friends. Not handsome, but very striking—now with shortish hair brushed up and back, a rather dashing clipped moustache, that shattering and uncomfortably steady gaze from under heavy eyebrows, cloaked, epauletted, his sword decorated with the ribbon of the order of St. Anne—he was a strange mixture of the exotic and the crude. Now he was brashly arrogant and assertive, laying down the law on matters of which he knew nothing; now he was all diffidence and charm. But the diffidence never lasted long. "What a delightful person, and what intelligence!" wrote Nekrasov to his friend, the critic V. P. Botkin, soon after his first meeting with Tolstoy. "A likeable, energetic, generous young man, a real falcon! Perhaps an eagle! I liked him better than his writing, and, God knows, that's good enough! He is not handsome, but he has an extremely attractive face, at once forceful and gentle. His glance is a caress."

Others liked him too. Ill-educated, almost perversely ignorant he might be, but at least his sceptical approach to all received opinion was a sign of a natural originality of spirit. And already that extraordinary power of animal magnetism, which had showed faintly in his student days, was gaining strength. It was the power that many years later was to cause one· of the teachers at his school in Yasnaya Polyana to write: "I have never met a man capable of firing another mind to such white heat. In the course of my spiritual relationship with him I felt as though electric sparks were striking into the very depths of my soul and setting in motion all kinds of thoughts and plans and decisions." *

Few were able to resist this magnetism, but within a very short time his new friends were asking themselves and each other, with varying degrees of irritation and exasperation, what on earth it was that made them put up with this exacting, imperious, sometimes even malevolent newcomer whom they so warmly welcomed to their fold and who rewarded them too often with derision and contempt. First he was quarrelling with the Westernizers, then with the Slavophiles. They were none of them, he would assure them, as he sprawled at his ease on a sofa in the homes of one or another of them, any good. All were chatterboxes, half-baked theoreticians

* Quoted in Troyat, *Tolstoy,* p. 220.

126

who knew nothing of life. One group would be censured for aping Western ways and turning their backs on the Russian tradition; another for turning their backs on the culture of the West and glorifying all that was disreputable and obscurantist in the Russian tradition. . . . Everywhere was insincerity, posing, idle pretension, and intrigue. Not a living soul among them had the least idea of the meaning of conviction.

But what, precisely, were the convictions of Count Leo Tolstoy? Nobody seems to have been bold or discourteous enough to ask this question to his face. Perhaps because it was clear that he had none. One of the Aksakov brothers, Konstantin, wrote to Turgenev after his first meeting with Tolstoy in Moscow: ". . . A strange person! Why does he behave so immaturely? Why so unsettled? . . . It seems as though there is still no centre in him."

It did indeed. He was writing quite hard throughout the year 1856. But there seemed to be no clear direction behind his talents. He completed *Youth,* and he demonstrated again and again his marvellous powers of observation and description in a number of sketches, notably *The Snowstorm,* which was based on an incident on his journey from the Caucasus to Yasnaya Polyana, where he had been lost, lucky not to have died, in one of those terrible Russian blizzards that obliterate the world and make it all but impossible to breathe. He tried his hand at a new form of contrived story-telling, *Two Hussars.* In *A Landlord's Morning* he produced a shattering commentary on the degradation of the Russian peasant. But even this was only a fragment of a novel that was never completed; and the ending, grafted on to a series of character studies, was unconvincing in the extreme. What would he do with these talents, now that he had, in effect, brought his autobiography up to date? What, apart from an obsessive and jealous insistence on his own total sincerity and goodness, as opposed to the insincerity and venality of almost everybody else, did he stand for? What, in any case, did all this talk about sincerity and love amount to? Sincerity about what? Love for whom?

With these misgivings went considerable bewilderment at his manner of life. For although the young Count from the Crimea spent a great deal of time in literary circles, he also aroused the suspicion of his new colleagues, no doubt also a certain envy, with his weakness for high society. For a man who held the establishment in open contempt, he spent a surprising amount of time in the aristocratic salons of St. Petersburg. Why? Even more extraordinary was his unconcealed passion for low life. He still gambled a great deal, and in fairly disreputable company. He still frequented brothels and pursued the gypsies. Turgenev had to bear the brunt of this from the very beginning. He had given Tolstoy the freedom of his rather splendid apartment and had been looking forward to long and stimulating conversation with the young genius late into the night. Instead, for much of the time, the young genius used his home like a hotel. One morning the poet Fet called on Turgenev and had to converse in whispers for fear of waking up Tolstoy, asleep in the next room: "It is like this all the time," Turgenev explained. "He came here straight from his battery at Sevastopol, moved in with me, and started going the pace. Drinking bouts, gypsies, cards all night long, and then he sleeps like the dead until two in the afternoon. At first I tried to quieten him down, but now I've given it up as a bad job." The wildness which Turgenev at first assumed was the sudden release of animal spirits after the hardships of the Crimea went deeper than that. Months later Tolstoy was still at it—and still recording the old self-disgust in his diary: "Horrible! But absolutely the last time," he wrote towards the end of April after a visit to a brothel. "This is no longer temperament but habitual lechery." And a few weeks later, of a visit to an amusement park: "Disgusting! Girls, stupid music, girls, an artificial nightingale, girls, heat, cigarette smoke, girls, vodka, cheese, wild shrieks, girls, girls, girls!"

It was no wonder that his new friends began to raise their eyebrows when this self-assured young man tore himself away from his orgies or turned up in their apartments the evening after a fashionable ball to instruct them in the worthlessness of their ideas. He had every reason to be determined not to be caught up in the world of second-rate intellectuals. But it was not simply impatience with the second-rate that drove the young Tolstoy to call down a plague on every house. Nekrasov himself, though his private life was squalid, was a gifted minor poet, and he strove with courage, persistence, and great intelligence to keep his *Contemporary* going as the forum and the citadel of liberal thought and respectable art in the teeth of a hostile and all-powerful government. The *Contemporary* had been founded by Pushkin, and Nekrasov saw himself as the guardian of a precious trust. The critic and gifted translator A. V. Druzhinin had done almost as much for Tolstoy, and, indeed, in his lucid moments Tolstoy respected him deeply, liked him, and allowed him, as he allowed nobody else, to criticize his work. Ivan Goncharov, who was to achieve immortality with his novel *Oblomov*, was far from being a second-rater.

The circle of writers associated with *The Contemporary:*
(seated, left to right) I. A. Goncharov, I. S. Turgenev, A. V.
Druzhinin, A. N. Ostrovsky; (standing, left to right) L. N.
Tolstoy, D. V. Grigorovich, 1856.

P. V. Annenkov, another critic and a close friend of Turgenev, was very much on the side of the angels. And yet Tolstoy could write in his diary of these men to whom he owed so much: "Goncharov, Annenkov—all disgust me; especially Druzhinin. And they disgust me because I want affection, friendship, but they are not capable of it."

He set about demanding affection and friendship in a very strange way, not merely by contradicting all the received ideas of liberal circles, but by attributing evil motives to all those who held them. Perhaps the most revealing of all his personal relationships was his friendship with Turgenev.

Turgenev, even though his major novels were still unwritten, was incomparably the greatest artist in prose then working in Russia. He was thirty-seven. He came of an old family with good connections, and his appalling mother, who had tyrannized over him as she notoriously tyrannized over her serfs, had left him a rich inheritance, far greater than Tolstoy's own. He had already suffered exile for offending the authorities with his obituary of Gogol. He already enjoyed great fame for his *Sportsman's Sketches* and he had produced a number of stories and plays that gave promise of the novels to come. He was manifestly a genius. With all this, he had travelled widely, and the cultural life of Europe was open to him as to no other Russian of that day. And he was the kindest, the gentlest, the most generous man imaginable. He gave to anyone who asked. His own nature was so open, he was so incapable of suspecting the motives of others until dishonesty, treachery, or bad faith was proved by their actions, that he was forever being exploited by the ignoble. And if this quality of innocence seems at odds with the sharpness of his perceptions as revealed in his writing, the explanation is that he accumulated a very extensive experience of human perfidy. He had a superb eye and also a powerful analytical mind which enabled him to draw exact conclusions from his experience. As Edmund Wilson has said, referring to Turgenev's remarkable insight into the psychology of a villain, once the villainy was recognized, "It was from observation of others that Turgenev had learned how such people behaved; his own character gave no key to their conduct, and it never at first occurred to him that there was anything sinister about them."

His humility was deep. Nobody was less of a poseur either to himself or others; nobody was less arrogant. Although he came to resent the desperate, almost life-long infatuation that held him in bondage to the singer Pauline Viardot, Maria Malibran's sister, and was aware of its ludicrous side, he never attempted to conceal his condition from the world. As an artist he lacked jealousy or envy. He welcomed new talent wherever he found it. He was to be the much loved friend of Gustave Flaubert, Georges Sand, Prosper Merimée, Henry James, and many others. When he came under attack, as he did, from his own co-nationals, it was because the conservatives saw in him a dangerous liberal, the liberals a reactionary.

It is desirable to dwell on Turgenev's nature because it was in almost every way the antithesis of Tolstoy's. Not to put too fine a point on it, the chaotic young man of twenty-seven was, for the first time in his life, about to enter the orbit of a man of great gifts who was manifestly his moral superior. His response to this test—for such it was—revealed a great deal: it was destructive in the extreme.

Turgenev was far from being a saint; he was simply a good man whose lack of pretension and unawareness of his own goodness only served to emphasize to the younger man's all-seeing eye his moral superiority. Tolstoy did not like it. He had basked in Turgenev's generous praise at a distance. From the Crimea he had dedicated *The Woodfelling* to the master and had been delighted by the generosity of Turgenev's response. He had eagerly accepted the invitation to stay with Turgenev when he got to St. Petersburg. But almost at once he started to behave so offensively that a lesser man than Turgenev would have shown him the door and refused to have anything more to do with him. Tolstoy never lost an occasion to provoke the older man into losing his temper or to humiliate him in public. This has generally been thought of as simply part and parcel of his, Tolstoy's, compulsive need to declare his own originality and incorruptibility by contradicting everybody, no matter what they said, by denying their gods, no matter what they were. And this need to challenge obviously entered into it. But it seems far more likely that vis-à-vis Turgenev, what Tolstoy was really doing was rejecting with all his force the knowledge, which he could not escape, that Turgenev was a better man. Sometimes working himself up into a fury, sometimes taunting coldly and maliciously, he knew how to drive poor Turgenev to distraction by pouring scorn on his dearest beliefs—and with that devastating stare from the little, half-closed eyes. Turgenev himself confessed to his old friend V. M. Garshin "that he had never experienced anything so disagreeable as that piercing look which, coupled with two or three venomous remarks, was enough to

131

drive a man mad unless he had considerable self-control." * It was the look of a man who seizes at a glance on the other's weaknesses, and often it would be accompanied by a slight ironical smile of ineffable superiority. It was a look wholly out of place among friends in decent society. "I know all your tricks," it seemed to say. "If you think you can pull the wool over my eyes, so much the worse for you!" It injected into any company in which Tolstoy found himself an element of vulgarity.

We have the famous story told to Fet by the short-story writer Dmitri Grigorovich of one of the quarrels in Nekrasov's apartment. Tolstoy has goaded Turgenev beyond endurance. The great giant of a man, gentle, physically soft, with his magnificent head and great eyes which simply could not comprehend the violence in the young man, "jumps up and marches up and down the room with enormous strides: 'I can't take any more of this! I've got bronchitis!' 'Bronchitis!' growls Tolstoy. 'Bronchitis is an imaginary disease! Bronchitis is a metal!' " Nekrasov, the host, stands there with a sinking heart. "He is as frightened of losing Turgenev as he is of losing Tolstoy, because both are pillars of *The Contemporary,* and he tries to steer a middle course. We are all at our wit's end and don't know what to say. Tolstoy is lying full-length on an oriental divan in the middle of the room, sulking. Turgenev, the skirts of his short jacket spread wide, keeps marching back and forth with his hands in his pockets through all the rooms of the apartment. Trying to ward off catastrophe, I approach the divan and say, 'Tolstoy, dear fellow, don't be so upset. You've no idea how much he loves you and respects you!' 'I shall not tolerate,' says Tolstoy with flaring nostrils, 'his malicious provocations. Look at him now, pacing up and down on purpose, wagging his democratic haunches at me!' "

When he was not being provocatively calm, he could put on a show of angry violence. He was in the mood to pull everything down to his own level, and his own level at that time was as low as it was ever to be. He did not content himself with attacking his new friends for their ineffective drawing-room liberalism. He attacked them through everything they loved. He was particularly violent about Shakespeare and Homer (Druzhinin was an accomplished translator of Shakespeare), who, he declared, were worthless phrasemakers. He was violent about Herzen, who, far from being an ineffective liberal, had twice suffered arrest and exile at the hands of the Third Section (secret police), and was now conducting his revolutionary campaign against the autocracy from London. He would actively seek out

* Quoted in Troyat, *Tolstoy,* p. 133.

Leo Tolstoy as an officer, ca. 1856.

the most wounding things to say—as once, knowing that Turgenev idolized Georges Sand, he announced at a dinner party given by Nekrasov that if her heroines had actually existed, the only thing to do with them would be "to lash them to the common hangman's cart and drag them through the streets of St. Petersburg." When Turgenev protested, Tolstoy was so rude that the poor man was prostrated for days afterwards. Even Nekrasov, the peacemaker, confessed on that occasion that he had been on the edge of a fatal quarrel with his young genius: "He disgusted us all and showed himself in his worst light," he wrote to their mutual friend Botkin. On another occasion Tolstoy coldly turned on Turgenev: "I refuse to believe that what you say expresses your conviction. Here I stand, with a dagger or a sword in my hand, and I say, 'So long as I live no one shall enter this room!' That is conviction. But you all try to hide your real thoughts from each other, and you call *that* conviction!"

"There is not one natural word or gesture in him," Turgenev one day complained. "He is for ever posing, and I cannot understand this ridiculous affection for a wretched title of nobility." *

Poor Turgenev—it was hard, it was impossible, to tell when the young man was deliberately posing, bullying, hectoring, with his very strong streak of sadism; or when he was quite carried away by black anger against the world for being what it was, against himself, against his new friends for putting up with him and refusing to quarrel with him. There was some sort of a volcanic movement brewing within him at this time. He was beside himself. Nobody could know, least of all he himself, that the internal pressures were beginning to build up for the stupendous and unheralded eruption that would be *War and Peace.* Seven more years were still to be endured before that seismic release. What was happening now, in the early months of 1856, was a premature, undirected, violent overflow of frustrated energy. Soon the movement was to be blocked by its own lava-flow, as it were, and for a number of years of travel and experimental activities of various kinds he and all those who admired his talents were to despair about his writing future. For six years, from 1857 to 1863, he virtually dried up. But at this time, when almost every night he had a quarrel to record in his diary ("Quarrelled with Turgenev, this time for good, I think"; "Insulted every one; Turgenev went home. . . . I am depressed"), he was writing very hard.

That his black mood went much deeper than the causes he attributed

* Quoted in Troyat, *Tolstoy,* p. 133.

134

to it was shown by his behaviour when his brother Dmitri (Mitya) died of consumption at Orel in January 1856. In some ways Dmitri was a caricature of Tolstoy himself, swinging from almost insane self-abnegation in youth to a life of uncontrolled debauchery, then insisting on setting up house with the prostitute, Masha, who had given him, at twenty-six, his first experience of the flesh. Now he was dying. Tolstoy went to see him as he lay tended by his Masha, but stayed only an hour or two. An hour or two was long enough to give him the scene he was later to use for the squalid death-bed scene of Levin's brother in *Anna Karenina*. When, three weeks later, Dmitri died, he did not go to the funeral. When the news reached him, he was intent on going out to a reception given by his relative the Countess Alexandra Tolstoy, his chief friend at the Petersburg Court. He sent round a note saying that he could not come because of a death in the family. But almost at once his resolution weakened: he dressed and went off to the party. We remember that moment in *War and Peace* when Pierre Bezukhov, having promised Prince Andrew not to go to the carousal at Anatole Kuragin's, broke his promise, arguing himself out of it like a sophist. To his hostess Tolstoy calmly announced: "What I wrote to you this morning was not true." Much later, in his *Recollection*, he was to write about his treatment of his dying brother: "I was full of conceit and had come to Orel from St. Petersburg, where I had been going out into society. I pitied Dimitri, but not very much."

Almost the only person who could manage Tolstoy at this time was indeed his so-called Aunt, Alexandra Tolstoy. She was in fact a first cousin once removed, only ten years older than Tolstoy, firmly entrenched at court as lady-in-waiting to the Grand Duchess Marya Nikolayevna, sister of the new Tsar, Alexander II. She was charming, elegant, sensitive, intelligent, and cheerfully devout. For years to come her tender but also critical and sharply astringent affection for her uncontrollable "nephew" was to mean for him in maturity what Aunt Tatiana had meant in youth —but with the difference of physical attraction. She could not only manage him and provide him with a refuge from himself, she was also the first woman who was not a whore or a peasant or a Cossack girl to whom Tolstoy knew how to talk. It is not too much to say that she was the only woman with whom he was ever to have a civilized adult relationship. He had proved himself incapable of forming an attachment of equals with any girl of his own class. He was able to come to terms with Alexandra

135

because, though sexually attractive, she was too old for him to think of marriage, too devout to think of a liaison. With her he was secure; and as though to buttress this security, he made a joke, which stuck, of addressing her always as "Grandmama"—*Babushka*. It was through her, more than anyone else, that Tolstoy was able to exploit the privileges of his rank and enter salons and drawing-rooms which would otherwise have excluded him because of his manners. It was thus to her more than anyone that we owe the marvellous pictures of St. Petersburg high society in *War and Peace*.

When Turgenev, enraged, once exclaimed, "Why do you come here among us? This is not the place for you! Go to your Princess," he was speaking more truly than he knew. For mingled with Tolstoy's impatience with chattering, loose-living intellectuals was the contempt of the aristocrat for the parvenu. Tolstoy might, when it suited him, ruthlessly expose the emptiness and falseness of the highest circles in the land. But to these circles he belonged, and from them the history of Russia took its meaning —aristocrats and peasant serfs living together in the intimacy of a symbiotic relationship which had no use for bourgeois sensibilities and aspirations. It is worth recording that the bored, cold, perfectly mannered Prince Vasili Kuragin, who dominates Anna Pavlovna's reception in the opening pages of *War and Peace,* is nevertheless a man who gets things done, a man who, when he reluctantly promises the widowed Princess Drubetskoy to have her son transferred to the Guards, remembers his promise and knows how to persuade the Emperor. At the same time, the manner affected by Prince Vasili is affected also by the younger Prince Andrew, with all his coldness and disdain, who represents certain elements in Tolstoy's own make-up: his worldly side, his fear and distrust of life, his contempt for the pretensions of others, his rejection of human relationships. It is noteworthy that it is only with Pierre Bezukhov, who represents the clumsy, uncontrollable, dreaming, violent, eager, but often uncomprehending elements of Tolstoy (an eternal adolescent, that is, who is also frightened), and with an enchanting child, Natasha, that Prince Andrew becomes a human being. And some of the conversations between Prince Andrew and Pierre reflect Tolstoy's own internal dialogue as revealed not only in his diary and his note-books, but also in his conduct.

Meanwhile, through that year of 1856, which had begun so badly with Dmitri's death and the bitter quarrelling with Turgenev, he continued

Countess Alexandra Tolstoy, Tolstoy's cousin, "Babushka." "As a ray of light may shine out from under some door into a dark corridor, so, when I glance back at my long, dark life, the recollection of Alexandra is always a bright ray."

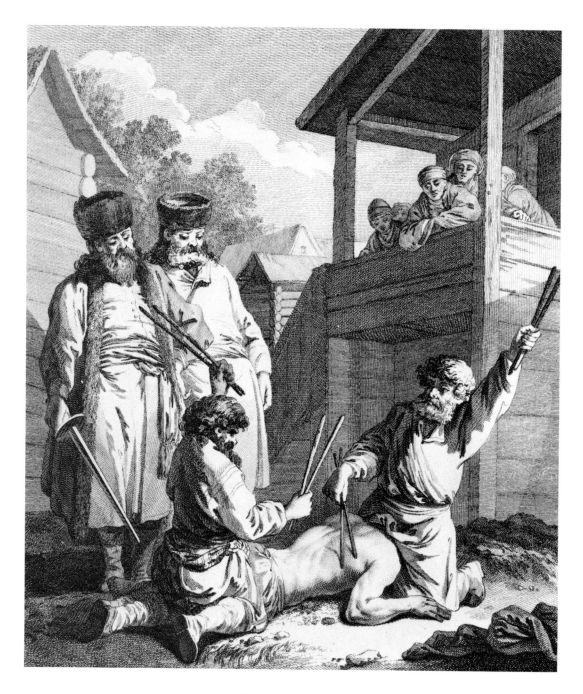

Punishing a serf.

to flounder. And there were two other major episodes which, in their very different ways, illuminated further aspects of that complex character: his attitude to the serfs, and his attitude to women.

In 1856 it was clear that very soon something, at last, was to be done about abolishing serfdom. Catherine had condemned the serf system at the beginning of her reign and ended by tightening the bonds as never before. The youthful Alexander I had ardently desired abolition, and then lost heart and fallen into reaction. Nicholas I, for all his absolutist temper, had perceived the necessity for action but allowed himself to be deflected by the power of vested interests and the fear of peasant risings. But Alexander II meant business. In March 1856 he announced that it was better to "abolish serfdom from above, rather than wait for it to abolish itself from below." He set up a committee to draft proposals for reform. And the obstructions immediately put in the way of that committee by a nobility supposedly obedient to the least wishes of the Tsar united all the liberal intellectuals, the conservatives too, in such an uproar of indignation that Tolstoy himself was forced to start thinking.

As usual with him, to think, or to half think, was to act; and to act meant to put himself out in front. He was surrounded by men who for years had been obsessed by the national disgrace of serfdom, while he had taken it for granted. His new acquaintance, the writer D. V. Grigorovich, had done a great deal to open the eyes of his countrymen with his tales of peasant life. Turgenev had not limited himself to writing *A Sportsman's Sketches,* which had had a powerful impact on the new Tsar himself. The moment he had come into his inheritance, he had acted quietly and without fuss to give his domestic serfs their freedom and to persuade his peasant serfs that they would be better off paying him rent for land they could think of as their own than toiling as bond labourers on their master's estates. Those estates, moreover, were far greater than Tolstoy's own inheritance: in addition to the Spasskoye property, which was the family seat, Turgenev owned ten other estates—some thirty thousand acres in all, with many thousands of serfs.

But once Tolstoy so belatedly decided that it was time to do something about his own few hundred serfs, it seems not to have occurred to him to discuss the problem with those of his new friends who had thought about it. On the contrary, it was up to him to take the lead in the matter of abolition and show others how it should be done. And to this end he very quickly prepared an elaborate project for his own estate, which he then proceeded to lay before the relevant civil servants as a model plan. Since these were not unnaturally non-committal, being actively engaged in working out the master-plan for the whole of Russia, which would take several years to mature, Tolstoy decided to act on his own. Off to Yasnaya Polyana he went, his heart brimming over with noble intent, and in the teeth of Aunt Tatiana's stubborn disapproval, gave orders for all the peasants to assemble next day to hear what he had to say. In his diary that night the scourge of the Petersburg liberals exclaimed: "When I compare myself as I now am with my old memories of Yasnaya, I see how far I have progressed towards a liberal approach. . . ." And, of Aunt Tatiana: "A hundred years of explaining would not make her see the injustice of serfdom." And again: "I am beginning to develop a silent hatred of my aunt, in spite of all her affection."

But the hatred was soon transferred to the peasants themselves. Tolstoy's plan for them was very like Turgenev's old abortive plan: immediate liberation, the landlord to be compensated by rent for thirty years, then their freeholds granted outright to all tenants. Tolstoy was shocked and outraged by the sceptical reception of this magnanimous plan. Turgenev had run into the same resistance some years earlier. And there was now additional cause for peasant suspicion. Since Alexander's announcement of his determination to do away with serfdom, one of those wild Russian rumours had swept into the farthest corners of the land: very soon, on the occasion of his coronation, the Tsar was going to free all the serfs absolutely and give them the land for themselves. So, the Yasnaya peasants began to mutter: what was the young master up to? Quite clearly he was trying to get a jump ahead of the game and trick them into paying him rent for what would be theirs for nothing if they waited a little longer. There was no resentment against the young master. Obviously he had a clever head on his shoulders, and good luck to him! But he was not the only one who could see round corners. So, no thank you—unless the barin gives us the land outright, no freedom for us. . . .

Tolstoy was furious, and he worked himself up into something like a panic, lashing out in letters to his Petersburg and Moscow friends at their absurdity, their iniquity, even, in pretending that the *muzhik* was fit for anything but slavery. He seems to have been genuinely frightened by the magnitude of the gulf between the peasant, in whom so many pretended to see the salvation of Russia, and himself and all his kind. And he

140

was driven to address an extraordinary letter to his acquaintance, Count Dmitri Bludov, a former Minister of the Interior, who had been working on the problems of abolition for nearly twenty years, warning him that the authorities had by their own temporizing allowed the situation to get out of hand, that if something (he did not specify what) were not done fast there would be a peasant insurrection on a colossal scale: "If the serfs are not free in six months, we are in for a holocaust. Everything is ripe for it. Only one criminal hand is needed to fan the flame of rebellion, and we will all be consumed in the blaze." *

Many years were to pass before Tolstoy finally identified himself with the muzhik, and then only as part of the process of denying the validity of everything that was comprehended in the slow and tortured movement whereby mankind had sought to raise itself from the mud. And during all those years he oscillated between impatient dismissal of the masses, something very like hatred of the people who would not allow him to help them on his own terms, and occasional bouts of abstract idealization. When he was at Yasnaya he continued to take the serf girls as his fancy took him; with one of them, Aksinya, a handsome married woman, who bore him a child, he became for a time infatuated. But this was a special case. Aksinya he saw as a human being, but the serfs as a class were irredeemable. The only hope lay in the children. Over them it might be possible to establish an influence before corruption set in. Thus it was that at the end of the decade he established the first of his schools.

Even in the Crimea, when he was living, suffering, and fighting with peasant conscripts, he was unable to get them into steady focus or develop a settled attitude towards them. At one moment they were "my nice little soldiers," in the next a rabble. In one mood they were thieves and looters in uniform, in another the salt of the earth, willingly going to their deaths in a cause they did not understand. Even while he was celebrating, in the *Sevastopol Sketches*, the virtues of the peasant in arms, he was beginning to write the novel—finally published, unfinished, as *A Landlord's Morning* —based on his observations during that brief period at Yasnaya when he had tried to reform his peasant's agricultural practices. This turned out to be, in effect, a series of sketches, devastatingly exact images of individual peasant squalor, bigotry, idleness, and degradation: immaculately accurate on the surface, immaculately heartless, absolutely hopeless. Yet while thinking on these lines he could still write in his diary: "The common people

* Quoted in Troyat, *Tolstoy*, p. 141.

are so far above us in the work they do and in the privations of their lives, that it seems wrong for one of us to write anything bad about them. Bad there is in them, but it is better to say of them (as of the dead) only what is good. . . . Who can be interested in the vices of this miserable but worthy class? There is more good than bad in them; it is therefore more natural and more generous to seek the causes of the former than of the latter."

This egregious passage, taken together with, on the one hand, the *Sevastopol Sketches,* and, on the other, *A Landlord's Morning,* highlights the profound fragmentation of Tolstoy's temperament. The peasant soldiers at Sevastopol—brave, cheerful, and long-suffering—are the same individuals as the peasants at Yasnaya—idle, bigoted, and sly. Both aspects of these people are shown in action, beautifully rendered, but exclusively from the outside. Only one thing is missing, and that is the human soul which somewhere—beneath all the surface appearances so perfectly rendered, beneath the crushing failures so pitilessly exposed—links all humanity in kinship: not only the peasants among themselves, but also "that miserable but worthy class" with Count Leo Tolstoy.

Compare for a moment Tolstoy's rendering of one of his exceptional peasants, the able, hard-working, and prosperous peasant Dutlov among his bee-hives in *A Landlord's Morning,* with Turgenev's presentation of Hor, much the same sort of individual, in *A Sportsman's Sketches.* Turgenev's powers of characterization are strong, but never the equal of Tolstoy's. Although we see Hor clearly enough, we do not see him with the same overwhelming immediacy as Dutlov. Both are successful creations. But with Turgenev's Hor we find ourselves humanly involved. He is one of us. He is an open-ended character. We have met him, are interested in him, guess a good deal about him, and want to know more. Dutlov, on the contrary, is a closed character. He stands before us, his appearance, his gestures, his tones of voice, even his motivation of the moment, perfectly rendered. As an object he is complete in himself. But an object he is. Tolstoy might have been describing with loving exactitude not a human being but an animal.

And, indeed, he was later to describe real animals in just this way. Enthralled by a story Tolstoy made up about an old, broken-down horse they saw on a walk together, Turgenev once said to him: "In a previous incarnation you must have been a horse." But in fact, if Tolstoy spoke of the broken-down horse as he was much later to describe with such spell-binding delicacy of perception Vronsky's thoroughbred in *Anna Karenina*, what Turgenev was admiring was not, as he imagined, true empathy—in the sense that Tolstoy could himself feel like a horse—but a rendering so exact of the appearance and behaviour of a horse, minutely observed, the details recorded with total recall, that it was Turgenev who was being made really to see a horse for the first time, so that he himself for a moment became that horse.

Consider the passage in *Anna Karenina* referred to above. There is no finer or purer example of the Tolstoy treatment: "Frou-Frou was a medium-sized horse, and by no means without faults. She was slenderly built. Her chest, though deep and powerful, was narrow. Her hindquarters fell away rather too much, and her forelegs, even more her hind legs, showed a marked inward curvature. Neither fore- nor hind-legs were particularly well-developed; but to make up for that she was exceptionally broad across the saddle. . . . Her cannon-bones, seen from the front, seemed no thicker than a finger, but were unusually thick when seen from the side. She possessed, however, in the highest degree a quality which made one forget all her defects: that quality was *blood*—the blood that *tells,* as they say in English. The muscles stood out sharply beneath the network of veins stretched in the fine mobile skin, smooth as satin, and seemed hard as bone. Her lean head with prominent, sparkling, lively eyes, broadened out at the nose to the flared nostrils with their bloodshot membranes. Her whole appearance, and particularly about the head, was spirited and yet gentle. She was one of those creatures who do not speak only because the mechanical construction of their mouths makes speech impossible.

"As soon as Vronsky entered she drew in a deep breath, and turning her prominent eyes so that the whites showed bloodshot, she gazed from the other side of the box at the newcomers, gave her muzzle a shake, and shifted restlessly from one foot to another.

" 'There—you see how nervous she is,' said the Englishman.

" 'Oh, you beauty!' said Vronsky.

"But the nearer he came the more agitated she grew. Only when he reached her head did she suddenly quieten down, and the muscles quivered beneath her fine and tender coat. Vronsky stroked her strong neck, smoothed back a lock of her mane that had got on the wrong side of her sharply defined withers, and brought his face close to her dilated nostrils, delicate as a bat's wing. Her extended nostrils loudly inhaled and exhaled

143

her breath; she set back one of her finely pointed ears with a start and stretched out her black firm lips towards Vronsky, as if wishing to catch hold of his sleeve. But remembering her muzzle she jerked it up, and again began shifting from one of her finely chiselled hooves to the other."

We read that passage with the joy of discovery. We know, we feel, what it is to be a race-horse being visited by its master in its box. But Tolstoy has not told us what it is. He has given us the image in a sort of ecstasy of delight in its uniqueness. The reader does the rest. It is the same with so many of Tolstoy's descriptions. For example, the unparalleled description of the view from the Russian lines of Borodino, swimming through the early morning mist as the sun goes up on the day of the great battle. We know what it was to be there; indeed, we are there, standing to and waiting for the onslaught of the terrible army that has never yet been beaten, while all the world holds its breath in that quiet dawn. Tolstoy does not tell us what we are to feel. He makes us *see*; we *feel*.

A horse, it is usually understood, has no soul; the Borodino countryside is an object. It is when Tolstoy offers us living human beings as though they were objects, and shows them to us in their various aspects, perfectly differentiated, but without entering into their souls—without, that is to say, giving us the spirit, strong and widely based in some, feeble or pathetically narrow in others, but common to all, which unites all humanity in an urge to transcend itself—that the Tolstoy treatment can be very disconcerting indeed. And this is so whether he is giving us a peasant of the most abject kind, or a politician (a real-life politician like Speransky), or a judge (an imaginary judge like the dying Ivan Ilych), or a frivolous feather-pate (like "the little Princess"), or even—but for the moment we hardly dare breathe the name—enchanting, enchanted Natasha.

For, not to put too fine a point on it, Tolstoy did not believe in people. The more closely his real characters—as opposed to the fictional projections of himself—are examined, the clearer it becomes that this celebrated moralist was a determinist, a materialist, a behaviourist. Although his eye for surface variations was so wonderfully acute that there is not a character in all his output who is not apparently unique, all are nothing but flesh, and all flesh is grass.

The second important episode in this restless, angry period was Tolstoy's first serious approach to matrimony. This entanglement—it can hardly be called a love-affair—started in the early summer, when Tolstoy had given up wrestling with his peasants. It ended in flight seven months later, but not before Tolstoy in his diary and his letters, to say nothing of his public conduct, had exploited the whole gamut of his uncertainties and his demands at the unfortunate girl's expense. She was Valerya Arsenev, an orphan of twenty, living with her two sisters in the care of an elderly aunt and a French duenna-companion, Mlle. Vergani. They lived at the neighbouring estate of Sudako, only five miles from Yasnaya. Tolstoy had known them for many years; but now, for the first time, he began to think seriously of Valerya.

The thought of marriage had been in his mind for some time. Now he was beginning to find it a little easier, perhaps because of the stimulus of his relationship with Alexandra Tolstoy, to get on with girls of his own class. Already he had been deeply stirred by an incident that had befallen him on his roundabout journey from Petersburg to Yasnaya via Moscow to liberate his serfs. In Moscow he had met the sister of his old Kazan friend, Dyakov. She was now married to a Prince Obolensky, and he fell head over heels in love with her. But it was a hopeless cause. Although he was sure that Alexandra Obolensky understood his feelings and was pleased by them, he himself felt relieved because she was safely married. Forgetting his feeling about Zinaida Molostvov at Kazan, he recorded in his diary that not since his first childhood love had he positively experienced "such a pure, strong, and good feeling. I say 'good,' because though it is hopeless, I rejoice in arousing it."

That was in May, and the experience must have stirred him up. Less than a month later he began to think seriously of Valerya as a bride. He rode off to refresh his memory of what she looked like. It was not very encouraging. "A pity she has no bone, no fire—a pudding. Sweet, though. Her smile is painfully submissive." But he could not leave her alone, kept on riding over to Sudako, kept on recording his changing moods. It was soon obvious to him that she was a silly, amiable, empty-headed provincial miss who would one day, no doubt, make a good wife and mother to a dull provincial official. "Valerya is horribly badly educated," he wrote "ignorant, not to say stupid." In some moods he found her physically repellent: "She was wearing a white dress and her arms, which are not good, were bare. This upset me. I begin to needle her so cruelly that she smiles uncertainly, tears with her smile. Then she played. I felt fine, but she was upset. All this I recognize."

He did not, at that time, realize much more. He wanted to marry. He

The Plowman.

wanted to fall in love. He wanted family life. Poor Valerya was as far from his ideal of a woman as it is possible to imagine. But she was young, unformed, pretty enough, and in spite of those thin, angular arms and elbows, there was clearly a physical attraction, and it was this that eventually destroyed his judgment. When she behaved naturally and did not dress for effect or try to be coquettish, he melted towards her. "For the first time found her *undressed*, as Seryozha would say. She was ten times better— above all, more natural. Has put her hair behind her ears, having understood that I like it so. In love with me(?). Seems to have a really loving nature. Spent the evening *happily*." And again: "It is strange that I am beginning to like Valerya as a woman, when it was just as a woman that formerly she was distasteful to me. . . . Yesterday for the first time I looked at her arms, which used to disgust me."

She was frivolous, by all means; but there were times when he was overcome with tenderness for her. It was always in her more childlike moments that he loved her best—while all the time asking himself if he loved her at all. Her great good fortune (for to be jilted by Tolstoy must be so regarded) was that, though still very young, she was in fact no longer a child. And soon it was to become quite clear that Tolstoy was incapable of marrying anyone but a child. The state of mind that he brought to Valerya Arsenev, and later, this time fatally, to Sonya Behrs, is, I think, well illustrated in the description of Kitty Scherbatsky as she appeared to Levin, Tolstoy's echo, in *Anna Karenina*:

"When he thought about her, he could picture her quite vividly, above all the charm of her small fair head, poised so lightly on the shapely girlish shoulders, and her expression of childlike serenity and goodness. That child-like expression, together with the slender beauty of her figure, made up her special charm, which he remembered always; but what struck him every time with a sense of the unexpected was the expression of her eyes, gentle, tranquil, true, and, above all, her smile, which transported him into an enchanted world, where he was filled with tenderness, as he could remember feeling on rare occasions in his early childhood."

Valerya could not quite make the grade. But it took Tolstoy six months before he finally abandoned the attempt to get her back into the nursery—or at least the school-room. The episode was complicated by manifestations of that strange, unexplained, fatalistic drift that conditions so much of the behaviour of Pierre Bezukhov in *War and Peace*—above all his sleep-walking acceptance of the various stages whereby he is pushed into

148

his marriage with Hélène Kuragin, even though his lust for her made him recoil in revulsion. As he went on deliberately courting Valerya through the summer of 1856, deliberately seeking to arouse her own desires, deliberately tormenting her, the pressure for marriage grew stronger. His friend Dyakov, who should have known better, had been the first to turn Tolstoy's thoughts in that direction. Aunt Tatiana urged it as hard as she dared. Mlle. Vergani never lost an opportunity to bring the two together. Even while he was recording his own oscillation between attraction and repulsion, tenderness and distaste, he could write: "Valerya is a splendid girl but she certainly does not please me. However, if we meet so often I may suddenly marry her. That would not be a misfortune, but it is unnecessary and I do not desire it." That was towards the end of June. In October he wrote: "I have become, without making a move, a sort of fiancé."

He had indeed. He had not formally proposed, but he had talked seriously of marriage with Valerya herself as far back as August, and since then had discussed with her all sorts of aspects of their domestic life together. He had taken her worldly education in hand and assumed the privileges of a fiancé of the most overbearing kind in telling her how to behave, what to wear and what not to wear. She had gone off in a great flutter of excitement and with trunkfuls of dresses to attend the coronation ceremonies of Alexander II in Moscow, and wrote back to Aunt Tatiana, partly in high spirits, partly to arouse his jealousy, long and glowing descriptions of her goings-on, her little successes with the Emperor's aides-de-camp, her dresses and her parties. She aroused his jealousy quite successfully—but also his blackest fury. She had reported ruefully that her best gown with a pattern of currants had been hopelessly crushed in the coronation throng. He was glad. It served her right. It sounded a hideous dress, and she must have looked a fright, done up to kill instead of dressing modestly.

"I try to restrain [Tolstoy wrote to Valerya] the mild hatred your note to my aunt has aroused in me. Not even mild hatred, but rather sorrow and disappointment. . . . Is it possible that a currant-pattern dress *de toute beauté, haute volée,* and Court aides-de-camp will always be for you the height of human happiness?

"To love high society rather than a man is dishonourable and also dangerous, for in that sort of society more rubbish is met with than in any other, and you even place yourself at a disadvantage, for you yourself are not high society, and so your relations with it, based on a pretty little face and a currant-pattern dress, cannot be very pleasant or dignified—*dignes*. As for Court aides-de-camp—there are in all some forty of them and I know positively that there are only two who are not rascals and fools, so there is not much pleasure to be got there either."

But when she came back, the extraordinary ritual dance continued. And when it was his turn to go to Moscow, he entered on a long correspondence about the meaning of love, about the difference between physical and spiritual love ("Your beauty I already love, but I am only beginning to love what is eternal in you and always to be treasured—your heart, your soul"), about the necessity for work, work, work if any human relationship is to be successful: "Everything has to be won by labor and hardship. But to make up for that, the severer the labor and hardship the higher the reward. And we have before us an enormous labor—to understand one another and maintain our love and respect for one another."

He went on to pour out a stream of advice, wildly punctuated, on everything under the sun:

"Please, *walk* every day, and whatever the weather. That is excellent, as every doctor will tell you, and wear your stays and put on your stockings yourself, and generally make improvements of that kind in yourself. Do not despair of becoming perfect. But these are trifles. The chief thing is—live so that when you go to bed you can say to yourself: today 1) I did good to someone, 2) I myself began to live a little better. Try *please, please,* to plan the day's occupations in advance and check them off in the evening. You will see what a tranquil and great pleasure it is to say each day to oneself: today I have done better than yesterday. Today I managed to do my threes against fours very smoothly, or I understood and appreciated a good work of art or poetry, or, best of all, I did good to someone and made him love and thank God for me. . . ."

That was on November 2. Whatever Valerya thought of the homilies, however apprehensive she may have been of the consequence of finding herself married to this most peculiar man, she had every reason for assuming that his intentions were honourable and serious. And, with various ups and downs, so it went on, surviving a passion of jealousy when he was told in Moscow that she had shown herself head over heels in love with a certain musician, recovering, going on to nurture her mind, finding time for more worldly instruction: "Alas, you are mistaken in believing that you have taste. . . . For instance, a certain style of dress such as a light-blue bonnet with white flowers is excellent, but it suits an aristocratic young lady who drives with fast trotters in English harness and ascends a stair-

150

case with mirrors and camellias, but with the modest surroundings of a fourth floor apartment and hired carriage, and so forth, such a bonnet is ridiculous—and still more so in the country driving in a *tarantass*. There is another kind of *élégance*, modest, shrinking from anything extraordinary or showy, but very particular about small details, such as shoes, collars, gloves, cleanliness of nails, neatness of the hair, etc., about which I stand as firm as a rock, provided it does not take too much attention from serious matters."

The future author of *War and Peace* is forever still observing, with that cool and *knowledgeable* eye. But he forgets himself for a moment at the end. "Farewell my turtle-dove, turtle-dove, thousand times turtle-dove, whether you're angry or not, I shall say it."

That was the peak. After that there are letters of increasingly cold and elaborate analysis of his and her feelings. On December 10 she hit back. She had had enough of his lecturing and preaching; would he kindly desist. This was just what he needed. On her own head be it! "Received an outraged letter from Valerya," he wrote in his diary, "and to my shame was glad." Two days later he replied: "We are too far apart. . . . Love and marriage would have given us nothing but misery, whereas friendship, I am certain, is good for both of us. . . . Then, too, I think I am not made for family life . . . even though it is what I most admire in the world. You know what a difficult person I am, suspicious and moody. . . . Of all the women I have known you are the one I loved most and still love most, but it is not enough." *

This long, drawn-out affair, although it had obsessed him for six months, left him quite unchanged. He had been enjoying his peasant girls at Yasnaya all the time. After the record of his very first meeting with Valerya in June, he wrote in his diary: "Sent for the soldier's wife." Immediately after he had finally extricated himself he attended a costume ball in St. Petersburg, and was attracted by a masked girl: "Sweet mouth," he wrote. "I pleaded with her a long time. She finally agreed, after much hesitation, to come home with me. Inside she took off her mask. As like A.D. as two peas, but coarser featured and older."

But the experience gave him a number of things. The most important was the short novel, *Family Happiness*, a fairly close reflection of his feeling about Valerya, but in the framework of marriage. It gave him, as

* Quoted in Troyat, *Tolstoy*, p. 154.

already mentioned, the first major experience of that sleep-walking fatalism that was to characterize Pierre Bezukhov in almost everything he did. Finally, some of the entries in his diary recording his disgusted reaction to Valerya when she dressed up to impress him might have gone almost verbatim into that memorable scene in which poor Marya Bolkonskaya allows herself to be dressed up so ludicrously by her sister-in-law, "the little Princess," and the silly, greedy Mlle. Bourienne for her first meeting with Anatole Kuragin.

It was time for yet another break. He had a hard enough task to justify himself in writing to Aunt Tatiana, who was not alone in reproaching him for his treatment of Valerya. It was more than he could face to return to Yasnaya, where the whole district was seething with scandalized indignation, until tempers had cooled off. The solution was to go abroad. He had already sent in his papers asking to be released from the army. Now he applied for a passport to leave Russia. And at the end of January he was off—five days by exhausting stage-coach to Warsaw, 180 miles a day. Then by train to Paris. And just as, six years earlier, he had set off for the Caucasus from Kazan carrying the memory of his brief involvement with Zinaida Molostvov, so, now, as he bowled and rattled along from relay to relay, he dreamed pleasurably of a certain Mme. Meugden, whom he had met and fallen at least half in love with in those last days at St. Petersburg. The timing was precisely right: when he met her he was already committed to departure, so he was safe. He wanted to write to her, but refrained. Instead, he made a remarkable entry in his diary on the way to Warsaw: "She is fascinating, and what joyful relations we might have. Why do I not feel such delight in my sister? Perhaps the whole fascination consists in standing on the threshold of love."

As if that were not enough thinking for one day, he records that he also wanted to write to Valerya's guardian "to show that the fault, *si fault il y a,* is not mine. . . ." It would have been interesting to read what he had to say about that. To Aunt Tatiana he wrote much later from Paris: "I never loved her with a real love. I was carried away by the reprehensible desire to inspire love. This gave me a delight I had never before experienced. . . . I have behaved very badly; I have asked God to pardon me, and I ask the same of all whom I have grieved, but to mend this matter is impossible, and nothing in the world can renew it now."

Valerya did not stay single for long. She soon married a young man called Talysin, who was to become a provincial magistrate.

5

GROWING PAINS OF GENIUS

Tolstoy's first travels outside Russia take up a good deal of space in the formal biographies, but we need not dwell on them. He was first enraptured by the brilliance and vitality of Paris, but he behaved like any other young Russian let out of his own country for the first time, except that his amazing energy and greed for experience enabled him to pack his days, and his nights, with an extraordinary variety of impressions. He saw all the usual sights and was disgusted with the elaborate pomp of Napoleon's mausoleum. He attended lectures at the Sorbonne and sat up late at *cafés chantants*. He took lessons in English and Italian. He enjoyed the brothels. But, apart from a few actors and actresses, he made few acquaintances among the French, spent most of his time with the large Russian colony, and allowed himself to fall half in love with two married Russian princesses—a Princess Lvov (to say nothing of her young niece) and a Princess Trubetskoy. Almost every night he dined with Turgenev, who was now living in Paris and cast into more-than-usual despair by the hopelessness of his love for Pauline Viardot. The spectacle of this very odd relationship struck Tolstoy in two ways. In the first place, it was a living proof of all he had said and thought about the demoralizing and enervating influence of women on pristine male integrity. In the second place, he was surprised to discover that Turgenev, who, he had repeatedly insisted, was incapable of real feelings, could in fact feel: "I would never have believed that he could love so deeply." He, Tolstoy, certainly did not know how to love deeply; how very strange that another could.

He had three months in Paris. Druzhinin and Botkin turned up for some of the time. But Turgenev was constantly there: they travelled together as far as Dijon and back. And day after day the diary recalls his ever-changing attitudes towards the man who, more than any other at any time in his life, seemed to get under his skin. Just as in Petersburg, so now in Paris, and so later again in Russia until the melodramatic rupture, he seems positively to have needed Turgenev, while angrily trying to reject this dependence. He needed him perhaps as a sort of walking conscience, or as the unacknowledged pattern for all that part of his nature which aspired to intellectual stability and artistic integrity. And he did his violent best to destroy the older man's hold on him by caricaturing his failings and, indeed, telling downright lies about him: Turgenev was cold. He was tired and worn out. He believed in nothing. He had never loved anyone, did not know what love was. He was dull, arid, void, a poor, flabby wreck of a man. Yet Tolstoy knew that Turgenev was none of these things and could not keep away from him. Turgenev for his part fell under the spell of the impossibly difficult young barbarian whenever they met. Months before this, he had written from Paris to Tolstoy, who was still in Petersburg, in a painful attempt to establish their relationship on a reasonable footing, and characteristically blaming himself: "You are the one and only man with whom I have had misunderstandings, and these happened just because, with you, I did not want to limit myself to a simple friendly relationship—I wanted to go further and deeper. But I went ahead carelessly, so that my clumsiness alarmed you, and then, seeing my mistake, drew back, perhaps too suddenly. . . .

"Your whole life aspires to the future, mine is built on the past. . . . You are too solidly planted on your own feet to become a disciple of anyone! I can assure you that I never thought you were malicious or dreamed that you were capable of literary jealousy. I saw in you (forgive the expression!) a considerable amount of confusion, but never anything evil. And you are far too perceptive not to know that if either of us has anything to envy the other, you are surely not the one. In a word, we shall never be friends in Rousseau's sense, but we shall love each other and rejoice in each other's success—and after you have settled down, and all that is surging around in you has subsided a little, then, I am certain of it, we shall

Tolstoy's passport, dated January 9, 1857.

An execution in the Place de la Roquette,
where Tolstoy saw a man guillotined in 1857.

meet again as joyfully and openly as on the day I met you for the first time in St. Petersburg."

Tolstoy's diary comment on that letter had been: "Received a letter from Turgenev yesterday, and it did not please me."

Now they were together again, and while Tolstoy pretended he could see only spiritual, moral, and physical decrepitude ("he no longer talks, he babbles") in the man who, at thirty-nine, had all his major novels in front of him, Turgenev at least understood that something was brewing in Tolstoy. "Tolstoy is beginning to lean towards forebearance and tranquillity," he wrote to Botkin and Druzhinin. "When this new wine has done fermenting, it will be a drink fit for the gods!" But to Annenkov: "No! After all my attempts to achieve a warmth of intimacy with Tolstoy I have to give up. We are too differently constructed. Whatever I like, he doesn't, and vice versa. I am uneasy with him, and he no doubt feels the same with me. He lacks tranquillity on the one hand, on the other the ebullience of youth. With the result *que je ne sais pas ou le prevoir*. But he will develop into a remarkable man and I shall be the first to applaud and admire him— from a distance."

Their friendship—Tolstoy's only attempted relationship with a man with whom he could have talked on equal terms—was saved for the time being by Tolstoy's decision to leave Paris. They could not have gone on much longer without a final quarrel. As it was, after saying his farewells, Tolstoy was moved to record in his diary: "When I came away from him I cried. I don't know why. I love him very much. He has made and is still making a different person of me." That was on April 8. It had been only two days before that he had written that Turgenev believed neither in people nor in reason nor in anything.

The immediate cause of his departure he made out to be the sudden wave of revulsion with which he was overwhelmed at the sight of a public execution. Obviously this spectacle shocked him. How could it not have done? In his diary entry for that night, a masterpiece of the laconic concrete, he wrote: "Got up at seven feeling poorly to see an execution. A thick white neck and chest; he kissed the Book and then—death. How senseless! Strong impression which will not go for nothing." To Botkin that same day he wrote a sharp diatribe against the cold violence of state power, symbolized by the calculated evil of "this ingenious and elegant machine by means of which a strong, fresh, healthy man was killed in an instant." And finishing: "Human law—rubbish! The truth is that the State

157

The Paris Opera Ball. Lithograph by E. Guérard, 1858.

is a conspiracy, designed not only to exploit but above all to corrupt its citizens. . . ." In after years, in the *Confession,* he was to write: "When I saw the head part company from the body and how they thumped separately into the box, I understood not with my mind but with my whole being, that no theory of the reasonableness of our present progress could justify this deed."

The execution may have been the last straw, but in fact he had already had enough of Paris. He had not taken violently against the French, and in some ways he was attracted to them. But, like Turgenev, they were heartless and empty. He adored Molière but abominated Racine "and others like him—the poetical plague of Europe." And above all there was no poetry in the French: "Their only poetry is politics." And he finished up with one of those silly observations that indicate how the dislocation of his mental and emotional processes—revealed in his attitude now to poor Valerya Arsenev, now to Turgenev—affected his perceptions of the world as a whole, perceptions that were marvellously penetrating and exact when faced with an arrested image of the moment, disturbingly incoherent in generalization or abstraction: "On the whole, I like the French way of life and the French people, but I have yet to meet the one man of real value, either in society or among the people." *

Now he was bound for Switzerland, and for another of those experiences to be made much of and reveal the man.

It was at the Hotel Schweizerhof in Lucerne, one of the first of the great Swiss hotels built in Victorian times, primarily for prosperous English tourists, that he had his encounter with the itinerant singer which was to give him his celebrated story, or sketch, *Lucerne.* He had been travelling about in Switzerland for some weeks before that, blissfully in the company of his adored Babushka, the Countess Alexandra, who was chaperoning her charge, the young Grand Duchess, on a tour of Western Europe. By the time he reached Lucerne he had taken against the English, who swarmed everywhere, and appeared to him dim and dull beyond redemption, as many of them no doubt were. Moving round and seeing the sights, insulated from the Swiss in a sort of travelling Russian circus, it does not seem to have occurred to him that the Russians, himself included, must have appeared as philistine to the English as the English did to him. The Countess Alexandra gives an amusing account in her memoirs of the activities of this circus on a day-trip to a beauty spot above Lake Geneva: How

* Quoted in Troyat, *Tolstoy,* p. 167.

160

Illustration for Tolstoy's *Lucerne* by N. V. Vereschagin. The scene is of the Tyrolean singer performing beneath the windows of the Hotel Schweizerhof.

the Russians livened things up! Tolstoy himself sat down at the piano in a tea-room packed with English and American tourists to urge his co-nationals into an improvised concert. "We sang *God Save the Tsar,* Russian and Gypsy songs, in short whatever came into Leo Nikolayevich's head. . . . It was a brilliant success. The foreigners crowded round us with compliments and thanks." No doubt some of them did; it was just what they needed to take their minds off the view and subdue the silence of the mountains. . . .

Not that Tolstoy was not deeply moved by the majesty of the mountains, the blue of the lakes, the brilliant clarity of the air. But the English spoiled them for him. And by the time he got to Lucerne he was hating them: "I have listened to more than five hundred conversations with the English, I have talked to them myself, but if I have ever heard a single living word from one of them . . . may I be struck dead by lightning." *

One evening (this is the real-life story of *Lucerne*) a wandering singer, a ragged Tyrolean, was performing so spiritedly in the street that Tolstoy urged him to come along and play beneath the windows of the Schweizerhof. Figures appeared on balconies and in windows, ladies in grand tenue, gentlemen "in detachable white collars"; down in the street itself a crowd gathered round, entranced. But when, after three songs, the poor man held out his cap for alms, all who had been listening simply melted away; nobody threw him even a sou. Tolstoy, furious and ashamed, ran after him, as he slunk away: "Come back to the hotel and have a drink with me!" The poor Tyrolean, ashamed of his rags, protested: It wouldn't do. But Tolstoy insisted. The dinner guests recoiled in horror. Supercilious waiters barred the way to the main lounge. Very reluctantly they allowed Tolstoy, by now every inch the Russian count, to shepherd the little man into the *Stuberl,* where he demanded wine. "Carafe of wine, sir?" "No, bring champagne, and bring your best!" It was an uneasy drinking party, the little Tyrolean embarrassed almost to tears, Tolstoy being grand, the waiters sneering. But Tolstoy was content. He had demonstrated to himself and everybody else his moral superiority and his nobility of soul; that he had humiliated the unfortunate little singer in the process was neither here nor there. He was not interested in the singer. He was interested in himself—in what he so frequently referred to in his diaries and his letters as his own self-perfection. Far from having second thoughts about this affair

* Quoted in Troyat, *Tolstoy,* p. 174.

next day, it never crossed Tolstoy's mind that there was anything questionable about his behaviour. He poured out the whole story to Countess Alexandra, who viewed his action with sceptical eye, and then built it up into the sketch *Lucerne,* into an indictment of man's inhumanity to man.

This is an important episode because it showed for the first time unequivocally in action, the real nature, already clear enough in his letters and diaries, of that love of humanity which was later to drive him to such excesses. There were to be plenty of similar incidents, notably the one recorded in *What Then Must We Do?,* written twenty-five years later, when he was pretending to be a peasant. Tolstoy was walking with a peasant friend when they met a beggar. The peasant gave the beggar three kopeks, Tolstoy gave him twenty and was immediately plunged into fearful distress: it suddenly occurred to him as in a moment of revelation that for him to achieve an act of charity and sacrifice comparable with that of the peasant who had given three kopeks, he should have given not twenty kopeks but three thousand roubles.

This is not the moment to relate these incidents to Tolstoy's view and conduct of life after his self-styled conversion in 1878. We are concerned immediately with the nature of the man who, without knowing it, was incubating *War and Peace.* And it seems to me important to an understanding of the limitations of this masterpiece that the introverted egotism —revealed in the diaries and in his relations with his peasants and with individuals as far apart as Valerya Arsenev and Turgenev—conditioned also the most fleeting and spontaneous actions. Of the incident with the beggar Rebecca West in her remarkable introduction to the story *Polikushka* quite justly said: "There is from start to finish no thought of the beggar. He might just as well have been brought into existence just for the moment when he held out his palm to Tolstoy. Not one second's consideration is given to the question of exactly what it is that the beggar most needs and how it could best be given to him from the point of view of his own and the general well-being. Tolstoy saw him purely as a means to his own salvation, and cared not a jot what happened to him otherwise."

There was some more Swiss travel—the usual contrasting of the clean, cold beauty of the Swiss landscape with the muddled humanity of the Russian one; the usual lusting after hotel chambermaids and landladys' daughters. Then Baden-Baden, where for ten days he fell into a passion of gambling, losing frightening sums at roulette, being bailed out by Botkin, who sent money from Lucerne, then by Turgenev, who turned up in the nick of time to rescue him—only to see his difficult young friend throw away all he had lent him, and more. "People all rotten," he wrote of the gambling-rooms the night before Turgenev's arrival, "and the most rotten of all is me." But he went on playing in a sort of delirium, and losing. Once more it was time to bolt. And the news that his sister Marya's marriage was breaking up made it still more urgent to get home. On the way, in Dresden, he viewed with dutiful enthusiasm the Sistine Madonna (which he was much later to deplore) and ran into Princess Lvov, whom, in Paris three months earlier, he had seriously thought of marrying. Now he found her too intelligent, as well she may have been. He no longer had the least desire to marry her, but he went on thinking about her, so much so that back in Russia he wrote to the Countess Alexandra in yet another passage of unconscious self-revelation: "I was in the right state of mind for falling in love, having lost at roulette, being dissatisfied with myself and completely idle (I have a theory that love consists of the need to forget oneself, and that is why, like sleep, it most often comes over a man when he is displeased with himself or unhappy)."

He went on: "Princess Lvov is pretty, clever, honest and kind-hearted. I wanted with all my might to fall in love with her, saw her often, and nothing! . . . What kind of a monster am I? Obviously I am lacking in something."

Ten days after writing that he was twenty-nine.

He was also more muddled than he had ever been before, but with a little added to the ingredients of muddle. At first Tolstoy was overjoyed to be back in Russia: he had spent much time comparing unfavourably the empty brilliance of western Europe with the warmth, spontaneity, and purity of the essential Russian existence. But now he saw Russian backwardness, dirt, brutality with new eyes, and they disgusted him.

He had been away only six months, but during these six months there had been a marked change of mood in St. Petersburg. There was a widespread conviction of the imminence of radical reform. In the autumn of 1859 the intellectuals of St. Petersburg and Moscow could think of nothing else; the only writing they were interested in was that which dealt more or less directly with social questions. So much so that Tolstoy, who was later to condemn all art as frivolity, now dug his toes in and stood up as the champion of art for art's sake. His mood was so black that even though he had to ally himself in public with the movement to emancipate the serfs, he refused flatly to admit that any good could come of either the workings of public opinion at large or the activities of the intellectuals in particular. While others were writing to congratulate Turgenev for his part in arousing the social conscience, Tolstoy remained silent. He reacted violently against the endless discussions in liberal circles—to the glorification on the one hand of the Emperor's nobility and enlightenment, on the other of the muzhik as a cult object. Artists had no business to play at politics, to meddle in affairs of state, that is. The State was, and must be, the enemy. As for the peasants, whom everyone was bowing down to worship, he, Tolstoy, knew them: he had lived with them.

But there was no consistency. The man who poured scorn on all those who saw in the Russian peasant the salvation of Russia and the world was very soon, on his second visit to western Europe, to overwhelm the nephew of the great educational reformer Friedrich Fröbel with the mystical intensity with which he proclaimed his conviction that the Russian peasant was indeed precisely this. In some ways this great original was very Russian. But it is encouraging to notice that it was not only foreigners who found themselves baffled by his increasing contradictions. After reading a letter to Botkin in which Tolstoy had suddenly and without warning announced that literature, as far as he was concerned, could be only a peripheral activity, Turgenev taxed him directly: "Sinner that I am, no matter how hard I cudgel my brains, I cannot make out just what you are, if not a writer: An army officer? A landowner? Philosopher? Founder of a new religion? Civil servant? Man of business? Do be kind enough to help me out of my predicament by informing me which of the alternatives I propose suits you best."

It is pleasant to see Turgenev showing his claws for once, but several years more were to pass during which neither he, nor anybody else, nor Tolstoy himself could see any settled pattern emerging. Between August 1857 and July 1860 he oscillated between Yasnaya Polyana, St. Petersburg, and Moscow. He made new acquaintances among the intelligentsia —notably the elder Aksakov, the satirist Saltykov-Shchedrin, the philosopher Boris Chicherin, the editor Mikhail Katkov (for whom he was to do a good deal of work). As usual, he was soon railing against all of them, as against his older friends. Not even the poet Fet, who was growing closer to him than any of his colleagues, escaped his censure for his "conceited and empty personality." He saw a great deal of Alexandra Tolstoy: even while they were travelling round Europe together he had decided that she was the finest woman he had ever met. Now he is rhapsodizing over her and seriously asking himself whether he should not marry her in spite of the great difference in age—only in the next breath to declare: "She has grown old and ceased to be a woman for me." He falls in love all over again with Dyakov's sister, Princess Alexandra Obolensky, hangs round her, tries to make her fall in love with him. "Beyond any doubt this woman tempts me more than any other." But not for long. Within a matter of weeks he is deciding that the daughter of the poet Fyodor Tyutchev is the girl for him. But she, too, is soon "ugly and cold." So back again to Princess Lvov, whom, in Dresden, he had decided he did not want at all.

In spite of his lack of personal elegance Tolstoy had now turned into something of a dandy, making a bid to be one of the best-dressed men in St. Petersburg. His old love of music had also been revived. It was a patchy, incoherent passion, but a genuine one all the same. Compositions and performers who caught his imagination were *ipso facto* important and great. Compositions and performers whom he did not know simply did not exist. For example, he was deeply moved by certain Beethoven trios; but it seems not to have occurred to him to find out more about Beethoven or to explore his other compositions. Years later, in 1877, Tolstoy attended a concert performance of the *andante cantabile* from Tchaikovsky's D Major Quartet. "Never in my life," wrote Tchaikovsky in his diary, "have I felt so flattered and proud of my creative ability as when Leo Tolstoy, sitting next to me, listened to my *andante* with tears coursing down his cheeks." But disillusionment set in when the great man started abusing Beethoven, Schumann, and Berlioz. "Not a demi-god but a garrulous old man," the composer decided. Tolstoy was then forty-nine, Tchaikovsky thirty-seven. . . . But Tolstoy had *War and Peace* and *Anna Karenina* behind him and was on the verge of his great change. Tchaikovsky, who wanted to idolize him, could never forgive him for holding forth about music, of which he knew nothing. Nevertheless, one of Tolstoy's few concrete achievements during the barren years now under discussion was to help found the Moscow Musical Society (together with Botkin and, oddly, Mortier de Fontaine, of whom he had been so jealous when Valerya Arsenev was said to have fallen in love with him little more than a year before), which was to grow into the Moscow Conservatoire under Rubinstein.

He also achieved, with no lasting results, one of his very rare flashes of self-illumination—as distinguished from the repetitive catalogues of sins of omission and commission. In a letter to the Countess Alexandra on Easter Monday, 1858, he unburdened himself:

"Christ is risen, beloved friend, *Babushka*, although I do not fast, and

A society ball in the late 1850s. Tsar
Alexander II and his wife are at center.

although I am sick of Petersburg, I feel so light of heart that I cannot refrain from chattering to you. When all is chaos inside me, you make me feel ashamed of myself, even when I can't see you. . . . Where does it come from, that warmth of yours that gives happiness to others and lifts them up above themselves? How happy it must make you to know that you can give happiness to others, so easily, so freely. . . . When I look at myself, I see I am still the same: a day-dreaming egotist, *incapable* of becoming anything else. Where is one to look for love of others and self-sacrifice, when there is nothing in one's soul but self-love and pride!" And he finishes: "My ambition is to be corrected and converted by you my whole life long without ever becoming completely corrected or converted." This spontaneous and accurate confession should be borne in mind when it is time to consider the celebrated *Confession* of just twenty years later.

Tolstoy's relationship with the Countess Alexandra would make a full-dress study in itself. It is clear that for him she was a woman to set above all others, and he accepted—indeed, positively demanded—her penetrating and astringent, but always affectionate criticism of his whole approach to life. But even though he felt for her a respect, as of one human being for another, which he felt for no other woman, the old familiar pattern was to repeat itself—in, as it were, a minor key: he could not resist the compulsion to dominate and to arouse feelings in her which he knew were best left alone. And, although Alexandra held herself on a very tight rein, he evidently succeeded. Then, at the height of this charade, once more he bolted, slipping off to Moscow without even telling her that he was leaving. Afterwards he wrote her a characteristic letter, explaining that living close to her in St. Petersburg had been so good that had he not gone away at once he might never have gone at all.

"Get married, my dear Leo," Alexandra replied, "and without delay, before egotism has quite dried you up. Having been very sparing when it comes to self-denial, you have much to give. . . ."

His heart was now set on Yasnaya. He had grandiose schemes, which came to nothing, for the re-afforestation of the Tula district. He had also determined that life held no more important task for him than to manage his estate—not sitting at a desk and working through his steward, but becoming a practising farmer and learning to plough and sow and scythe with the best of the peasants. He was also beginning his long emotional involvement with Aksinya, the wife of one of his own serfs, who seems to have accepted the situation philosophically. Tolstoy was far from philo-

168

sophical. Aksinya was to become an obsession with him. Already in May 1858 (before the visit to St. Petersburg that drove him to bolt from Countess Alexandra) he had written in his diary: "Today, in the big old wood. I'm a fool. A brute. Her red, sunburnt neck . . . I'm in love as never before in my life. Have no other thought." He had a son by her. So deep was his infatuation that there were times when he seriously considered arranging for her husband to divorce her and marrying her himself. It was while he was under the spell of Aksinya that he managed to distance himself by composing the short novel *Family Happiness*, which was to be the only considerable work to come out of the artistically barren years from 1857 to 1862. The essential basis of this story was an imaginative projection of what would have happened had he married Valerya.

He was ashamed of *Family Happiness*. It was "shameful offal—a blot," he wrote to Botkin, and tried to cancel publication of the second part in Katkov's *Russian Herald*. But it received surprisingly good notices, chie y because of the idyllic descriptions of the countryside at Yasnaya Polyana, which are as good as anything Tolstoy was ever to do, and the delicacy of perception into the heroine's feelings. As a novel it was trite, awkward, stiff, contrived, and shapeless, petering out into nothing. It was understandable for Tolstoy's well-wishers, who had been distressed by the inferior quality and undirected content of his three recent compositions (*Lucerne*, *Albert*, and *Three Deaths*), to rejoice at the reappearance of some of the positive qualities of his earlier work. It was also understandable for Tolstoy to despair. He was trying to do something he simply could not do: to make up a story in which characters and situation illustrated a text—in this case his early conclusions about the nature of marriage (which were later in real life applied to his own marriage and, in imagination, to the marriage of Pierre and Natasha in the more than questionable Epilogue to *War and Peace*). *Family Happiness* fails because Tolstoy was not content to repose his fiction on the faithful relation of two observed characters, Valerya and himself, viewed from the outside and exhibited against the background of an observed society. He chose to present the story and the background through the eyes of the heroine, a device that would have been permissible had he limited his vision accordingly. But he could not bring himself to do this and was unable to refrain from endowing her with some of his own qualities of thought and vision, with results that are absurd. He knew he had failed. What he seems not to have known is that he also managed to convey, as never before in any fiction anywhere, and with spell-binding precision, the almost wordless spontaneity of communication between husband and wife. We see, perhaps, the first fruits of all his seemingly sterile brooding, his headlong advances into, and equally brusque flights from, the orbits of so many women of so many different kinds.

Tolstoy himself, knowing that he had failed, and not perceiving where his true strength lay, was in a mood to give up writing altogether. He could not do well what he had set out to do; therefore he could do nothing. When Fet, to whom he felt ever more closely drawn—if only because the poet held aloof from radical thought and had decided to become a country gentleman and, as it were, a Sunday poet—announced his intention of settling down on an estate near Yasnaya Polyana, Tolstoy wrote, in almost total confusion: "To write stories is stupid and shameful. To write verses— well, write them; but to love a good man is very pleasant. Yet perhaps against my will and intentions, not I but an unripe story inside me compels me to love you. It sometimes seems like that. Do what one will amid the manure and mange one sometimes begins to compose. Thank heavens I have not yet allowed myself to write and will not do so. . . . Druzhinin is appealing to me as a matter of friendship to write a story. I really want to. I will spin such a yarn that there will be no head or tail to it." *

And so on. That was in October 1858. This mood of incoherence, which seems to have amounted almost to a mild form of nervous break- down, persisted all through the following year. He was depressed when he contemplated the talents of others. He felt empty and sterile. He could not even make sense of his chosen domestic life and quarrelled with everyone around him. He was supposed to be finding salvation in, as it were, cul- tivating his own garden and turning his back on writing. But there was no salvation: "I am being ground down in the mill of domestic problems again with all their stinking weight." But who was the "I" that was being ground down? "This year nothing can awaken any response in me. Not even sorrow. My one impulse is to work and forget, but forget what?" And work at what? "I am not much use as a writer any more," he wrote to Druzhinin. "I have written nothing since *Family Happiness* and I don't think I shall ever write again. . . . If at least there were some subject that was really nagging at me, demanding to take shape, impelling me to be bold, proud and strong. Then, yes! But really, to write novels that are charming and entertaining to read, at thirty-one years of age! I gasp at the thought!" †

* Quoted in Maude, *Life of Tolstoy*, p. 200.
† Quoted in Troyat, *Tolstoy*, p. 193.

Nobody had asked him to write novels that were "charming and entertaining to read." What his friends hoped in vain to see was a mobilization of those tremendous gifts in a major work which should be demanding and compelling. But he preferred in this mood to pretend that all writing was frivolity. "I shall write no more fiction," he wrote again to Fet. "It is shameful, when you come to think of it. People are weeping, dying, marrying, and I should sit down and write books telling 'how she loved him.' It's shameful!" *

It seems to me impossible to stress too heavily this period of abdication. Because here, in essence, was a foreshadowing of the celebrated and much longer abdication twenty years later, after the completion of *Anna Karenina*. The tremendous and world-famous figure at the summit of his powers, who turned his back on fiction, on all art indeed, and erected upon this "renunciation" a philosophy, or life-style, which he was strong and grand enough to impose on countless others, was moved in much the same way and for much the same reasons as the thirty-one-year-old writer who had, quite simply, dried up. Drying up, or, if the term is preferred, running into a block, is a common enough phenomenon among writers and artists of all kinds. It may be a temporary block; it may be long-lasting; it may be permanent. It is accompanied as a rule by feelings of despair. But, also as a rule, the afflicted recognize it for what it is, learn to live with it, and are not moved to pull down with them the whole fabric of the arts. We have seen enough of the young Tolstoy by now to understand that it was unbearable for him to contemplate exclusion from the temple as the result of his own failure. He had to prove that the temple was a sham. All that he was later to write when he fell sterile after composing two immortal masterpieces, scorning the very concept of art and slighting his own greatest achievements into the bargain, was forecast in one sentence in a letter to his friend Chicherin, early in 1860: "I am working at something that comes as naturally to me as breathing and, I confess, with culpable pride, enables me to look down on what the rest of you are doing." †

What he was working at was teaching in a village school.

In suggesting that Tolstoy's enthusiasm for learning to plough, for getting mud on his boots and trying to live like a working peasant, then for persuading, in face of stubborn resistance, his serfs to send·their children

* Quoted in Troyat, *Tolstoy*, p. 193.
† Ibid., p. 194.

to be taught by him at the big house, was in the nature of an alibi to cover his temporary collapse as a writer, I am not in the least questioning the genuineness of his new impulse. He was not alone among workers by brain to be deeply attracted by the open-air life and physical labour and to pride himself, justifiably or not, on manual skills; or in being overcome by the conviction that to be a doctor, or a vet, a farmer, or a forester was a worthier occupation than writing stories. Where he was lucky—or unlucky —compared with others before and since was in being so placed that he could indulge his nostalgia for the simple, useful life without having to toil from dawn to dusk to keep body and soul together—from, indeed, the firm base of a seigneurial position with assured power over a considerable community of bond-slaves. The establishment of a village school in his own house was a Tolstoyan variation on a fairly common-place theme. It offered him a chance, up till then denied him, of achieving domination over a chosen arena, however small that arena. For the first time, also, he was able to crystallize at least some of the burning notions hitherto held in turbulent suspension. The interesting thing is that domination brought out the best in him. Being the unquestioned and unquestionable master of the village children, looked up to by them, even adored, he could at last relax entirely, allow free play to all his compelling magnetism and charm, and cast aside that defensive arrogance which afflicted his relations with the adult world. Many years later, as an old man, he was to write to his official biographer, P. I. Biryukov: "I owe the brightest time in my life not to the love of woman but to love of people, to the love of children. That was a wonderful time. . . ."

Some of his ideas were stimulating to a degree, even inspired, though carried, as might be expected, to extremes. He exercised his dominance by refusing to dominate at all in the accepted sense. The children were not to be taught: they were to teach themselves: "No one brings anything with him, neither books nor copy-books. No homework is set them. Not only do they carry nothing in their hands, they have nothing to carry even in their heads. They are not obliged to remember any lesson, nor any of yesterday's work. They are not tormented by the thought of the impending lesson. They bring only themselves, their receptive nature, and an assurance that it will be as jolly in school today as it was yesterday." *

And again, after describing the skirmishing and rough-and-tumbles

*Quoted in Maude, *Life of Tolstoy*, pp. 250–251.

172

Tolstoy at his school, painted by A. A. Plastova. "When I enter the school and see this crowd of ragged, dirty, thin children with their bright eyes and, so frequently, their angelic expressions, a sense of alarm and horror comes upon me such as I experienced at the sight of drowning people. . . . I desire education for the people only in order to rescue those Pushkins, Ostrogradskys, Filaretovs, Lomonosovs who are drowning there. And every school teems with these." (Tolstoy in a letter to Countess Alexandra Tolstoy.)

that marked the beginning of every class, while the teacher patiently waited for the children to subside, he goes on:

"In my opinion this external disorder is useful and necessary, however strange and inconvenient it may seem to the teacher. . . .

"First, this disorder, or free order, only frightens us because we were ourselves educated in and are accustomed to something quite different. Secondly, in this as in many similar cases, coercion is used only from hastiness or lack of respect for human nature. We think the disorder is growing greater and greater and has no limit. We think there is no way of stopping it except by force; but one need only wait a little and this disorder (or animation) calms down of itself and calms down into a far better and more durable order than any we could devise." *

The children responded. They had the time of their lives. They may not have learned much in the conventional sense, but they would have learned nothing at all without Tolstoy's school—or schools, for he was soon to establish quite a network of them, staffed as a rule by eager university students, who came for what they could get to eke out their penurious existences and then fell under the master's spell. And their imaginations were stimulated in a manner undreamed of in the Russian state schools of the time.

This first spell as a schoolmaster (not counting the brief experiment on the eve of his journey to the Caucasus) did not last long, a matter of months. He still could not settle down for long. Having organized the school, won the affection of the children, overcome the worst of their parents' resistance, he was off and away again, this time to Prussia. Apart from the familiar restlessness, the main motive for this second and last journey outside Russia seems to have been to get away from Aksinya, not because he was tired of her but because he was coming to love her too much. "I am afraid when I see how attached I am to her. The feeling is no longer bestial, but that of a husband for his wife," the diary records. It would not do. He must go away. And the opportunity was there. His beloved elder brother Nikolai was ill with galloping consumption, the disease poor Dmitri had died from and which Tolstoy feared in himself. Sergei had taken Nikolai for treatment to Soden, a little German spa. Tolstoy decided to follow them, taking with him his sister Marya, herself ill, and her three children. There was another good reason for going to Germany. It was inconceivable for Tolstoy to start a school at Yasnaya without

* Quoted in Maude, *Life of Tolstoy*, pp. 252–253.

174

immediately seeing himself as the heaven-sent messiah engaged in establishing a model for a new educational system for the whole of Russia. To prepare himself for this new role he needed to see for himself what was being done in Western Europe.

In July 1860 Tolstoy left for Berlin. He was to be away for nine months, and when he returned to Russia in April 1861 he had lived through a traumatic experience which was to affect his whole life. This was the death of Nikolai in his thirty-eighth year.

Tolstoy had gone to Germany with the express purpose of rallying to Nikolai's support; but for a long time he could not bring himself to go near him. First, with Marya and the children, he arrived in Berlin more concerned about his own health, and Marya's, than about Nikolai. He was seized with the idea that he also had consumption, and it was not until he had been examined by a distinguished lung specialist that he put aside his fears. Then it was decided that Marya should go herself to take the waters at Soden, while Tolstoy, whose teeth were now in a shocking state, but who refused as always to go to a dentist, should go for a cure at Bad Kissingen. But first he treated himself to an educational tour, which took him as far as Dresden and Leipzig; he despised what he saw. He visited the novelist Berthold Auerbach, who shared his views on education. Then, arrived in Kissingen, he met Julius Fröbel, nephew of the creator of the kindergarten. But there was no meeting of minds. The younger Fröbel had his own ideas, believing that certain constraints had to be imposed in the classroom. Tolstoy could not dominate here and decided that Fröbel was an arid chatterbox, moreover, "nothing but a Jew." After that, excursions into the Harz Mountains, to Luther's Wartburg, anything but to Nikolai in Soden. Nikolai, fast dying now, was hurt and bewildered, but gentle as always, even though he complained in a letter to Fet. In the end it was Nikolai who dragged himself over to Kissingen, and although Tolstoy, shocked by his appearance and stricken with remorse, vowed never to leave his brother's side again, the very next day he allowed Nikolai to travel back alone to Soden and stayed hanging about in Kissingen for another two weeks before he pulled himself together and forced himself to join his brother. It was late August now, and a wet, cold summer. In a final effort to stave off death Nikolai decided to seek the sun in the south of France. The whole family, less Sergei, who had gone back to Russia after losing all his money at roulette (Tolstoy was now trying to devise a scheme for the abolition of roulette), traipsed off on the long, last journey. Two weeks later Nikolai was dead.

"On 20 September he died, literally in my arms [Tolstoy wrote to Fet]. Nothing in my life has made such an impression on me. It is true, as he said, that nothing is worse than death. And when one seriously reflects that, when all is said, it is the end of everything, then there is nothing worse than life. Why strive, or try, when of what was Nikolai Tolstoy nothing remains for him? He did not say that he felt the approach of death, but I know he watched each step of its approach and knew just how much time was left. Some minutes before his death he drowsed off, but then suddenly awoke and whispered with horror: 'What is that?' That was when he saw it—the absorption of himself into nothingness. And if he found nothing to cling to, what can I find? Still less!"

After describing his brother's last hours, he goes on: "All who knew and saw his last moments say: 'How wonderfully calmly, peacefully, he died'; but I know with what terrible pain, for not one feeling of his escaped me.

"A thousand times I say to myself: 'Let the dead bury their dead.' One must make some use of the strength which remains to one, but one cannot persuade a stone to fall upwards instead of downwards whither it is drawn. One cannot laugh at a joke one is weary of. One cannot eat when one does not want to. And what is life all for, when tomorrow the torments of death will begin, with all the abomination of falsehood and self-deception, and will end in annihilation for oneself? A nice sort of joke! Be useful, be good, be happy while life lasts—people tell each other; but we, and happiness, and goodness, and usefulness, consist of truth. And the truth I have learned in thirty-two years is that the position in which we are placed is so atrociously fraudulent and evil that we could find no words for it (we liberals) if men were placed in such a position by other men. . . . 'Take life as it is.' 'Not God, but you yourself have put yourself in this position.' How? I take life as it is. As soon as man reaches the highest degree of development, he sees clearly that it is all nonsense and deception, and that the truth—which he still loves better than all else—is terrible. That when you look at it well and clearly you wake with a start and say, with terror, as my brother did: 'What is that?' "

Profoundly affected as Tolstoy was by his brother's death, it drove him to no extremity, and he allowed his contradictory thoughts about life, death, and a future life to remain in suspension. He brooded a good deal

176

A "maison de santé et de plaisance" in Hyères, in the south of
France, where Tolstoy's brother Nikolai died in 1860.

A. I. Herzen, whom Tolstoy visited in England in February 1861. Portrait by N. N. Gay.

and based his indeterminate thinking on a very idiosyncratic premise—the human demand for justice as the primary need:

"Justice forms the most essential demand of man from man. And man looks for the same in his relation to the universe. Without a future life it does not exist. Adaptability! This purpose is the sole, the unalterable law of Nature, say the naturalists. But in the best manifestations of man's soul: love and poetry—this is not to be found. These things have all existed and have died, often without expression. Nature far overstepped her aim when she gave man a need for poetry and love, if adaptability to purpose be her sole law."

But although, perhaps more sharply than hitherto, his state of mind was foreshadowing the state he was to reach in later years, he went on living for another two months at Hyères in his sister's pension, where he enraptured the children with his games and fairy-tales; then came a two-month tour of Italy, which seems to have left no lasting impression; then he went to London, where he was overwhelmed by the personality of Charles Dickens, lectured on education, listened dutifully to Palmerston in the House of Commons, was impressed by the museums at South Kensington, and discovered that Herzen, whom he had despised, was a likeable and heroic little man. Much later Tolstoy was to declare that no good could ever come of Herzen and his friends because their personal morals were so loose. He was, of course, aware that his own personal morals were quite spectacularly loose, but, as he once said when condemning his Russian writer friends for the contrast between their public exhortations and their private lives, he himself was admittedly a sinner, had never pretended otherwise, and had never sought to tell others how to live.

As for Herzen's impressions of Tolstoy, he wrote to Turgenev: "I am seeing a great deal of Tolstoy. We have already quarrelled. He is stubborn and talks nonsense, but he is naive and good." *

At the end of his London visit, on March 17, 1861, the Imperial decree proclaiming the Emancipation of the serfs was published. It left Tolstoy notably unmoved. He would have to do something about it when he got back to Yasnaya, but the Emancipation was an act of state, and he made a point of looking down his nose at all acts of state. He was just off to Belgium, and there was no need to hurry home. And it was in Belgium that he had his celebrated meeting with Pierre Joseph Proudhon which was to give him, among other things, the title of *War and Peace*—which Proudhon was using for his treatise on the nature of war. The records of

* Quoted in Troyat, *Tolstoy*, p. 203.

179

the conversations between the two men throw a rather startling light on the Russianness of Tolstoy. This supreme idealist who in so many ways achieved total honesty found it necessary not only to conceal from a distinguished foreign philosopher his thoughts about the regime, on the one hand, and the Russian peasant, on the other (which would be understandable for reasons of discretion: Proudhon was a political refugee from France and a marked man), but positively to lie about them, insisting that the Emancipation decree was a model of enlightened generosity, that all cultivated Russians were behind it and put their faith in education as the foundation of a strong and prosperous state. Proudhon was moved to report to a friend: "Russia is jubilant. The Tsar proclaimed his Emancipation decree in agreement with the boyars and after consulting all concerned. The pride of these ex-nobles must be seen to be believed. A highly educated man, Mr. Tolstoy, with whom I have been talking in the past few days, said to me, 'That is what I call real emancipation. We are not sending our serfs away empty-handed, we are giving them property along with their freedom.' " *

In fact Tolstoy's ideas on education were getting more and more eccentric. He was condemning all formal education without exception. One of the features of French life that struck him most was the literacy and political awareness of the ordinary man in the street. He wrote better, knew more, understood more than any child at school. Why was this? Obviously he had learned nothing at school but had educated himself by reading the newspapers and arguing in bars and listening to satirical songs in *cafés chantants.* All schools must therefore be useless—except his own school at Yasnaya, which must be reproduced all over Russia. He still did not hurry back. He wandered a little more in Germany, visiting schools and behaving like an emissary from the Tsar himself. On one occasion he appropriated all the copy-books in a certain classroom to take back to Russia as samples of German school-work. When the teacher objected that it was a little hard on the parents, who had to pay for the books, he went off to a stationer and came back with armfuls of paper, demanding that the pupils copy out their lessons for him, announcing, "I am Count Tolstoy of Russia." In April he was home.

The first thing he did was to quarrel, melodramatically—and decisively —with Turgenev, who had invited him over from Yasnaya to Spasskoye.

* Quoted in Troyat, *Tolstoy,* p. 205.

180

Leo Tolstoy in Brussels, March 1861.

Turgenev had just finished his first major novel, *Fathers and Sons,* which, with its picture of the nihilist Bazarov (it was in this novel that the term nihilist was introduced), was to become the centre of virulent controversy. He wanted Tolstoy to read it, but after a few pages Tolstoy fell asleep over the book. What he had read he did not like, but he was in no position to say so and was angry with himself. Turgenev, who had come in to find him asleep, said nothing, and the matter was never referred to again. But the air must have been full of unspoken hostility, and the storm broke two days later when the two men went to visit Fet and his wife at their new country estate. They got to talking about Turgenev's illegitimate daughter, Paulinette, who was being looked after by an English governess in the Paris home of Pauline Viardot. Turgenev was on the defensive. He felt that he was being silently criticized for not bringing up the child in Russia. He sang the praises of the governess. For example, she had insisted not only that Paulinette must take an interest in certain poor people and be given an allowance to spend on them, but that she must go personally to visit "her poor" and collect their clothes to mend herself and take them back again. Tolstoy had taken no part in the conversation. Now he turned that familiar, dreaded glare on poor Turgenev:

"You think that is a good thing?"

"Of course it is a good thing. Only in that way can the giver learn to understand the meaning of real poverty."

Tolstoy exploded: "Well! What I think is that a little girl sitting in fancy dress with dirty, stinking rags on her knees is putting on a hypocritical, theatrical farce!"

Turgenev turned pale with fury: "If you speak in that way I shall punch your head!"

"Why shouldn't I say what I think?"

"So you think I am bringing up my daughter badly?"

"I am saying what I think, without any personal allusions."

Beside himself, Turgenev clutched his head and rushed out of the room. He was back in a moment, apologizing to Fet's wife, not to Tolstoy: "I beg you to forgive this scandalous behaviour, which I deeply regret." He then left the house. Tolstoy stayed on for a quarter of an hour and then himself went off, leaving the Fets to contemplate the void.

He set off for Nikolskoye, the estate he had inherited from his brother Nikolai. On the way he brooded, and his grievance grew beyond all bounds. He stopped at another friend's house and wrote out a formal chal-

Ivan Turgenev, in an undated sketch by Pauline Viardot.

lenge which he sent off by a servant, ordered to gallop with all speed. Turgenev must either write a formal apology that he, Tolstoy, could show to Fet, or else come in person to the next staging post and fight a duel.

Turgenev did write a most handsome apology, without reserve, begging forgiveness. But Tolstoy never received it, because he had already moved on to the next staging post. There he was waiting, lashing himself into ever increasing anger as the hours went by, and finally wrote another letter: a duel there must be, not one of those parodies of a duel where the principals fire to miss and end up drinking champagne together, but a real fight to the death, and with no seconds to restrain them.

The next morning, at dawn, the messenger at last arrived with Turgenev's first apology, soon afterwards another messenger with an answer to the second challenge:

"Let me say without beating about the bush that I would willingly stand up to your fire if I could thereby erase my truly insane words. It is so contrary to the habits of a lifetime for me to have spoken as I did that I can only attribute it to the irritation caused by the excessive and constant clash of our views on every subject. . . . That is why, in parting from you forever—for such occurrences are indelible and irrevocable—I believe it my duty to say once again that you are in the right in this affair, and I in the wrong. I add that what is here in question is not the courage I wish or do not wish to show, but an acknowledgment of your right to call me out to fight, presumably in accordance with the accepted rules of dueling (that is, with seconds) and also your right to pardon me. You have made the choice that suited you, and I have only to submit to your decision."

To this, according to the Countess Tolstoy, the reply was sent: "You are afraid of me. I despise you and want no more to do with you." Poor Fet, who made a further attempt to reconcile the two, also got badly bitten. To him Tolstoy wrote: "Turgenev is a scoundrel who deserves to be thrashed. I beg you to transmit that to him as faithfully as you transmit his charming comments to me." *

Four months later Tolstoy himself decided that it would be proper for him to show forgiveness. "If I have insulted you, forgive me," he wrote to Turgenev, then in France. "I find it unendurably hard to think that I can have an enemy." † But the letter went astray and did not reach Turgenev for another three months, during which kindly friends in St. Peters-

* Quoted in Troyat, *Tolstoy*, p. 212.
† Ibid.

184

burg had told him that Tolstoy had been circulating copies of his letter calling Turgenev a coward. It was now Turgenev's turn to issue a challenge. Tolstoy denied the charge. Turgenev was ready to make it up again, but this did not suit Tolstoy's mood. He had been prepared to make a grand apology in his own way and his own time and in a lofty spirit of *noblesse oblige*. But now he was haughty again. And so, through a comedy of misdirected letters, the estrangement persisted. It was to continue for fourteen years—from 1861 to 1875.

For some reason it has been widely agreed that in this quarrel Turgenev was the original offender—though those who believe this admit that Tolstoy pushed his reaction to offence too far. But there are limits, surely, even to Russian openness and directness, and in Tolstoy's gratuitous remarks about Turgenev's daughter those limits would seem to have been passed. It is worth remembering in this context that, while Tolstoy attacked Turgenev for the faulty upbringing of his daughter—his illegitimate daughter, whom he acknowledged to all the world and on whom he lavished infinite care—he, Tolstoy, had at Yasnaya a three-year-old son by his peasant mistress Aksinya, whom he did not acknowledge publicly and on whom he lavished no care at all: a little boy who was to grow up to be a coachman on the Tolstoy estate.

If this story appears to us now to show Tolstoy in a sad light, some idea of the inescapable impact of his personality on his contemporaries is shown by the way they rushed to make excuses for him. And it has to be remembered that they were making excuses not for the author of *War and Peace* and *Anna Karenina*, but for a difficult and troublesome writer, ten years Turgenev's junior, who at that time had for all practical purposes dried up. Thus Botkin could write to Fet: "The scene between him [Turgenev] and Tolstoy at your house made a sad impression on me. But do you know, I believe that Tolstoy really has a passionately loving soul; he wants to love Turgenev ardently, and finds his spontaneous warmth of feeling evoking no more than mild, good-natured indifference. It is to this that he finds it impossible to reconcile himself."

Tolstoy's love again. . . . We shall be returning to it. Reading Botkin's words about Turgenev's "mild, good-natured indifference," we recall Turgenev's own letter to Tolstoy, accusing himself of loving Tolstoy too much. And we may move forward in time to Turgenev's death-bed appeal to the old friend and enemy who had then produced his masterpieces and sworn to have no more to do with art:

"Good and dear Leo Nikolayevich, I have not written to you for a long time because I was and *still am,* to tell the truth, on my death-bed. I cannot get well—it is useless even to think of it. I write to you chiefly in order to tell you how happy I am to have been your contemporary—and to make my last, sincere appeal. My friend, return to literature! You see, that gift came to you from the same source as all other gifts. Oh, how happy I should be to think that this appeal might have some influence upon you! I am done for. The doctors don't even know what to call my illness. It bores me even to talk about it! My friend, great writer of the Russian land, listen to my appeal! Let me know if you receive this scribble, and allow me to embrace you once more, hard, very hard, you, your wife, and all your family. I cannot go on. I am tired."

Tolstoy was away when that last letter arrived from France at Yasnaya Polyana; but Turgenev lingered on for another two months, and Tolstoy could have replied, but did not. He was then extremely busy being a peasant saint. When the news of Turgenev's death reached Russia, he was filled with remorse and threw himself into a reading, or rereading, of everything Turgenev had written, so much of which he had angrily dismissed: "I think of Turgenev continually," he wrote. "I love him terribly. I pity him, I read him, I live with him." That was in September 1883, when Tolstoy was fifty-five.

We return to 1861. After the quarrel with Turgenev towards the end of May, Tolstoy took up his life as a working, teaching squire at Yasnaya Polyana more intensively than ever before. He had brought back with him from Germany a young teacher to work with him in the school, and very soon he had collected round himself enough helpers to start up similar schools in a number of separate villages. They lived simply, on subsistence wages. Although many of them arrived with their heads full of revolutionary ideals, such was Tolstoy's magnetic power that he was soon able to infect them with his own conviction, about which he protested too much, that no good could come of politics in any shape or form; more than this, that it was useless, indeed deleterious, to try to teach the peasant children to enjoy and appreciate the fine flowers of civilization. "Civilization perverts healthy minds. And even though we are all products of civilization, we must not contaminate the common people with this poison; instead, we must purge ourselves through contact with them." Contact with "them" meant, among other things, disowning Beethoven and Pushkin, whom he had previously so far forgotten himself as to admire. The peasant children were bored when he read them Pushkin, and they had no ear for Beethoven's Ninth Symphony. This, surely, could mean only one thing: since civilization was corrupt and the peasant children were pure, he must be guided by them. "Perhaps they do not understand and do not want to understand our literary language simply because our literary language is not suited to them and they are in the process of inventing their own literature." They loved the "Song of the Volga Boatman"; therefore this must be better than Beethoven, whose symphonies were admired "not because they are expressions of absolute beauty but because they flatter our hideously over-stimulated sensibilities and our weakness."

But while, head down, in his compulsive urge to systematize and push to their apparently logical conclusions a handful of quite salutary insights, he was intellectually bulldozing everything in sight that stood a little above the common level, he also found time and occasion to assume certain official duties of the kind he most denigrated in the service of a government he despised.

This government had called into being a corps of Arbiters of the Peace, provincial worthies whose job it was to preside over the implementation of the Emancipation decree and sit in judgement over the redistribution of land, balancing the claims of the freed serfs and the landowners. Tolstoy agreed to serve as an Arbiter of the Peace for the Tula district. In so doing, inevitably, he made himself unpopular with both landowners and peasants: with the landlords because he stood against them when they tried to cheat their peasants; with the peasants because they tended to regard the whole concept of the Emancipation as a confidence trick. Although he tried to do his duty conscientiously and well, his heart was not in the business of serving the state, an activity that contradicted all his avowed principles. And instead of fighting back when local landowners intrigued against him, he soon retired on the pretext of ill-health. It is worth recording that even during this brief interlude when he was actively engaged in an official reformist movement and working on the side of the angels with other men of good will, he contrived to dissociate himself from the general enthusiasm and to put the whole business of the Emancipation into a perspective painful not only to all those intellectuals who had been crying out against serfdom for so long, but also to the more enlightened landowners. Thus, at a banquet in Tula attended by all his fellow Arbiters of the Peace, when the toast of the Tsar was proposed he turned to his neighbour and remarked: "I drink this toast with particular pleasure. No others are needed, for in reality we owe the Emancipation to the Emperor alone."

His attempts (they were few) to work for the common good inside the administrative machine were doomed to failure. He lacked the patience; he lacked the will to compromise; he rejected root and branch the whole idea of a state endowed with coercive powers; he questioned the validity of political and institutional reform of any kind. His attitude is fixed in that short passage in *War and Peace* in which Prince Andrew, who has allowed himself to be caught up in the reforms proposed under Alexander I between 1807 (Tilsit) and 1812 (Napoleon's invasion), suddenly comes to his senses. His colleague, Bitsky, is rhapsodizing about the new Council of State, and Andrew reflects:

" 'What does it matter to me or to Bitsky what the Emperor was pleased to say at the Council? Can all that make me any happier or better?'

"And this simple reflection suddenly destroyed all the interest Prince Andrew had felt in the impending reforms.' "

Above all, of course, Tolstoy was unable to interest himself for more than a moment in any idea he had not himself originated or in any movement that owed anything to others.

At this period, in the early 1860s, the climate of Russian politics was very different from what it had been for so long under Nicholas I. Then indeed there had been little or no scope for enlightened laymen to influence the administrative machine. But in the first part of the reign of Alexander II the air was full of hope. Just how far things had moved may be illustrated by a small incident in Tolstoy's own life. Early in 1862, he brought out the first number of his famous educational review *Yasnaya Polyana,* with its call to arms: "Let it be established that in education there is only one criterion: freedom!" Not unnaturally the then Minister of the Interior, Count P. A. Valuyev, soon smelled subversion and ordered a discreet enquiry into the activities of Count Tolstoy. The consequent report, although critical of certain aspects of the Yasnaya school, was quite remarkably imaginative and understanding: "To establish a simple, easy and independent relationship between master and pupil; cultivate mutual affection and trust; free lessons from constraint and learning by rote; transform the school into a kind of family in which the teacher acts as parent: what could be more desirable and profitable for all?" * The report was accepted by the Minister of Education, who forwarded it to Valuyev with the comment that

* Quoted in Troyat, *Tolstoy,* p. 221.

Count Tolstoy's educational activities could only command respect and that it was the duty of the Ministry of Education to help him and encourage him, even though it did not share all his ideas.

In a word, at this period at least, the Imperial authorities were more ready to cooperate with Tolstoy than he was ready to cooperate with them. Tolstoy's attitude may be criticized not because he decided that it would be a betrayal to collaborate with a regime that allowed a Minister of Education to close down the Yasnaya school if he saw fit, but because it never occurred to him even to consider the question in the light of the people's needs. And here Tolstoy the original, like so many other Russian originals, merges into the Russian absolutist tradition, expressed by men as far apart from him as Herzen and Saltykov-Shchedrin, to mention only two: the Russians are free as no other people are free because though they bow before the tyrant's *force majeure,* they have never betrayed themselves—as, for example, the English have betrayed themselves by accepting freely the imposition of a constitutional government hypocritically disguised as an expression of the popular will. Tolstoy himself was to state this position much later in his life: "Those Englishmen who come to Russia feel themselves much more free here. At home they are bound by laws which they make themselves through their representatives, and which they obey, imagining all the time that they are free men. Now in this country it was not I who made the laws: consequently I am not bound to obey them—I am a free man."

His attitude was not always so loftily bland as that. In the spring of 1862 he was feeling ill, and on doctor's advice went off to take the *kumiss* cure among the nomad Bashkirs who lived in their felt tents in the open steppe to the east of Samara (now Kuibyshev). Here, living in a tent himself, drinking immense quantities of kumiss, or fermented mare's milk, eating mutton and dried horseflesh with his fingers, he was delighted to recapture some of the old joys of his early existence in the Caucasus, showing off his strength in wrestling matches and his skills in riding. But in his absence, terrible things were happening at Yasnaya Polyana: without warning, poor, aging Aunt Tatiana was being subjected to all the humiliation of a formal police raid, with a house-search of the most rigorous kind. One of the landowners whom Tolstoy had offended as Arbiter of the Peace was getting his own back by laying information with the authorities, alleging that Tolstoy had been engaging in subversive activities: a secret printing press, illegal manifestoes, all the paraphernalia of revolutionary activity. The raid was instituted by the then head of the Gendarmerie, Prince Dolgurokov, who covered himself by consulting the Tsar. Nothing, of course, was found, and apologies were made. But when Tolstoy returned in July, bursting with health and mare's milk, he exploded.

No talk about being a free man now. His beloved Countess Alexandra had to bear the brunt of it; as a lady in waiting at Court she knew how to approach the Tsar to obtain an immediate and public apology—and she also, simply because she lived at Court, was at least partly responsible for the villainous outrage: "One of your friends, some filthy colonel, has read the letters and private diaries I intended to leave at my death to the person dearest to me in the world. . . ." Tolstoy raged. "It was my good fortune, and that of your friend, that I was not at home at the time—I would have killed him!" Life for him would from now on be intolerable. He would have to shut himself away in a monastery, not to pray to God—"a waste of time in my view"—but simply to get away from "the moral ignominy of these people swollen with conceit and this society with its epaulettes and crinolines."

All was lost. "Everything that was a source of joy and satisfaction to me has been ruined." The peasants were rejoicing to see him treated as a criminal; all the confidence he had won from them had gone for nothing. Either he must have a public reparation, or he would leave the country for good. "I shall not hide, and I shall make it known to all that I am selling my property to leave Russia, where nobody can be sure one minute that he will not be thrown into irons and flogged the next, along with his sister and wife and mother." Or he might kill himself. "There are loaded pistols in my room. I am waiting until the matter is decided one way or the other."

The row rumbled on, gradually subsiding. Alexandra Tolstoy did her best to soothe him and went to extreme lengths to win reparation for him. In August he received a personal message from the Tsar, via the Governor of Tula, saying that although subversive material had in fact been found in the possession of some of his students, there would be no charges and he, Count Tolstoy, would not suffer further inconvenience.

A violent explosion of this kind was evidently just what Tolstoy needed. It was the immediate prelude to his first great change of life. By August 22 he had calmed down sufficiently to write a formal and entirely deferential appeal to the Tsar. On September 16 he proposed to the eighteen-year-old Sonya Behrs. On September 23 he was married.

190

A Bashkir tribesman. Russians like Tolstoy who took the kumiss cure at Samara would often live with the tribesmen in their tents or caravans.

It had been Dr. Andrei Behrs, a physician attached to the Moscow Kremlin, who had advised Tolstoy to take his kumiss cure in the spring of that year, and it seems likely that in making the journey to Samara and beyond Tolstoy was repeating his familiar manoeuvre of bolting from an entanglement that might lead to the marriage he insisted he ardently desired. There were three Behrs daughters—Lisa, Sonya, and Tatiana. Lisa was twenty, Sonya eighteen, Tatiana sixteen. Tolstoy had known them all their lives. Their mother, who had married very young, had, indeed, been his childhood sweetheart, only three years older than Leo, who had once pushed her off a balcony in a fit of jealousy. She was now thirty-seven, Tolstoy thirty-four. For some time past this visitor from another world, already famous and very grand, had been showing obvious pleasure in the warmth and gaiety of the Behrs household, and it was coming to be understood that he might at any moment ask for Lisa's hand. Lisa was set on it. And Sonya, who was also at least half in love with him, although he was old and rather disgracefully toothless, and quite intoxicated with his fame as a writer and his knowledge of the world, was already in the process of allowing herself to become engaged to a rather conventional young guards officer whom she did not really love.

For Tolstoy, his genuine and delighting love of children conjoined here with his leaning towards immature young girls, the attraction of the young and boisterous family was irresistible. The Behrs were not wealthy, and they divided their lives between a ramshackle apartment in the Moscow Kremlin, full of servants and hangers-on and eager young suitors, and a country villa just outside the city. This gay and youthful atmosphere—with its excitements, its crises, its flirtations, its living warmth—was to be translated in *War and Peace* into the immense town house of the Rostov family. And the existence of the Rostovs was a running together of the liveliness of the Behrs with the riotous extravagance of Tolstoy's own grandfather's establishment before it fell on evil days. Lisa Behrs, with her unimaginative, calculating eye for the main chance, and her chilly beauty, was to be the model for Vera Rostov (and there was a memory of her in Hélène Kuragina's meaningless smile and passive, unquestioning acceptance of admiration); Tatiana, the youngest, gay, funny, emotional, irrepressible, hopelessly spoiled, with her gleaming black eyes and her singing, was Natasha.

It was Sonya who was, after all, to be the Countess Tolstoy. Lisa was too cold, too priggish, too self-consciously cultivated. Tatiana was too

Lisa Andreyevna Behrs, Sonya Behrs's older sister
and, for a while, her rival for Tolstoy's affections.

young; one may suspect also that she was too much of a person, able to look after herself and give as good as she got, for Tolstoy to see her as someone who could be moulded by him into the wife of his dreams. Sonya appeared to be just such a girl. She was graceful, dark-haired, given to romantic melancholy, but with a dazzling smile, and the beauty of her large, dark eyes was enhanced and made a little mysterious by the misty blankness that so often goes with short-sightedness. She was a clever and serious girl, without being a blue-stocking. She read avidly, scribbled stories, painted in water-colour, played the piano. Both she and her sister Lisa had worked for a university diploma qualifying them as teachers. Dr. Behrs had encouraged that. (Tatiana was to be trained as a professional singer.) But although Sonya was genuinely interested in teaching and had a talent for it, which was to come in useful with her own children, she lived for marriage. And even now, in the summer of 1862, when she found herself falling in love with the great man who, it was understood, was destined to marry Lisa, she herself was already half engaged to her brother's friend, Mitrofan Polivanov, a cadet in the Horse Guards.

The story of the two months from July, when Tolstoy returned from Samara to learn of the police raid at Yasnaya, to his marriage in late September reads like a passage in a novel, and a Tolstoy novel at that. Twelve years later, when Tolstoy came to write *Anna Karenina*, he looked back on his own betrothal and marriage; and the details of Levin's proposal to Kitty —from its first preliminaries, when he traces in chalk on the green baize of the card-table the initial letters of the fatal words he shrinks from uttering, and Kitty immediately divines what they stood for, down to the non-arrival of the bridegroom at the church, because his man has packed all his shirts, leaving him nothing to wear—were close transcriptions of what took place between himself and Sonya. The words conveyed by the initial letters written down by Tolstoy for Sonya at her grandfather's country house read: "In your family a false opinion exists about me and your sister Lisa; you and Tanya should destroy it." And again: "Your youth and need of happiness today remind me too strongly of my age and the impossibility of happiness." By some miracle Sonya understood, and with very little prompting. But in their moment of breathless communion the spell was broken when Sonya's mother called out crossly that it was time she was in bed. We know all this not only from Sonya's own narration, but also from the memoirs of Tatiana, who had run into the card-room to hide because she was not in a

194

mood to sing and, not daring to reveal herself, overheard the whole fantastic exchange.

It was not a proposal as such. But it was a sort of promise, and Sonya took it as such. Dr. Behrs and his wife were still convinced that the difficult young suitor was dangling after Lisa, and they were getting impatient, because people were talking and Lisa herself was unsettled. It was partly to force the issue that Madame Behrs had decided to take all three girls to visit her father, who lived at Ivitsi, only thirty-five miles from Yasnaya—giving her the excuse to call on Tolstoy's sister Marya, a very old friend, on the way. But it was there, at Yasnaya, acting the gay, benevolently avuncular host on his own ground, making up Sonya's bed with his own hands, mounting her on one of his own horses to ride off on one of those idyllic summer picnics in the hayfields, that it became clear to Lisa, to Sonya too, and to Tatiana—but not to Madame Behrs—that his eyes were for Sonya. Two days later the Behrs family drove off to Ivitsi. And on the very next day Tolstoy surprised them all and put them into a flutter by riding the thirty-five miles after them. The little scene in the card-room took place that evening.

But still nothing happened. After a few days the family returned to Moscow. Tolstoy insisted on going with them, managing to keep close to Sonya nearly all the time. Lisa was now feeling desperate, and showing it. Madame Behrs was upset, though she still assumed that her old friend the Count was simply trifling, unable to bring himself to the point with Lisa. And so it went on, with Tolstoy walking the eight miles every day to Pokrovskoye, so that Sonya herself was in despair, and set herself to make him jealous by flirting with another admirer, a university professor the same age as Tolstoy. Father Behrs was now angry, and not concealing it: what on earth was this conceited young oaf doing, making life a misery for Lisa and upsetting the whole household?

What the young oaf was doing was living out his own personal drama and confiding its progress with more than usual confusion to his diary. It was as though in these two months he lived again in compressed form and with accelerated tempo through all the emotions, all the fears, the doubts, the longings and the despair, the agonizing uncertainties, that he had ever experienced in face of women—such a variety of women—now all centred on the dark head of an eighteen-year-old girl. Was this real love? Or was it being in love with love? He did not know. Was Sonya as tender and true as she seemed? Or was there an element of vulgarity in her make-up? So on, endlessly, all the time becoming increasingly possessed. Sonya herself had written a story about a young girl torn between two lovers (the story was destroyed; later Tatiana was to write that "in it in embryo appeared the Rostov family: the mother, Vera, and Natasha"). Tolstoy himself was pictured as one Dublitsky. When, feeling a little more sure, Sonya gave it to him to read, he was startled by the coolness of her eye. Dublitsky, he read, was distinguished by an "usually unattractive appearance" and "unstable judgement." All his old self-consciousness about his ugliness and clumsiness were revived.

He still oscillated wildly. But by mid-September he was head over heels in love and calling on God to help him. His diary entries are one long cry of agony: "I am in love as I did not believe it possible to love. I am a madman and shall shoot myself if it goes on like this. Was there this evening. She was enchanting in every way. But I—the unattractive Dublitsky." And the next day: "Every day I think it is impossible to suffer more and be happy at the same time, and every day I become more insane. Once more I left her with anguish, repentance, and happiness in my soul. Tomorrow I will go as soon as I am up and say everything, or shoot myself."

There was no reason for it "to go on like this." He had only to speak. He had already written a letter of proposal, which he had taken more than once to the Behrs home and brought away again. He seems to have worked himself into a genuine fury of despair over his age, his toothlessness, his ugliness: he imagined that Sonya could see nothing else—although in her Dublitsky story she had spoken of the tremendous spiritual strength that looked out of his eyes. All this must really have been a rationalization of his fear of being cornered.

At last, on September 16, he acted. Tatiana was singing, accompanied by Sonya. She was singing superbly, even for her. Sonya was clumsy at the piano. Tolstoy slipped into her seat and took up the accompaniment to perfection. The song, a waltz, reached its climax on a thrillingly high note, which Tatiana triumphantly sustained. Tolstoy burst out in extreme agitation, "How you sing today!" Nobody knew, but he had engaged himself in one of those compulsive gambling tests he used so often when trying to come to a decision: he had vowed, if Tatiana takes the high note well, it means that I must give Sonya my letter today; if not, not. . . . He gave Sonya the letter when Tatiana went off to make tea.

It was all over, or nearly. Poor Lisa, desperate to know what was going

196

on between the two, burst into Sonya's room, where her sister had gone to read the letter. When Sonya told her, she burst into tears and screamed: "Refuse! You must refuse!" Father Behrs at first forbade the marriage, but gave way under pressure from his wife. There was further outrage when, having taken years to make up his mind about marriage, months to decide about this particular marriage, Tolstoy insisted that the wedding must take place in a week's time. It was indecent. It was impossible. What about the trousseau? "My wife will need no trousseau; she looks very well as she is!"

More seriously, and with dire implications for the future, there was a testing time for Sonya, and for Sonya alone. With heaven knows what confusion of motives—his own image of total honesty, the determination to ensure that his past should never catch up with him unawares—this extraordinary fiancé gave into the hands of his eighteen-year-old bride, who regarded him as a paragon of virtue, the complete diary he had kept since his student days at Kazan, and commanded her to read it. She read it with incredulity at first and then a sickening sense of shock. She lay awake in tears all night, then, red-eyed, decided to forgive and forget. But of course she could not forget; nor, when it came to it, could she ever completely forgive.

There was one more shock. After the wedding in Moscow, itself hair-raising enough when the bridegroom failed to appear (he had to borrow a shirt from his father-in-law), the bride and bridegroom set off for Yasnaya in a special sleeping coach, or *dormeuse*, which had been ordered for the occasion. Sonya had left her whole family in tears. She herself was worn out with emotion and nervous exhaustion, and alone for the first time, as the great coach lurched and rumbled along, with this marvellous but terrifying creature with the monstrous past. Tolstoy could not wait. That night, at the primitive inn where they broke their journey, he virtually raped her. She resisted. She cried out. Her tears came in floods. When she was asleep he found time to note down in his diary: "She knows all. Simple. . . . Her terror. Something morbid."

We recall the diary entry after the guillotining in Paris: "Got up at seven feeling poorly to see an execution. A thick white neck and chest; he kissed the Book and then—death. How senseless! Strong impression which will not go for nothing."

Sonya recovered, as she had recovered after reading the diary, and soon both his diary and his letters to Countess Alexandra are filled with expressions of almost intoxicating happiness: "I love her when she gets angry with me, and suddenly, in the twinkling of an eye, she is a little sharp in thought and speech: 'Leave me alone, you bore me'; but the next minute she is smiling shyly at me; I love her when she does not see me and does not know that I love her in my fashion; I love her when she is a little girl in a yellow dress and sticks out her lower jaw and tongue at me; I love her when I see her head tilted backwards, her serious and frightened and childlike and passionate face. I love her when . . ."

He never asked—this can be said with certainty—what his own fashion of loving amounted to. Not once in either his courtship or the rapturous moments of his early married life did it ever cross his mind to ask what he could do, how he should be, to make Sonya happy. And this had been true of all his previous affairs. His was the happiness sought. All those other girls had been considered as instruments for the achievement of his happiness and had been discarded. Sonya had been chosen. Sixteen years later, in the *Confession,* he was to write of his marriage: "The new conditions of happy family life completely diverted me from all search for the general meaning of life. At that time my whole existence was centred on my family, my wife, my children, and therefore no concern for the increase of our means of livelihood. My striving after self-perfection, and for which I had already substituted a striving for perfection in general, for progress, was now again replaced by the effort simply to secure the best possible conditions for myself and my family."

Poor Sonya. . . .

6

"GREAT WRITER OF THE RUSSIAN LAND"

Tolstoy's marriage took place on September 23, 1862. On June 28 of the following year the first child, Sergei, was born; and by the early autumn Tolstoy was deep in the novel that was to become *War and Peace*. "I have never felt my mental and even moral powers so free and able for work," he wrote to the Countess Alexandra in October of that year. "And the work is there. All this autumn I have been completely taken up with a novel about the years 1810 to 1820."

Throughout the next six years of furious labour Sonya plunged herself into the self-appointed tasks of managing the household, protecting her husband from the outer world, copying and recopying from Tolstoy's very difficult handwriting that immense manuscript with its seemingly endless rewritings and revisions. During those six years of *War and Peace* she bore three more children and was six months gone with the fifth when the last words were written. She had some very disturbing passages to copy. Thus, almost at the outset of the novel in its settled form, and after only a year of marriage, she had to copy Prince Andrew's outburst to Pierre on the very subject of marriage: "Never, never marry, my dear fellow! That's my advice: never marry until you can say to yourself that you have done all you are capable of, and until you have ceased to love the woman of your choice and have seen her plainly as she is, or else you will make a cruel and irrev-

Leo Tolstoy at the time of his marriage, 1862.

Sonya Andreyevna Behrs in the same year, 1862.

ocable mistake. Marry when you are old and good for nothing—or all that is good and noble in you will be lost. It will be wasted on trifles. . . . Tie yourself up with a woman, and like a chained convict you lose all freedom! And all you have of hope and strength merely weighs you down and torments you with regret."

Prince Andrew was a character in a novel, by all means. He was, moreover, married to "the little Princess," pretty, vapid, her feather-head full of nothing but parties and gossip. But Prince Andrew was more than an ordinary character in a novel: he represented certain elements in Tolstoy's own nature. This proud, aloof, demanding man who could dream of glory, who was ready to sacrifice himself if he could find a cause worthy of that sacrifice, who did not know how to love until it was too late, represents the dismissive aristocrat in Tolstoy that never found expression in action. And the relationship between this splendid figure, who nevertheless feared life, and Pierre Bezukhov, also noble, but clumsy, eager, desperately honest, torn between his lusts and dream of universal love, self-perfection and self-imitation, reflected Tolstoy's own internal dialogue.

His relations with Sonya were very different from Prince Andrew's relations with the little Princess, but in certain moods Prince Andrew's feelings were his own, and he did not hide them. Sonya herself, though plunging with almost fanatical dedication into the career of practical helpmeet to a genius, at times cried out in her heart against the loneliness and monotony of life at Yasnaya Polyana and sighed for pretty clothes and the gaieties of social life in the city to which she belonged. She got no sympathy from her husband, who could be terrifying in his condemnation of her frivolity—as one would imagine after reading his earlier injunctions to poor Valerya Arsenev. And his conception of frivolity was extensive, comprehending far more than the conventional vanities and nonsenses of a young bride. His character was at last crystallizing out, his views becoming set—not all at once, far from it, but stage by stage. Up to now he had had, as it were, no firm base: his challenges to received opinion, to his seniors, to authority itself, had been spasmodic—aggressively defensive in character and, except perhaps in the matter of village education, ineffective save in a purely destructive sense, because he lacked the power to compel. Now at Yasnaya with Sonya, and with a family on the way, master of his own dominion, including his young bride, with all his contradictions at last finding resolution in the writing of his first masterpiece, he could begin not only to lay down the law but also to command it.

One of the first manifestations of the maturing Tolstoy—the man who was to emerge as the bearded prophet hurling thunderbolts, the teacher who at all cost had to dominate, the man of whom Gorky was to say there was no room for God and Tolstoy in the same universe ("they were like two bears in one den")—occurred absurdly enough after the birth of little Sergei. Tolstoy attended that birth and much later described it with clinical detachment in *Anna Karenina*. He was full of solicitude. But when Sonya discovered, to her own great grief, that she could not breast-feed the infant, he was outraged. Sonya had done her best, suffering an agony of pain, and persisting until her nipples were fissured and the doctors commanded her to stop. Tolstoy lost his temper. It was inconceivable that any wife of his should allow herself to become so soft, so corrupted by civilization that she could not feed her own child. And when at last Sonya gave in and the child was handed over to a wet-nurse, her husband sulked and growled and refused to go near the nursery.

The "correct" note was struck by Sonya's father, who chivvied his daughter and his son-in-law impartially and briskly: "I see you have both lost your wits," he wrote to his daughter from Moscow. "Be reasonable, dear Sonya, calm yourself, don't make a mountain out of a molehill. . . . As for you, dear Leo Nikolayevich, rest assured that you will never be transformed into a real muzhik, any more than your wife will be able to endure what a Pelageya can endure. . . . And you, Tanya, do not let your mad sister out of your sight for one moment, scold her as often as possible for her crazy notions that are enough to try the patience of the Lord, and pitch the first object that comes to hand straight at Leo's head, to knock some sense into it. He is a great master at speechifying and literature, but life is another matter. Let him write a story about a husband who tortures his sick wife by forcing her to nurse her baby. He will be stoned by every woman alive." *

Very much the correct note. Tolstoy was by all means a clown: he had indeed the makings of a great comic character. But he was also a giant, and comic giants are dangerous. Directed at this remarkable pachyderm, Dr. Behr's cool wisdom and edged but humourous teasing were meaningless and void.

Given a steady, imaginatively cherishing, quietly self-assured and undemanding husband, Sonya could have indulged her romantic fantasies, her wildly oscillating moods, her sense of self-importance, her fear of sex,

* Quoted in Troyat, *Tolstoy,* p. 267.

203

occasionally beating the wings of her sensitive spirit against conveniently padded bars of philistinism. Then, endowed as she was, beneath all her self-dramatization, with marked practical sense, she might have matured with motherhood and added years into a stimulating and contented wife. Tolstoy was the last person in the world she should have married, and the experience in due course drove her out of her mind, although for years she kept madness at bay by turning herself into an obsessive manager who was also a slave.

A great deal has been written in attempts to determine just how long the marriage could be considered a happy one and, when it manifestly ceased to be happy, who was most to blame for the failure. Nothing could be more profitless than arguments of this kind. The marriage was doomed from the start; it ended in spectacular disaster; and the disaster was long prepared. When Tolstoy, eighty-two years old, the universal sage, or guru, laden with honours, finally ran away to die in the station-master's house at Astapovo, with Sonya in full pursuit, forbidden access and pressing her face against the window in full view of the throng of onlookers and journalists, this was only the final reduction to terrible farce of a situation that had been latent from the first days of the marriage and fully developed for years before the public catastrophe. The details are irrelevant to any further understanding of Tolstoy, who behaved throughout his marriage precisely as he would be expected to behave by anyone with some knowledge of his previous development. He was, to repeat, a giant and a supreme egotist who lacked any control over his emotions. Sonya was dwarfed by him but could never bring herself either to surrender to *force majeure* or to run away. She loved him wildly, and hated him, and could not let go. She made herself indispensable to him, and he was caught forever by his own sense of responsibility for her and their growing family. From the earliest days, even when Sonya was still intoxicated and he himself rejoiced in the total possession of a child-wife, they tormented each other. Sonya, too, kept a diary, but, as a rule, wrote in it only in moments of bitterness and despair—pouring out, for example, her fearful, suicidal jealousy of the peasant girl Aksinya, who was still living close by, and later of her own sister Tatiana, who at times her husband seemed to prefer to her. And just as Tolstoy had made Sonya read his own diary on the eve of their marriage, so he now read hers—and continued to show her his own, to which he resorted only occasionally now. Towards the end of her first pregnancy she was particularly difficult, moody, inconsequent in her conversation, desperate in her diary. It never crossed her husband's mind that perhaps he should make allowances for her pregnancy. He simply knew that he could not stand Sonya's tears and silly chatter. And only ten days before Sergei's birth he wrote in his own diary, for her to see:

"Where is it—my old self, the self I loved and knew, which still springs to the surface sometimes and pleases and frightens me? I have become petty and insignificant. And what is worse, it has happened since my marriage to a woman I love. Nearly every word in this notebook is prevarication and hypocrisy. The thought that she is still here now, reading over my shoulder, stifles and perverts my sincerity. . . ." He goes on to elaborate on his despair at the state he is in, reduced to drink and gambling after only nine months of marriage, and then continues: "I must add words for her because she will read them. For her I write not what is not true, but things I should not write for myself alone. . . . It is appalling, dreadful, insane, to allow one's happiness to depend upon purely material things, a wife, children, health, wealth."

But that "sincerity" which was stifled and perverted by the thought of Sonya's hurt and offended eyes found a new and splendid outlet: no longer the endless self-contemplation of the diary, which dwindled and quite vanished, but the great novels of his prime. Towards the end of his life he was to write of this marvellous period a sort of requiem for Sonya and all she stood for:

"Then comes a third, an eighteen-year period which may be the least interesting of all (from my marriage to my spiritual re-birth) and which from a wordly point of view may be called moral: that is to say, during those eighteen years I lived a correct, honest, family life, not indulging myself in any vices condemned by public opinion, but with interests wholly limited to selfish cares for my family, for the increase of our property, the acquisition of literary success, and all kinds of pleasure." *

Sonya, of course, now herself fifty-nine and a lost soul, had to read that too.

Marriage and the birth of Sergei completed the immense accumulation of the experience, the weight of which released the springs of genius. Tolstoy had now lived through everything that he needed for the writing of *War and Peace* and *Anna Karenina*. His mind, moreover, had worked through all the processes that were later to crystallize into his renunciation

* Quoted in Maude, *Life of Tolstoy*, p. 296.

of the world. There was to be no change in kind, only in magnitude and intensity. Nothing was to be added; much was to be excluded. The first thirty-five years of Tolstoy's life, when contemplated in some detail, are seen to comprehend all the elements that went to make up the towering figure who was to dominate his age. Only the genius that quickened all those elements is missing. And although his contemporaries could not have foreseen the range and power of that genius which now suddenly took fire, we, with hindsight, can look back and see it coming.

After his sterile years, and immediately after the death of his brother Nikolai, he had begun seriously, though half-heartedly, to write again. To Fet he had written from Hyères that he would not, could not write again: "Art is a lie, and already I am no longer able to love a beautiful lie." But even as he wrote those words he was trying. At first he could do nothing. Then, suddenly, "For the last three days I have been invaded by a host of images and ideas, such as I have not had for ten years." He even started a novel about the Decembrists, the conspirators of 1825 who had plotted to destroy the Autocracy and had themselves been grimly broken by Nicholas I in the moment of his accession to the throne. Although this novel came to nothing, its conception marked a moment of critical importance in Tolstoy's development as a writer: for the first time he was breaking out of the limited field of strict autobiographical concern and planning a major work which was not in the narrow sense about himself. But still he was not ready to embrace the world and enter into a universe of which he was not the centre. And the impulse to write was itself uncertain and soon overlaid when he returned home in April 1861 to quarrel with Turgenev and throw himself into his schools. But in Brussels he had started the story *Polikushka,* based on an incident in peasant life told him by a friend, and in the year of his marriage he returned to yet one more passage in his own past life. Long before he had started the long story, *The Cossacks,* about his Caucasian experience. He had tinkered with it inconclusively over the years, and now, in urgent need of money to pay a gambling debt, he undertook to finish it. But he was still not ready for the final challenge. *The Cossacks* belonged to his past. He managed to finish *Polikushka* in the first months of his marriage, under pressure from his literary friends, who were afraid he would never write again. And he started the famous story about a horse, told in the first person, *Kholymoster,* which he was to lay aside for more than twenty years. Then, apparently quite suddenly, after the birth of Sonya's first child, all inhibitions began to melt into the air, like morning mist, to reveal, spread out to the horizon and beyond, the vast, the stupendous landscape of *War and Peace*.

Not that Tolstoy himself was at first aware of the scale and extent of that landscape. *War and Peace* arose directly from his preoccupation with the Decembrists. He found he could not write about these idealistic, recklessly courageous, ineffective young aristocrats who had dreamed of saving Russia from the dead hand of Autocracy without illustrating their background. Their background was the 1812 campaign against Napoleon and the subsequent Russian entry into Paris. They had got to know the Russian peasants serving as conscript soldiers; they had seen with their own eyes the backwardness of their country when compared with the West. They were determined to change all that; they formed secret societies to hammer out a new and liberal constitution and draw up plans of action. There were a handful of civilians among them, but the majority were army officers (for young aristocrats at that time the army offered almost the only available career), and they included representatives of some of the most ancient and noble families in the land. After the ignominious failure of their conspiracy, five of the ring-leaders were hanged, the rest sent off to Siberia, where they remained throughout the long reign of Nicholas I. It was the return of some of these men and their wives from exile over twenty years later, early in the reign of Tsar Alexander II, that stimulated Tolstoy to plan a novel about them. Instead, as time went on, he became fascinated and engrossed by the panorama of the Russia from which they sprang, the Russia of his own grandfather and father. And so, in the autumn of 1863, he started again. The new novel was to be called *Russia in 1805*, this being the year of the first Russian confrontation with Napoleon and the disaster of Austerlitz. But soon it was clear that this would not do: as the novel grew, it expanded into a monumental epic that would sustain its great cast of characters, and the unfolding of Russia's destiny, all through the uneasy peace and the Tsar's alliance of expediency with Napoleon, to the renewal of hostilities and the final defeat of Napoleon in the 1812 campaign. As the narrative progressed, Tolstoy racked his brains for a new title, and remembered the philosophical essay he had seen in Proudhon's apartment in Brussels some years earlier: *War and Peace*.

The writing of that novel, which is over 2000 pages long, took just six years. It was not merely a matter of organizing and writing down the equivalent of six major novels in six consecutive years: there had to be a

The entry of the French army into burning Moscow, in 1812.

vast amount of reading—what is nowadays loosely called research—to support the historical aspects of the narrative, from the intimate details of a battle to secret diplomatic exchanges. And, of course, besides visiting the critical battlefields where he could, he consulted and questioned many who in their youth had survived the retreat to Moscow, the terrible battle of Borodino, *la Moskowa*, and the occupation and great fire of Moscow itself.

The uniquely direct, matter-of-fact, inelegant, sometimes congested style of the whole gives at first sight the impression that the author of *War and Peace* was a man who had no particular feeling for words, but who nevertheless saw what he needed to describe with such edged and luminous clarity that the words arranged themselves. A reader knowing only that Tolstoy in middle life turned his back on art might be forgiven for assuming that this was a natural progression in a man who showed himself in his greatest creations deaf to the poetry of prose. But at second sight it becomes clear that the apparent artlessness conceals the most arduous art; that the deadly precision of the four-square prose reflects a vision of reality that would only be blurred and obscured, not heightened, by techniques employed by other writers whose less certain grasp of the concrete is recompensed, or even transformed into a virtue by the mastery of the evocative cadence and subtle combinations of vowels and consonants —above all by keeping open their eyes and ears, all their senses, very much their hearts, to an infinity of associations and allusions. This unblinking, in a sense blinkered, concentration on the particular object, unique and unrepeatable, the particular scene, the particular character, is shared in some degree by many other Russian writers and had a great deal to do with the almost stunning impact on the West, at the turn of the century, of what was called Russian realism. It depends what one means by realism. In Tolstoy, who carried the Russian approach to an extreme never attained before or since, it is as though he was afraid of losing touch with reality if (to confine ourself to his characters) he departed for a moment from the exact representation of the individual or allowed the outlines of the particular to be blurred or distorted by any reference to the general. This intent, this almost hypnotized concentration on the physical and psychological features of each separate character allows him to achieve a focus so clear and stereoscopic that the effect on the reader is one of total revelation (the scales fall from our eyes). When a score of major characters and a hundred minor ones have been presented to us in this way—their destinies interwoven, their personal relations elaborately explored, their individual lives, their miseries and joys, caught up in the great movements of history, dissolved, re-formed, dissolved and re-formed again under the sweep of armies marching and counter-marching, advancing and retreating across the face of Europe from the upper Danube to the heart of Moscow, a Europe dominated always by the presence of the great Russian plain; when all this is behind us, when martial strife and personal conflict have ebbed away, and the upshot of it all is that Napoleon is destroyed, Prince Andrew is dead, and Natasha has a baby—we are left with the sense that for two thousand pages we have shared these destinies, lived through them in the most complete and minute detail, experienced the life of a whole people, and apprehended its meaning as never before. Leaving aside as an irrelevance, as nearly everyone after a first reading of *War and Peace* is inclined to do, the author's undisguised intrusions, his explicit moralizings, or philosophizings, about the making of history, the nature of war, and the absurdity of the claims of great men to influence the course of events, we are ready to agree with the critic N. N. Strakhov, Tolstoy's friend and unqualified admirer: "What mass and balance! No other literature offers us anything comparable. Thousands of characters, thousands of scenes, the worlds of government and family, history, war, every moment of human life from the first mew of the new-born babe to the last gush of sentiment of the dying patriarch. . . . And yet no person is hidden by any other, no scene or impression is spoiled by any other, everything is clear, everything is harmonious, in the individual parts as the whole." *

And we may also echo E. M. Forster: "After one has read *War and Peace* for a bit, great chords begin to sound, and we cannot say exactly what struck them."

Those great chords, Forster decided, gathered their resonance and their spread from Tolstoy's sense of space, "from the immense area of Russia, over which episodes and characters have been scattered, from the sum-total of bridges and frozen rivers, forests, roads, gardens, fields, which accumulate grandeur and sonority after we have passed through them." No doubt this, as far as it goes, is true. The whole of the vast activity presented, the self-absorbed activity of innumerable individuals marvellously realized as physical, sentient beings, is planted in the earth from which it springs, to which it will return; and it works itself out beneath the vast arch of the eternal sky. Forster felt that this celebration of space

* Quoted in Troyat, *Tolstoy,* p. 302.

210

carried with it a sense of liberation, of opening out. In fiction he constantly sought expansion, not completion, and he believed he had found it in *War and Peace,* which for him also held, to borrow Joseph Conrad's phrase, "the magic suggestiveness of music, which is the art of arts." But Conrad himself would not, I think, have found this quality in *War and Peace,* nor do I think it is there. It seems to me that this great book, far from opening out, is very firmly closed. Forster's great chords are real, they are almost palpable, but they are not struck by Tolstoy. They are struck by the reader himself, at first unconsciously, and they arise from the conflict between his unexpressed acceptance of the mystery of life and Tolstoy's obstinate, furious refusal to have anything to do with it.

He could not bear mystery. We have seen this quality in him, as exposed in *Childhood* and *Boyhood,* even in the school-room. We have seen it grow. The thought that something might be hidden from him made him almost beside himself. There had to be an answer to everything, and that answer must be lucid and clear-cut. What would not conform with his answers he distorted to fit them. Those questions which it was clear even to him could never be answered he sought to ignore. But these are the very questions that matter. They have to be asked, and the way we ask them is the way we live. Tolstoy did in fact ask some of these questions, but then he made nonsense of them by pretending that universal truth consisted in abstaining from alcohol, meat, tobacco, violence, and sex. This prescription may or may not be a sovereign remedy for private discontent and public woe: Tolstoy was not the first to be convinced that it was, and he has not been the last. But it has nothing at all to do with the mystery that exists, pressing in on us, quickening or wounding our consciousness, the mystery that Tolstoy refused to acknowledge, from which he fled.

Let us be clear about this. Tolstoy did indeed ask questions about life and death. We have seen him doing so in youth and early manhood; he was to continue to do so until he died. But they were the wrong questions, or he asked the right questions in the wrong way. Elizabeth Gunn has a beautiful and penetrating passage on this matter when she takes up Tolstoy's flat, self-blinded statement in *War and Peace:* "A Russian is self-assured because he knows nothing and does not want to know anything, since he does not believe that anything can be known." She accepts, provisionally at least, the generalization about the Russian nature, but turns Tolstoy's meaning against him by considering its application first to Dostoevsky, whose "belief that it is impossible to know . . . is precisely what allows him to admit the co-existence, the inextricable mixture of good and evil," then to Chekhov and his characters: "The questions they ask themselves resemble Natasha's questions; they are questions that remain unanswered, thrown up like so many tiny glimmering balls against the night, against the background of the universe; questions that do not seek to wrest the truth from God, that, with whatever degree of desperation, accept the unknown. . . .

"Dostoevsky and Chekhov, unlike Tolstoy, do not fear the unknown; they do not fear to see their questions glimmer, flicker a moment and die, since nothing can be known. Whereas Tolstoy is frightened of the dark. He does not want to know, since nothing can be known. . . . But at the same time he wants it both ways. He not only asks: What is the meaning of life; not only does he ask, he actually, in the bargain, wants to determine the answer in advance."

It was not until long after *War and Peace* that Tolstoy began systematically to lay down the law, as it were, to God. But the tendency was always there, and the spirit behind this tendency is manifest in his great books, though in them he has not yet committed himself to "wresting the truth from God" but, rather, as far as his fictional characters are concerned, to the simple assertion that life holds no mystery.

In *War and Peace* we are faced, as in no other novel, with the harsh and terrible fact of mortality. Mortality is the absolute. Generation after generation lives and dies—to what purpose? Leaving what behind? We recall that magical passage in which Prince Andrew sees that the gnarled and venerable forest oak, which he thought was blasted and dead, has again put out tender young leaves to mingle indistinguishably with the quivering canopy of green in yet another spring. Prince Andrew is transported by this revelation and stirred to believe that life, after all, still holds something for him. By all means. . . . But this, though touching, is facile. He appears to forget that one day the great tree itself must die and put out no more leaves. What is it for? There is, there can be, no answer for those who, like Tolstoy himself, cannot see life on this earth as a preparation for an after-life. Here Tolstoy does not even ask the question: *this*, he says, is all. It is his supreme achievement to make us see the colour and wonder of the physical world with a heightened consciousness far transcending our normal awareness, and, at the same time, to bring us, to keep us unremittingly, face to face with death. And to make sure that we do not break back into life he seals the exits for the living. Thus Natasha, the embodiment, the very emblem, of triumphant, heedless life, the principle of vitality, must also die. But she is still young and healthy when the novel draws to its close, and likely to live for many more years. What to do? She could be made to die in an accident, in childbirth, or of some lethal disease striking out of a blue sky; but this would be too arbitrary. The very fact of accident in the particular context of Natasha's life and death would destroy the sense of inevitability, replacing it with pathos. And Tolstoy is wholly taken up with the sense of inevitability—as indeed is proper in a man who, at least since the death of his once-adored brother, had been obsessed with the terror of death and the conviction that there is "nothing worse than life" because it ends in death. So Natasha's mortality is exhibited to us in another way: we see her married to Pierre—still young, but changed into a matron, her figure, her delight in pretty things, her eagerness for life all gone, wholly wrapped up in the primitive business of suckling her young, joyfully coming forward (in that passage that has caused so much distress) to hold up her sick baby's nappy to show that the stains are now a healthy yellow, no longer green. Natasha too, as we knew her, is dead.

Very well, we all of us are born, rejoice, suffer, and die. And nobody knows what it is about. *War and Peace* for a time seems to be developing into the great Stoic novel. Certainly Tolstoy, with his wonderful eye for the surfaces of life and his scarcely less wonderful intuitions for the feelings of individuals about other individuals, was supremely equipped to write it. But he was not a Stoic. He could not face up to acknowledgment of the mystery that the Stoic stares in the face. He tried to suborn the mystery, or to conjure it away. He knew very well that behind every discovery of cause behind cause there must be still another cause, and so on to infinity. But he could not live with this question-mark eternal. There must be a meaning and there must be a way.

In *War and Peace* he was able, largely, to ignore the question-mark. Life is a fact, and much of the book is a paean to sheer animal vitality, a rejoicing, all darkness banished. (But darkness for Tolstoy included all manner of aspects of life that stood between him and his obsessive concern with self-perfection, including sex, very much including sex, and all that complex network of adult responsibility that obstructs the unhindered contemplation of the self.) Death is also a fact. And the basic conflict of the book reflects the internal conflict of a man magnificently equipped to

Anton Chekhov, 1897. "I dread Tolstoy's death," Chekhov wrote. "If he died, a large vacuum would be formed in my life. . . . When Tolstoy is part of literature, it is easy and agreeable to be a writer. . . . As long as he remains among the living, bad taste in literature, all vulgarity, insolent or tearful, all harsh, embittered vanities, will remain remote and in deep shadow."

Opposite: Fyodor Dostoyevsky, as portrayed by V. G. Perov in 1872. Tolstoy and Dostoyevsky never met, but Tolstoy wrote in a letter that when he heard of Dostoyevsky's death, "It was as though one of my supporting pillars had suddenly buckled. I had a moment of panic, then I realized how precious he was to me and I began to cry. I am still crying."

rejoice in the richness of life, who yet hated it because it went hand in hand with death. O grave, where is thy victory . . . ? For Leo Nikolaye-vich Tolstoy this victory was absolute.

The great paradox of *War and Peace* is that this immense canvas, which appears to include the whole of life, is in fact steeped in the spirit of exclusion. Mystery is out. George Moore, in one of those brilliantly perceptive essays (wise even in their sometimes tiresome flippancy) which have temporarily been forgotten, put it very well: "Tolstoy is lord over what is actual and passing; he can tell better than anybody how the snipe rise out of the marsh, and the feelings of a young man as he looks at a young girl and desires her, but his mind rarely reaches a clear conception of a human soul as a distinct entity; his knowledge of the soul, except in the case of Pierre, is relative and episodic."

Nothing, it seems to me, could be more true of the man whom we have been observing in his human relations from childhood to maturity. It has been only in the Countess Alexandra and the novelist Turgenev, two exceptionally strong and highly developed characters, that he has shown the faintest awareness of a complete and untouchable inner core, of an individual human being to be respected as such, of a personality as valid as himself. He was to quarrel with Alexandra as he had already quarrelled with Turgenev. All the other people in his life hitherto were seen by him only from the outside or, at most, as extensions of himself.

"The actual and the passing. . . ." Every passage, every sentence, every word, is contrived with almost overwhelming effect to fix the read-er's eye and mind on what is immediately under his nose. The actuality is so blindingly exact that all the senses are filled with it, leaving no room for reflection—because, if reflection is permitted, one will see that this is indeed not all. No writer, not Flaubert himself, ever worked more obses-sively and tirelessly for the exact word—but for the definitive, the closing word, not the quickening, the releasing word to open long and spirit-lifting vistas for the imagination. Tolstoy wrote and rewrote and filled the mar-gins of his drafts in the restless search for this literal truth of the actual and the passing. When he touches on the universal mystery, as sometimes in the thoughts of Pierre, or in Prince Andrew's flickers of awareness of forces alive and working behind the actual and the passing, it is only, as with Andrew, to dismiss it with a sigh of regret, or as with Pierre, to insist that the mystery can be solved by the practice of universal love and the achievement of moral perfection—and therefore is no mystery at all. Natasha is allowed to dream a little, but in the end she too is put almost brutally in her place. The other characters are themselves unaware of the existence of a mystery, gloomily selfish when they are unsympathetic, like the old tyrant Prince Bolkonsky or the stiff and arid Prince Kuragin; or, when sympathetic, moving through life with self-satisfied smiles—self-satisfaction in one form or another being for Tolstoy synonymous with happiness. All are totally absorbed in the actual and the passing, never for a moment dwelling in their thoughts, as every human being in the history of the world has sometimes dwelt, on the unanswerable questions to do with life and death.

In an early chapter I said that Tolstoy described his peasants in *A Landlord's Morning* as though he were describing animals in a zoo, and I suggested that when we came to look at *War and Peace* and *Anna Karenina* we should find that he extended this treatment to most of the characters in those novels. And so he does. They are magnificent animals, some of them, sometimes ravishingly beautiful, sometimes ugly brutes, some dull and plodding, others mettlesome and high-spirited, some limited and dour, some gentle, some vicious. They are presented, as a rule, to perfection (it is not too much to say) as seen from the outside—and from many angles. A number of writers have dwelt upon the brilliant effect Tolstoy knew how to achieve by showing us a given character as he appears in his various aspects to the different individuals, or circles, surrounding him and in which he moves. Very much in the round, they are presented to us, put through their paces, embroiled in testing experiences designed to show off their points, as it were—and then it is all over with them. They are destroyed. And it does not matter in the least whether they die, a ruined hulk with a great barrel chest, unconscious and suffocated by the weight of the pomp and hypocrisy that surrounded them in life, as Count Bezukhov early on in the novel, or in terror, after an illusory revelation of the meaning of universal love, itself a death-wish, as Prince Andrew towards the end. It does not matter because throughout the great narrative there has been no sense that these characters, unique and exactly differentiated as human animals, are united at precisely that level that distinguishes humanity from the animal world: their apprehension of the unknown.

I hope it is understood that I am not in this volume undertaking a critique of *War and Peace* as a novel—or a description of it. Many have written about its splendours and some have analyzed cogently enough its limitations. The book is there for all to read, and the most recent writings about it, as about Tolstoy himself, have been among the best. Thus, just as Henri Troyat has lately offered the best detailed biography of Tolstoy, so John Bayley, in *Tolstoy and the Novel*, provides the finest study of his achievement as an artist, and so Miss Gunn goes deeper than any other writer in English into his contradictions as an artist. What we are concerned with in these pages is the nature of the man who wrote *War and Peace* and *Anna Karenina*, and afterwards denied them. Certain aspects of those masterpieces bear directly on this concern. Conversely, a deeper understanding of Tolstoy as a man is an aid to a livelier appreciation of the imperfections, as well as the triumphant felicities, of the work. When he had completed *Anna Karenina*, Tolstoy gathered together all those threads in his character that seemed to him relevant to his eternal quest for self-perfection and did his best to exclude all others. Then, still unable to bear mystery, he applied himself with all his superb vitality to destroying it and forcing life to conform to his own pattern. Thus in due course he came to reject orthodox Christianity and suffered excommunication because he inveighed against the Church and denied the Resurrection. But he clung to, and magnified, a Christian-Judean-Syrian ethic, taking what he needed from the teaching of Christ and St. Paul because they corresponded with aspects of his own personality. He was a sensualist with a sense of guilt, a womanizer who held woman responsible for his own lust, a violent man who, as time passed, became convinced that force was evil, an aristocratic landowner who preferred to be a moralist, a moralist without a practical goal. In the period of *War and Peace* and *Anna Karenina*, the fifteen years between thirty-five and fifty, all these attitudes, though latent, were not yet clarified. And he was still proudly and consciously an artist.

I have tried to suggest that the clumsiness and congestion of Tolstoy's prose derives not from insensibility to the beauty of words but to his fixed determination never to allow his words to develop a life, a poetry of their own. The reader is to be directed every inch of the way. There are to be no overtones or undertones to raise echoes in the mind of thoughts and feelings existing apart from the object of Tolstoy's immediate attention; no heart-catching modulations, elisions, suggested associations, fleeting allusions, which may kindle trains of thought or feeling over which the author has no control. Everything is presented with perfect clarity, with no shadows, no ambiguities. All this huge talent is directed towards making us see precisely what Tolstoy saw, no less—and certainly no more! It may be the wounded Prince Andrew watching the surgeons at work removing Anatole Kuragin's leg after Borodino—a picture from the field dressing station at Sevastopol; it may be the moment when Pierre is first made aware of Hélène Kuragin as a woman, a passage that strikes with almost numbing force because it is the sole direct reference in the whole of the book, a book teeming with men and women falling in and out of love, to sexuality:

"Hélène stooped forward to make room, and looked round with a smile. She was, as always at evening parties, wearing a dress such as was then fashionable, cut very low at front and back. Her bust, which had always seemed like marble to Pierre, was so close to him that his short-sighted eyes could not but perceive the living charm of her neck and shoulders, so near to his lips that he need only to have bent his head a little to have touched them. He was conscious of the warmth of her body, the scent of her perfume, and the creaking of her corset as she moved. He did not see her marble beauty forming a complete whole with her dress, but all the charm of her body only covered by her garments. And having once seen this he could not help being aware of it, just as we cannot renew an illusion we have once seen through.

" 'So you have never before noticed how beautiful I am?' Hélène seemed to say. 'You had not noticed that I am a woman? Yes, I am a woman who may belong to anyone—to you, too,' said her glance. And at that moment Pierre felt that Hélène not only could, but must, be his wife, and that it could not be otherwise."

"The actual and the passing" . . . Hélène is there before us, physically, and with an immediacy that is almost suffocating. There is no room for anything else. There is no room for *us*. We see as we are directed to see, and then, his purpose achieved, Tolstoy confronts us with the next object, the next picture, and so on and forever. It is not until we raise our eyes from the book, or put it down, that the great chords begin to sound. It is then that, at last, our own consciousness of the mystery behind this teeming, brilliantly rendered life, breaks in on us. If we could read the two thousand pages at one sitting we should never, while our reading lasted, break out of Tolstoy's world, which is a closed world.

How different from Shakespeare, whom Tolstoy said he despised. To leap across a continent, to leap from one art to another (one has to make that sort of convulsive jump to get away from Tolstoy's eye), perhaps it is worth reflecting on the difference between Goya and Velásquez, or Velásquez's follower, Manet. Consider Goya's great nude, the *Maja*: I can never look at it without thinking of Hélène Kuragin. Compare the *Maja* with Manet's *Olympia*. Both are magnificently painted for what they are; but the one is a final and definitive statement about a particular naked woman: this is how she is; what the eye sees is all. Whereas *Olympia*, and also the Rokeby *Venus* of Velásquez, no less brilliantly rendered as physical objects, as statements, that is, are also question-marks which set the mind ranging where it will. The same, it seems to me, is true of Goya's terrible painting of the firing-squad, compared with Manet's *Execution of the Emperor Maximilian*. The subject of the Manet painting is even more precisely localized than the subject of the Goya; yet Goya gives us only the overwhelming and inescapable aspect of a single, specific moment of horror, while Manet gives us a comment, universally applicable, on the human tragedy. Or, to return to Velasquez himself, nothing at all could be more precisely limited and defined than any one of his series of paintings of the child Infanta, Margarita Theresia of Spain. A particular child stands there, looking at nothing, with a ribbon in her hair, heavily and stiffly dressed like a grown-up lady of the Court. There is nothing else. But there is everything else. Here, indeed, great chords are struck, by a painter who touches that formal portrait with the whole mystery of life. And now compare the infinitely complex, infinitely tender suggestiveness of that stupendous painting *Las Meninas* (The Maids of Honour), an arrested moment by all means, but not at all "the actual and the passing"; every line, every shadow, every recession, every figure in that painting—from the child whose portrait is being painted, to the distanced figures of the artist and the king and queen, from the grotesque Court-dwarf to the tender leaning-forward of the maid of honour on the left, the Doña Maria Augustina Sarmiento— combine to arouse an almost intolerable sense of the wonder and beauty and tragedy behind all the pomp and majesty. This is what life is and we are part of it. . . . But we are not part of the life of the Rostov family in *War and Peace*, no less miraculously drawn: we are lookers-on, and we look where we are told.

We are part of the life of *Hamlet* and *King Lear*, though no such lives ever were. Tolstoy in old age turned *Lear* into an absurdity and denied the validity of *Hamlet*. He did this with devilish cleverness on two levels. First he set out to prove that Shakespeare lacked any power of characterization. He did so by taking to pieces some of the nonsense written about Shakespeare's characters by scholars who, while they might have known a great deal about Shakespeare, lacked any idea of what is meant by char-

220

acterization. Then he took *Lear* itself to pieces by the process of "making it strange," to use the Russian critic Shklovsky's phrase. That is to say, he summarized what actually happens in *Lear*, the bare bones of the "plot," ignoring the poetry; and, of course, he had no difficulty in showing that it made no sense at all. Monarchs do not suddenly and without warning announce that it has come into their heads to abdicate and divide their kingdoms among their daughters, the shares to be determined by the degree of their filial love. No conceivable father would turn upon and disinherit the most dear of his daughters because she declares in all honesty that, deeply as she loves her father, she will love her future husband too. Tolstoy goes on and on like this with solemn perversity, conducting the flagging reader through scene after scene of the play. It is impossible to take it seriously, and yet one must, since it is offered as a serious contribution to aesthetics.

Nothing, in a word, could be more dishonest. The question is, why does Tolstoy find it necessary to lie about Shakespeare as he does? Why does he have to pretend that in *Lear* Shakespeare tried to write a realistic play with a cast of characters taken from life, and failed for lack of elementary competence? I suspect the answer is that if Tolstoy allowed himself to surrender to *Lear, Hamlet, Macbeth, The Tempest*, he would lose his footing; he would be swept along like the rest of us by the mysterious and irresistible power of Shakespeare's vision—and, unlike the rest of us, who surrender and let ourselves be swept we know not where, he would fight against it and drown.

Let us try another tack as we circle round the great works of Tolstoy's great period. We have seen his destruction of Natasha's youth as an aspect of the novel's insistence on mortality. But this transformation, which is surely false as well as ugly, also fulfills a secondary purpose. No longer in accordance with the laws of mortality, but now in accordance with nothing but Tolstoy's own idiosyncratic view of moral imperatives, we are asked, we are instructed, to believe, that Natasha's deterioration fulfills a higher morality. It is the duty of a wife to bear children, suckle her own young, feed her husband—and nothing else; not only must she neglect her looks, her hair, her clothes, she must also put behind her her music if she sings or plays, her painting if she paints, her dancing if she loves to dance. All this she must do in opposition to what Tolstoy calls "the golden rule advocated by clever folk, especially the French, which says that a girl should not let herself go when she marries." And she must do it because every-

221

thing that was alive, pretty, enchanting about her before marriage, everything about her that was enjoyable or enjoying, was calculated to one end: to fascinate men in general and her future husband in particular. In the case of Natasha even her singing, we are told in effect, had been corrupt (and this, by implication, must also have been true of Tolstoy's adored sister-in-law Tatiana): Tolstoy will not allow that she sang because she loved singing for its own sake, or music for its own sake. She "had at once abandoned all her witchery, of which her singing had been an unusually powerful part. She gave it up just because it was so powerfully seductive."

For the moment leaving aside the question of the validity of this outlook, we may now ask what Tolstoy's views have to do with the great, endlessly repetitive drama of the human destiny. What, indeed, have Tolstoy's views on a great many things, from the reforming politics of a Speransky to the megalomania of a Napoleon, to do with this great theme which for much of the time he handles so superbly?

The usual, indeed natural, response to Tolstoy's moralizing about the nature of history, politics, and so-called great men is that these are extraneous to the novel as such, to the human drama represented by the non-historical characters. In a word, the man who showed himself such a great artist in his representation of the unfolding lives of a host of characters taken from life itself could not restrain himself from pushing those characters aside from time to time, advancing to the front of the stage, and haranguing a captive audience with whatever thoughts on quite irrelevant matters happened to be uppermost in his mind at the time. But, as Isaiah Berlin has shown, Tolstoy's views on history are far from irrelevant. And in fact a second look shows that he treats his historical characters in precisely the same way that he treats his imaginary ones. He comments on *all* his characters, without exception, telling the reader what to see and what to think about them. There is no difference in kind between the manner in which we are shown the thoughts of Nicholas Rostov before Austerlitz and the thoughts of Napoleon before Borodino. That is to say, Napoleon is woven, or intended to be woven, into the seamless fabric of the novel —not, as it appears, superimposed upon that fabric. The reason why Napoleon sticks out like a sore thumb (apart from the technical difficulty of, as it were, neutralizing a celebrated historical character about which every reader already knows, or thinks he knows, a great deal) is that Napoleon is an outsider, a hated character, an enemy who embodies an attitude that Tolstoy abhors.

For *War and Peace,* besides being an essay on mortality, is a patriotic novel. And just as we may ask what Tolstoy's views on the place of women in the home have to do with "the slow, sad music of humanity," so we may ask what patriotism has to do with that music, unless viewed with compassion as one of the nobler elements in man's drive towards self-destruction. We have already noticed how, with all the violence of his rejection of Russian attitudes and institutions, Tolstoy nevertheless gloried in his Russianness. This is no place to explore the reasons why the fine scepticism of so many of the most luminous and lofty Russian spirits, from Pushkin to Solzhenitsyn, is blunted by the simple and touching belief that Russians in spite of their shortcomings (perhaps because of them) are the chosen race. It is necessary only to record that Tolstoy submitted to this illusion. He believed quite passionately not only in the special Russian virtues, which manifestly exist, but also in their superiority to all other virtues. And the struggle with Napoleon could be, and in *War and Peace* was, presented as a defensive fight to the death between the invading and inferior foreigner, seen as representative of a corrupt system (all systems, of course being corrupt, but the French more corrupt than others), and the resisting Russians, seen not as representative of any system but as a family drawing together, composing its family quarrels, and closing ranks in face of an intruder, an outsider.

In one of his most stimulating passages Bayley has come near to the truth about this. But he himself is so entranced by the Russian family, so almost completely absorbed by it, that he does not see how preposterous this attitude is. Those closed family circles in the novel, interlocking without really opening into each other, embrace individuals of many kinds, splendid and shabby, good and bad alike (even the rascal Dolokhov is, most improbably, sacrificially devoted to the sustenance of an aged and beloved mother); all send their children to the wars and are thus united in a struggle that is a family affair from start to finish. This is made easier to present because of the peculiarly open, shared nature of Russian family life and the freedom of communication between people who characteristically give uninhibited expression to their emotions and their thoughts, who are alien to reticence and have no secrets from one another unless for a specific purpose, usually ulterior. And behind the aristocratic family stands the immense, unseen host of the peasants, themselves now seen as part of the great family, distilling their instinctive wisdom into the words of the peasant philosopher Karatayev, a wisdom also embodied in the atti-

First drawings of Pierre as illustration for *War and Peace,* by
M. S. Bashilov. Tolstoy commented, "His face is all right; you
ought to give his forehead a greater tendency for philosophizing
—a wrinkle or bump over the eyebrows. But his body should be
broader and more corpulent."

The ball at the Rostovs. Illustration for *War and Peace*, by M. S. Bashilov.

tudes of Kutuzov as commander-in-chief under the Tsar. Tolstoy in his middle thirties might inveigh against the system, the regime, and pour scorn on Court circles and his fellow aristocrats, but when coming to the test, when his countrymen are face to face with the insolent, invading foreigner, all are good Russians, and their stern and benevolent father is the Tsar.

This presentation indeed upset many contemporary Russian readers of *War and Peace*. The novel, as so many ardent reforming intellectuals indignantly pointed out, is a celebration of the Russian nobility, a nobility with its black sheep by all means, but essentially a nobility that stood for Russia, the Russia that destroyed Napoleon. It is a picture of life as seen from the drawing-rooms of St. Petersburg and Moscow and the rambling country houses of the provinces; and the fighting itself, with all the un-romanticized exactitude of its presentation, is the fighting as seen through the eyes of the products of these drawing-rooms. There is not the faintest suggestion, even when Tolstoy is at his most caustic about the frivolous and corrupt representatives of his great Russian family, that this social apparatus was a glittering superstructure raised upon the bare backs of innumerable slaves.

This is a major aspect of *War and Peace* which needs thinking about. Tolstoy is not writing about the horror and absurdity of war, although his treatment touches upon both. He is celebrating, to borrow a contemporary Russian phrase, a great patriotic war. Just as he tells us what we are to think about his characters, so he tells us what we are to think about that war. We must take sides. This is not a poet's war, it is a propagandist's war. Tolstoy can say what he likes, and does, to prove his point, about the great unseen forces that set nations in arms against each other; but this is simply talk. What he *shows*, with an unparalleled splendour of presentation, is the destruction of the insolent invaders by the great Russian family of brothers.

Let us glance again at Shakespeare, this time at *Henry V*. Nothing on the face of it could be more stridently patriotic than the attitudes struck by the English as they prepare to do battle with the French. And yet when we read the great speech on St. Crispin's Eve, English virtue and French perfidy are quite forgotten. We are raised to a great height, far above the squabbles between nations, and carried into the very heart of the mystery of human endeavour and self-sacrifice. The same is surely true of Hector going out to his certain death beneath the walls of Troy. Homer and

Shakespeare were alike in being more concerned with human beings than with causes. But for Tolstoy the war with Napoleon was a cause. And it was won by the great Russian family not because of superior arms, or superior numbers, or superior generalship, but because they were *better people*. In a less exalted context the word for this attitude would be smug.

The disconnected, the fragmented, the wholly erratic make-up of Tolstoy the man thus shows itself at every turn at war with Tolstoy the artist. *War and Peace* is a statement about mortality by a man who hated life, which enthralled him, because it ended in death and nothingness. But his inconsistency was extreme. If life is no more than a tale told by an idiot, why worry about peasant education, about Valerya Arsenev's taste in clothes, about Sonya's inability to breast-feed her children? Why worry about the great Russian virtues, about the pretensions of Napoleon, about the "uselessness" of Speransky's reforms? But Tolstoy worried very much. And with his obsession with the meaninglessness of life and the terror of death, which drove him in the end into a quasi-mystical escape into the wilderness, there went, as we have seen, that no less powerful obsession with theories of behavior which drove him, from his university days, perpetually and in vain to systemize his ideas. Nothing must be left open. And this applied no less to ethical convictions about sex and violence than to philosophical convictions, largely the products of an emotional reaction of an original, sceptical, but untrained mind against conventional opinion: that the pretensions of great men to influence the course of history were ludicrous and vain, that institutional reforms were useless, perhaps worse than useless, so long as the men and women functioning within the institutions remained imperfect. These philosophical convictions led him, of course, into many contradictions: thus, if Napoleon was a vain and ludicrous pretender, so were all others in authority, including Napoleon's adversaries Kutuzov and the Emperor Alexander I. So historical truth had to be distorted—the real Kutuzov had to be transformed into something like the inert instrument of the national, the popular, will; Alexander into the symbol of sacrificial patriotism.

Tolstoy sells the pass. It was as correct as it was bold to make Napoleon a central figure of his great panorama. But by singling him out for a personal attack Tolstoy contradicts his own general thesis that men are puppets of forces greater than themselves. Napoleon is attacked and held up to derision precisely for believing that he was in command of his own destiny—but so, to a greater or less degree, was every other character in *War and Peace*. George Moore observed that "it is during the retreat from Moscow that we begin to understand that the hero of the book is Destiny. For everybody in the book sets out to do something, and everybody does something, but no ones does what he sets out to do." And this is true as far as it goes. But in some degree this truth must be the theme of all art, which broods upon and illuminates mystery. It does not require a Tolstoy to tell us that neither Napoleon nor any other celebrated master of men, nor, for that matter, private persons leading private lives, are inevitably themselves the victims of the forces they seek to control. This is at the root of all tragedy, all comedy.

If I may interject a personal note for the sake of clarity, let me say that I find the Napoleon of history detestable. But I find him detestable not because he believed he was in control of events, not because he thought he was influencing the course of history, but because of the nature of his actions and because his character was inferior. Seen with the distancing eye of a great artist, Napoleon himself must appear no less than anybody else as a member of the human family, as a victim. Instead Tolstoy treats him as an outsider, first as a Frenchman who intruded on the great Russian family, then as an offender against his theory of history. Any picture of Napoleon in the round must exhibit his meanness, his coarseness, his destructiveness, his lust for power—as well as his charm, his creative vitality, his courage. Tolstoy could have exhibited him in this way, and to marvelous effect. But he is not exhibited, he is caricatured and condemned.

There is another character in *War and Peace* who is held up to obloquy, this time a Russian. Tolstoy's formidable technique is brought unscrupulously and crushingly to bear on the unfortunate figure of Count M. M. Speransky, who lives in history as one of the handful of men round the young Alexander who toiled devotedly to draft far-reaching, desperately needed constitutional reforms. The passages about Speransky are brief and totally dismissive. Tolstoy uses his superb evocative skill to destroy him in two or three phrases, leaving nothing but a flabby handshake, a blank stare, and a false laugh as the monument to a man who, though notorious for his failings, worked hard against overwhelming odds for the common good and was broken because of it. Speransky was a Russian, but in Tolstoy's eyes he did not belong to the great family. He was an outsider, as Napoleon was an outsider, because although benevolent in intention he shared Napoleon's belief that action could achieve foreseen results. He was

Tsar Alexander I. A contemporary print of the Emperor whom
Napoleon challenged in 1812. The confrontation of Russia and
France forms a central theme of *War and Peace*.

a foreign body in that great, cosy, almost mindless family whose members did not hold with active politicians.

We are brought back to that reflection of Prince Andrew's, quoted earlier in a different context, during his conversation with Bitsky about the inauguration of the new Council of State, which had been set up on Speransky's recommendation in 1810: "What does it matter to me or to Bitsky what the Emperor was pleased to say at the Council? Can all that make me any happier or better?"

It is the casualness of this astonishing observation, slipped into the middle of Book Six, nearly halfway through the novel, that sends prickles down the reader's spine. Tolstoy is not labouring a point or proclaiming a revolution in moral attitudes: he is commenting on what he took to be self-evident. Prince Andrew has been attracted and then stirred by the power and range of Speransky's intellect and his passionate conviction that will combined with reason can change the world. For a moment, at Speransky's insistence, he throws himself into the work of a committee concerned with judicial reform (we remember how Tolstoy himself served briefly, before his marriage, as Arbiter of the Peace with the task of implementing the Emancipation Act of 1861). But very soon reaction sets in. Admiration of Speransky's intellect, incorruptibility, and drive is lost in revulsion from his personal shortcomings. Prince Andrew himself is one of those people who cannot breathe the air of insincerity that surrounds all politicians. Very well, he could not stand much of Speransky at close quarters. We are not surprised. But instead of saying: "I personally cannot stand this man, though no doubt he is meaning well and doing good," or "I cannot stand him and I believe no good at all can come of such inferior material," he asks, "What does it matter to me. . . . Can all that make me any happier or better?" As though the movement and object of all human activity must be to secure the personal well-being and happiness of Prince Andrew Bolkonsky. What is one to say of egocentricity pushed to this degree?

It is the voice of Tolstoy himself. It is a most disconcerting voice. We remember those diaries and letters, with their obsessional concern with the pursuit of personal happiness. Even the quest for moral perfection, for auto-beatification, is powered by the unappeasable desire for happiness. And this adolescent conception of happiness remained with him until the end when, in his eighty-third year, he ran away from Sonya and Yasnaya, still in pursuit of happiness.

230

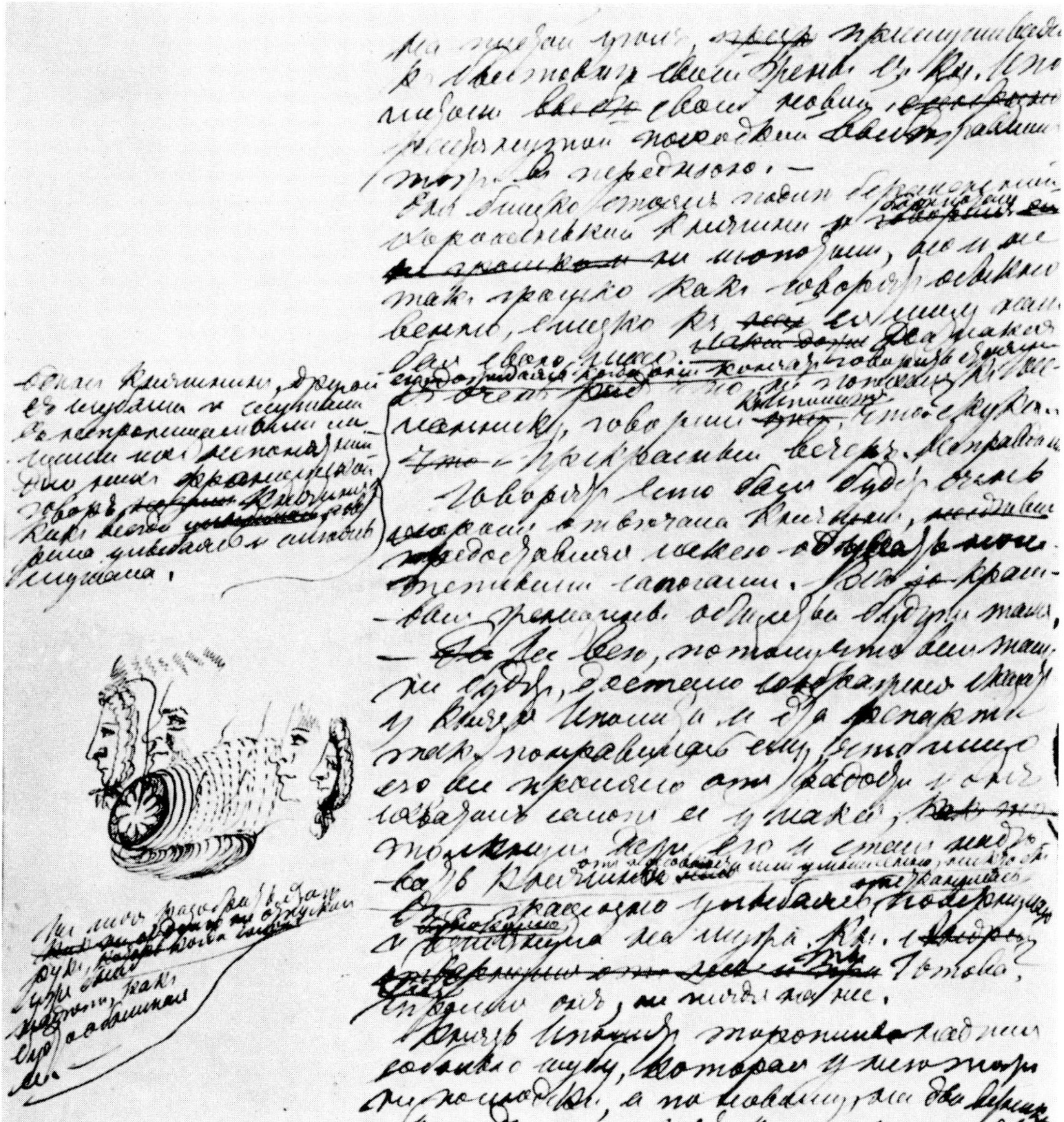

A page from the manuscript of *War and Peace*.

Here is a great flaw at the heart of this extraordinary man, so magnificent in his visible attributes, so strong, so bold, so formidable—and so willful. He was willful in the manner of the gods of antiquity, and, like them, sometimes childish: now exultant, now sulking, now in a rage at being crossed, sometimes whimpering in the night because he was unhappy. How could a man of this stature—with such power of intellect, so much originality, such stupendous vitality, with his blazingly, excruciatingly exact perceptions of the physical world—how could such a man, with his immense experience of the world, persist all his life in thinking of personal happiness in terms of the nursery and the school-room? I want, therefore I must have. . . . And the fact that what he wanted, the object of his intolerable longing, was not, except intermittently in his earlier years, material possession, or even worldly fame and glory, but self-perfection, only underlines the paradox: he thirsted for self-perfection as greedily as a certain kind of man thirsts for office or great riches, as a certain kind of woman thirsts after the biggest diamond in the world.

The flaw at the heart of the man was also a flaw at the heart of *War and Peace*. And it is reflected in the form, or lack of it. The formlessness of the book, which has worried many critics, which so afflicted Henry James that he could not bring himself to regard it as a great novel and threw up his hands in despair, is commonly regarded as an unfortunate accident arising from a technical or artistic failure, all too understandable: failure to control or order the huge mass of material, the host of characters. But this is far from being the whole answer. Tolstoy's technical equipment is so powerful and his eye for shape and pattern so exact that it would be dangerous to say that there was any limit to his virtuosity, that there was anything he could not achieve in the way of presentation when he set his mind to it. In the separate chapters of mingled dialogue, description, and comment he moves through the maze he has created with the breath-taking certainty of a sleep-walker. And just as I have already suggested that the nature of Tolstoy's prose style derives not from insensibility to words and cadences but, rather, from his determination to pin the reader inexorably and inescapably to his own immediate vision of the arrested moment, so the formlessness of the whole, which contains innumerable passages quite beautifully formed, reflects his refusal to acknowledge mystery.

For what is form in a complete work of art but the line drawn by the artist to demarcate the outer limits of his own experience and understanding? "Within these limits," he is saying in effect, "I am at home; and where I am at home is on ground won hardly from the immense unknown. I believe (I can do nothing else) that this territory, this novel, this painting, this arrangement of sounds which I have created must in some way reflect, however dimly, hesitantly and imperfectly, at least some small aspect of universal truth, of what is commonly called the underlying reality governing all things and all men. And my task is so to shape and burnish the reflecting surface, and so to light it, that the reflection is as complete and true as I can make it." The complete and perfect work of art, then, is inseparable from its form, which thus acknowledges its limitations while transcending them. There are not many complete and perfect works of this kind, but there are many that aspire to such completeness and perfection, even though the artist himself may be, at best, only faintly or intermittently aware of the nature of the force that drives him on.

But what happens when, as with Tolstoy, the artist does not know the meaning of humility? What happens when he refuses to acknowledge the validity of what he cannot understand? What happens when he says, in effect, I recognize only what I see, I acknowledge only what I can prove by reason; all else is delusion, at best a sentimental dream, more probably a fraud? What happens, with the best will in the world, is that his creation, which cannot comprehend the totality of all things seen, is bound to be episodic, is bound to sprawl.

George Moore, who knew less about Tolstoy's early life than we know now, gets to the heart of the matter but makes a joke of it: ". . . The reader must be a very casual reader indeed if he fails to ask himself if it were Tolstoy's intention to transcribe the whole of life. His intention seems certainly to have been to include all the different scenes that come to pass in civilised life, and no doubt he ran them over in his mind, for a scene of ladies in a drawing-room taking tea is followed by a scene in a ballroom with ladies dancing, and this is followed by a scene in a barrack-room with a quarrel among the officers. Scene after scene! . . . We turn the pages; but alas, there are more pictures, and curiosity taking the place of the pleasure of art, we ask ourselves how it was that Tolstoy forgot to include a description of a yacht race. . . . For no writer ever tried harder to compete with Nature than Tolstoy. Yet he was a clever man and must have known he would be defeated in the end; but he is one of those men to whom everything is plain and explicit except the obvious, and *War and Peace* is so plainly the work of a man with a bee in his bonnet that, despite the talent manifested in every description, we cannot help comparing him to a swimmer in a canal challenging a train going by to a race."

This, of course, is not the whole of it. For Tolstoy, violently as he rejected the unknown, was divided against himself. And very soon, in *Anna Karenina,* he was to display the depth of that division.

Sonya Tolstoy, with Tanya and Sergei, 1866.

7

THE ENEMY OF LIFE

For six years, while he wrote *War and Peace*, Tolstoy's conscious spiritual development was at a standstill. The diary was laid aside; while he was creating at fever-heat there was no need for the eternal self-reproach, "nothing done." As for sex, there was Sonya. And there is every reason to suppose that Sonya's partial frigidity, or at least her lack of enthusiasm for sex, was well suited to his own particular need. Sonya was dutifully, even tenderly, available and ready to bear a long succession of children, bemoan her frequent pregnancies as she might and did. For a man beset by cyclonic seizures of lust, which would give way to self-disgust the moment it was satisfied, this was obviously the best possible arrangement. Tolstoy was soon at odds with poor Sonya not because she could not satisfy him sexually but because he could not bear to live under the same roof with anybody who made claims on him or expected to be treated as a human being in his or her own right. And Sonya, in love but often hating, tore herself to pieces, then tore in vain at him, in her refusal to recognize the sheer magnitude of her problem. Because she was incapable of seeing her husband as the genius he was, but only as a famous writer, everything she did was wrong. Deciding that the only way she could get close to him and make herself indispensable was through his work, she had cast herself as the Author's Wife, acting as his manager, his guardian, and his amanuensis. But what happened when the author stopped work? Nothing but tears and frustration. The absurd situation was reached at the end of 1869 when, with *War and Peace* finished and her husband on the edge of nervous exhaustion, instead of rejoicing over the end of the great ordeal and encouraging him by all means in her power to rest and lie fallow, Sonya urged him to start a new novel at once.

It is true that Tolstoy's lying fallow took an idiosyncratic turn. He idled a good deal, as only a Russian with adequate means and a house full of servants knows how to idle. But he had plenty of generalized energy, even though his creative powers were for the time being burned out.

What happened now was, after a short-lived false start on what was to be a great historical novel about Peter the Great, first a great burst of reading in philosophy, chiefly remarkable for Tolstoy's discovery of Schopenhauer, whose organized pessimism at that time seemed to fortify and illuminate his own unorganized sense of the futility and terribleness of life; then a sudden, unheralded enthusiasm for Greek, which possessed him entirely (the speed and thoroughness with which at forty he mastered this difficult language was an indication, if one were now needed, of his formidable powers of concentration and the intellectual toughness he could bring to a given subject within a recognized horizon) and was to condition his approach to the writing of *Anna Karenina*; then another burst of educational zeal, which involved setting up more schools and also the production of a series of *Readers* based on innumerable stories and anecdotes created and told for the occasion.

All this activity, interrupted only by family excursions to the Bashkir country to drink kumiss, race horses, and buy more land, was regarded by Sonya with blank and exasperated incomprehension. Publishers were offering him unbelievable sums; he ignored them. Sonya was not merely distressed: she was a grown-up woman now, the mother of five, and prematurely responsible for the management of what would nowadays be called a valuable literary property—one in which she had also sunk all her emotional capital. Her newly discovered managerial competence, her distress at her husband's neglect, her inarticulate sense that she had been left far behind, are all reflected in a letter to her sister Tatiana: "It is not so much the money; the main thing is that I love his literary works, I admire them and they move me. Whereas I despise this *Reader*, this arithmetic, this grammar, and I cannot pretend to be interested in them. Now there is something lacking in my life, something I loved—it is Leo's work I am missing, that has always given me so much pleasure and filled me with such respect. You see, Tanya, I really am a writer's wife, I take his work so much to heart." *

Sonya had stopped growing, and she was hardening into the woman who, thirty years later, was to go to almost any lengths to secure the then-glittering property for herself and her children when her husband wanted to give it all away, and to involve herself in a squalid comedy of deception and intrigue, theft and counter-theft, as she fought for possession of her aged husband's diaries and for the position she had long before lost to his sinister disciple and spiritual gaoler, V. G. Chertkov, and her own youngest daughter, Sasha.

But towards the end of 1872 her spirits began to rise. Tolstoy was back again with Peter the Great, toiling at the new task, devouring all the material he could lay hands on, and making elaborate notes in separate note-books about every aspect of life in early eighteenth-century Russia. He was in despair. Everything about Peter and his court sickened him: how to write about this uncouth and hateful monster without, by implication, pillorying Russia? This he could not bear to do. Perhaps Catherine the Great would make a better subject? He tried it and rejected it. The manners of the times were too remote. It was impossible for him to put himself into that period as he had put himself into Alexander's Russia. And then suddenly, out of the blue, his nerves strung to breaking point, he found himself thinking of a very recent local tragedy which had nothing to do with grand historical perspectives. The mistress of a friend and neighbour had thrown herself under a train on the new railway, driven out of her mind by jealousy when she found that her lover was having an affair with his children's German governess. Just as, in his insatiable quest for experience, years earlier the young Tolstoy in Paris had watched a public execution, so now he had gone to watch the post-mortem on the mangled corpse of this unfortunate woman. And suddenly the memory of that scene connected in his mind with an earlier idea for a novel about an upper-class woman guilty of adultery. Two days later he happened to pick up Pushkin's *Tales of Byelkin* and started looking through it. One of the stories began, "The guests were arriving at the country-house. . . ." and Tolstoy's heart leapt with the choking joy of recognition. This and this only was the way to begin a story! No fussing, no preliminaries: pick up the reader with perfect economy of effort and drop him into the heart of

* Quoted in Troyat, *Tolstoy,* pp. 335–336.

238

the story. He was away. This was what he had to do, and he went to his study and wrote: "After the opera the guests reassembled at the home of the young Countess Vrasky." *Anna Karenina* was born.

That opening was soon changed, of course, and the scene to which it referred buried deep in the novel. In the end *Anna Karenina* was to open with that dubious but finely incantatory statement: "All happy families are alike, but each unhappy family is unhappy in its own way." But the Pushkin influence was still there, with its directness and economy, the familiar given a new edge by Tolstoy's recent immersion in Greek, which was to affect not only the language and form of this novel but also, far more improbably, Tolstoy's attitude to fate and the human tragedy. Reading *War and Peace*, it is easy to see the emergence of the man who was later to turn his back on art, and a number of critics have found it hard to understand how the man who wrote the Epilogues to *War and Peace*, to say nothing of the propagandist who is never far from the reader's elbow for the greater part of that book, could suddenly, and on the eve of his great surrender to didacticism, throw himself into the composition of a story finely and elaborately wrought, which, instead of seeking to embrace and command the whole panorama of human existence, limits itself to the exploration of a single tragic situation.

Or, to look at it from another angle, how could the Tolstoy who saw Hélène Kuragin as the eternal whore, corrupt destroyer of masculine integrity, the Tolstoy who transformed Natasha overnight into a loving housewife, lose himself in rapt contemplation of an image of worldly elegance and beauty, a woman who even before she sinned stood for everything he held, or said he held, in contempt—and, when she did sin, deserting child and husband, behaved in a way he utterly condemned?

Of course, she was made to suffer from it. She had to end her life under the iron wheels of a train. But it is not enough to say of this, as was said by George Moore, that *Anna Karenina* "was written to prove that if a woman lives unhappily with one husband, and leaves him for the man she loves, her moral character will disintegrate; and he foresees no end for her but suicide." Tolstoy assuredly believed that adultery was wicked; but he knew very well that few adulterers commit suicide and that most undergo no visible change of character. His subject is not, in fact, the wages of sin, even though on the title page he printed the words "Vengeance is mine, and I will repay." The subject is the self-destruction of a particular woman of unusual radiance, charm, and even nobility of character who, by betraying her husband and abandoning her child, betrays herself—her consciousness of self-betrayal not being forced upon her but existing and growing in her own mind.

We do not know what Tolstoy had in mind when, two years before the suicide of his neighbour's mistress, he told Sonya that he was contemplating a novel about a woman guilty of adultery, that already a whole cast of supporting characters was grouping itself around the central figure. But we do know that when he started *Anna Karenina* he had a heavily didactic purpose. To judge by existing fragments of early drafts, this was to demonstrate the demoralizing and destructive, the evil, power of female sexuality. There was nothing cool, lovely, radiant, about Anna as he first saw her. Vronsky was not to be intoxicated and corrupted by a beauty and charm over which Anna had no control: he was to be ensnared by the force of evil. In the original notes about Anna's appearance we read: "She is unattractive, with a narrow, low forehead, short, turned-up nose—rather large. If it were any bigger she would be deformed. . . . But, in spite of her homely face, there was something in the kindly smile of her red lips that made her likeable." * And as this unpromising heroine was to ensnare Vronsky, so she had already ensnared her husband. Both men—Karenin in the original draft an eager, sensitive, rather feeble but wholly likeable creature, and Vronsky, upright, honest, and warm-hearted—are caught up in the toils of a devourer of men.

All that was changed. Karenin becomes the pedantic civil servant with ears that stick out and the habit of cracking his finger joints; Vronsky is a brilliant example of the conventional Guards officer, dashing and self-satisfied, crackling with animal vitality, anything but steady and straightforward. He is attracted to Anna at sight "not because she was very beautiful, not because of the elegance and the modest grace of her whole figure, but because there was something tender and caressing in the expression of her lovely face as she passed him. As he looked across at her, she too turned her head. Her brilliant grey eyes, darkened by thick lashes, gave him a friendly, attentive look, as though she were recognizing him, and then turned to face the approaching stream of people as though in search of someone."

And so it begins, with Anna on her way back to Petersburg and her child and husband after a swift visit to Moscow to help save her brother's marriage—already unknowingly caught by her fate, even as Vronsky,

* Quoted in Troyat, *Tolstoy*, p. 350.

240

Opposite: Leo Tolstoy, painted in 1873 by Ivan N. Kramskoy while Tolstoy was writing *Anna Karenina*. Kramskoy served as the model for the painter Mikhailov in that book.

la Moskowa, le 7 Septembre 1812.

A scene from *Anna Karenina*, painted by Leonid Pasternak in 1899.

Preceding page: The Battle of Borodino, an account of which forms a major section of *War and Peace*. Painting by Louis François Le Jeune.

smitten to the heart, abandons poor Kitty and embarks on his fatal pursuit. Far from being the man-eater, she is the sacrificial victim. She is given every excuse to turn from her husband, every excuse to surrender to Vronsky. She appears to us as a beautiful, tender, and honest creature pursuing her chosen way unquestioningly, delighting in her child, regarding her husband if not with passion, then with tender and sometimes amused affection, suddenly caught up in a storm not of her making, and thrown off course. The working out of her tragedy follows because she makes no excuses for herself: she is too honest and she cannot bear the deceptions forced upon her by a clandestine affair. We may see her as the victim of Karenin on the one hand and Vronsky on the other; but she sees herself, carried away by passion as she is, as responsible for her own actions.

Nothing, indeed, could be further from the line of thought that Tolstoy had been developing for more than twenty years and to which, even as he wrestled to bring the novel to a close, he was irresistibly drawn back. In the story of Anna's passion he has for the first time been able to forget himself. At last he is humbled, declaring in effect: here is a corner of a mystery which I accept as such. He was not to approach this mood again until nearly thirty years later, when, his whole outward life absorbed in religious prophecy and angry lecturing, he sat down and wrote that amazing story about a Caucasian hero who also betrayed his people and himself, *Hadji Murad*—and then pulled down the blinds on this last vision of mystery and human tragedy.

Anna's own story, of course, is only part of the book, which it dominates. As the novel progresses Tolstoy begins to operate on two distinct levels. For while Anna's story is allowed to develop in accordance with its own inner logic, which owes everything to the author's implicit acceptance of life and little or nothing to his moralizing and philosophizing, the parallel story of Levin and Kitty has little or no organic connection with the main theme. Here we are back with the Tolstoy we know, moving through episodes taken directly from the author's own life (the betrothal, the wedding, the birth of the first child, the death of a brother), and bombarded with his old familiar preachings. The Levin story appears to be designed only partly as a foil, leisurely, healthy, and sane, to the passionate intensity of Anna's tragedy, almost wholly as an excuse for Tolstoy to dramatize his thinking about life and death. In his handling of the relations between Anna's sister-in-law, Dolly, and her cheerful and endearing rascal of a husband, Tolstoy demonstrates the marvellous skill with which he can interweave a sub-plot into the main story and use it to lessen or increase the emotional temperature and anchor Anna's madness to the day-to-day reality from which it grows. For a time the story of Kitty and Levin is also so woven. But as the novel wears on, it becomes increasingly plain that the Kitty-Levin relationship has come to represent far more than one thread in a complex web of human relations. What we are watching now is a painful working out of Tolstoy's own internal conflict. Levin, in effect, is usurping the novel.

When Tolstoy still entertained his first view of Anna as a force for evil, destructive of both Vronsky and her husband, Levin with his search for moral rectitude and certain knowledge of the true, the only way, had his place at the opposite pole from corruption. Anna and Levin could have, must have, been seen as exemplars of the bad life and the good. But when Tolstoy started to fall in love with Anna, which he did, more absolutely and self-forgettingly than he did with any woman in real life, and began to tell her story, she at once assumed a reality compared with which Levin appeared as a construction, an embodiment of some (but far from all) of Tolstoy's qualities and notions. It says wonders for his technical mastery that he was able to keep Levin in the book at all without making him appear quite wooden; but the conflict is there. Anna is life—as, at a lower degree of intensity, Dolly, Stiva, Kitty even, are also life. Levin is an artifact. He comes to life because everything that Tolstoy touched came to life, even the characters in that life-destroying horror *The Kreutzer Sonata*. It is indeed astonishing the violence Tolstoy could do even to his most completely established characters without shattering the illusion—as, for example, the sudden shriek of hysteria when he watches Vronsky for the first time making love to Anna. ("Vronsky felt what a murderer must feel when he looks at the body he has robbed of life. . . . And as with fury and passion the murderer throws himself upon the body and drags it and hacks at it, so he covered her face and shoulders with kisses.") With Levin it is far easier because the key is low. And although Levin is no more than a vehicle to convey a moral, the major episodes through which he is built up are real because they are themselves taken from life, Tolstoy's own life. Somehow, although we frequently wonder what on earth Levin-Tolstoy's thoughts about problems of peasant agriculture have to do with the working out of Anna's tragedy, we are ready to accept the tale of Levin's progress because it is beautifully told.

Until Anna is dead. . . . Clearly the novel cannot end with Anna's

246

A page from the manuscript of *Anna Karenina,* and a
fine example of the lines which Sonya had to decipher.

suicide. The story is life, life which existed before her and continues after her in its all-comprehending sweep, its vertiginous depths. It begins in the Oblonsky household before Anna so radiantly appears and it must go on when she is gone. When Vronsky shakes off his nightmare and goes off to fight as a volunteer for the Serbs against the Turks, broken but alive (and with raging toothache to prove it), this is fitting, indeed inevitable. Anna is dead; so much beauty is dead, slowly and relentlessly ruined by the violence it has done to its own nature long before the formal act of self-destruction. Vronsky—and the rest of us—go on living. Well, so we go on, Dolly and Stiva, Karenin and Seryozha, Levin and Kitty too. The book must show this, must suggest in its closing pages the imperceptible, inexorable formation and growth of the scar tissue over the wound.

But in fact the ending of *Anna Karenina* is not like this at all. It is as though with Anna dead Tolstoy had broken the spell that held him, had, once for all, committed an act of exorcism. Not only Anna is crushed beneath those iron wheels. All that part of Tolstoy himself that was at last beginning to respond with resignation to the beauty, the horror, the multiplicity, the mystery of life died with her. In that final section it is as though Tolstoy has turned his back on the poetic vision which sustained him throughout the novel, and returned to that obsessive contemplation of himself, of his own place in the universe, which dominated him from adolescence to his thirty-sixth year, when he started writing *War and Peace*. Anna herself—the very sense of wonder at the infinite complexities of the human spirit, of the relatedness of all things on this lonely planet as it spins eternally among the stars—all this is quite simply blotted out. And the mystery of existence is suddenly reduced to that sad "I want, therefore I am," to a solitary figure, Tolstoy-Levin, oblivious of everything but his own unappeasable self-love: "I cannot live without knowing what I am and why I am here. And that I cannot know, so therefore I cannot live."

And this is indeed what was happening, as far as it can be pieced together.

For twelve years the tremendous creative force in Tolstoy, the contemplation of innumerable aspects of life outside himself, and the exercise of his unparalleled skill in rendering those aspects—and with all this, too, pride of family, delight in outdoor activity, and the thirst for fame and land —had kept at arm's length his need to think about himself, or, to put it in another way, had switched his egotism into productive channels. When he came to write *War and Peace* he had for the time being abandoned his quest for the key to universal understanding—or, rather, adjourned it *sine die*. And this, as Isaiah Berlin exposed so beautifully in *The Hedgehog and the Fox*, was what his theory of history, one of the driving forces behind that novel, was about. "A Russian is self-assured because he knows nothing and does not want to know anything, since he does not believe that anything can be known."

History, as always understood, is nonsense, because real history is the sum total of all the human, indeed all the organic, activity that makes up life on earth. If it were possible for an individual to comprehend this totality then there would be no mystery. It is not possible. But this only means that what men call mystery is due simply to the mechanical shortcomings of the human brain. *There is no mystery;* there is only lack of knowledge. Therefore let us stop inventing mysteries and systems and admit that we know nothing. Here in this novel which I call *War and Peace*, Tolstoy is saying, let me demonstrate at least some of the innumerable inter-related, pre-determined human activities that, unlike the posturings of so-called great men, are actually the stuff of the real history that can never be written.

And this he did—not seeing that it might have been expressed in a single phrase—for example, Paul Valéry's observation that history can prove anything because it contains everything. The doing released in him all his creative genius, so that it is perhaps not too much to say that the very act of dwelling so intently for so long on things seen and felt and transcribing what he saw and felt with such fanatical faithfulness and precision must in some degree have broken down his own defences and exposed as never before those quivering nerve endings, so that for once he was vulnerable and approaching a condition in which he would be forced to admit, tacitly if not explicitly, that there were indeed things under the sun that could not be accounted for even if the human brain was infinitely extensible. He was open to feeling—in a word, to love. His first impulse as we have seen, was to write a second historical novel—until suddenly he was set alight, reading those simple words of Pushkin's, by spontaneous combustion. And the fire swept through him, burning away all preconceptions of Anna as the female principle of evil, and left him face to face with the hard, inescapable fact of sheer delight in a woman and a sinner—a woman of the kind who had so disturbingly attracted him in life, but from whom he had always fled (Countess Alexandra? Princess Obolensky? Princess Lvov?) And he used her story, or was used by it, to declare what he had always denied and was soon to deny again, that life is something we *can* know about, but only by living it with and through others, seen for what they are, not merely in relation to ourselves—our own private woods consisting entirely of trees.

At some stage he revolted. During the writing of *Anna Karenina* he was under great strain. Death was all round him. The fear of it had never been far away. In the immediate aftermath of *War and Peace*, exhausted and lost, on his way to the Penza region to buy more land and give himself a change of scene—to get away from Sonya, too—he had undergone that shattering experience in the wretched inn at Arzamas which he was later to relate in *Notes of a Madman*. Then, in the depth of the night, already distressed by a sense of dire premonition, he had awoken to find the room filled with an overpowering presence from which he could not escape, even when he groped his way to the hall where the doorkeeper and his own familiar servant were sleeping peacefully.

"Why have I come here?" he asked himself. "Where am I going? From what and whither am I fleeing? . . . What do I fear?"

"Me," answered the voice of death. "I am here!"

And the spectre would not leave him until he had roused his servant, packed his bag, and fled into the night.

Now death was real. Between 1873 and 1875 old Aunt Tatiana died, and then his guardian from his student days, Aunt Pelageya. Then, one after another, three of his own children—Petya, Nikolai, and little Vavara. While the infant Petya lay dying, Sonya was already pregnant with Nikolai, who died within the year. Sonya herself, not unnaturally, was shattered, so that Vavara was born prematurely and died at once. At the height of Sonya's physical prostration and mental agony Tolstoy was moved to write to a friend: "There is no worse situation for a healthy man than to have a sick wife."

Already in 1874 Sonya was commenting in her own diary about her husband's increasing preoccupation with religion. This was when *Anna Karenina* was still going well. At the same time he was supervising his schools—no fewer than seventy of them now—and planning a seminary for training peasant teachers. And in spite of domestic tragedy, or perhaps because of it, he would take his family to Samara in the summer, where he was building up a stud farm that at one time contained 400 horses. In a word, he was once again all over the place, plunging wildly, as he had been before his marriage, before *War and Peace*—with the difference that he

250

Sonya Tolstoy around 1875.

was now grand, famous, very much the great writer, very much the barin. *Anna Karenina* was becoming a chore, in the way *War and Peace* had never become a chore. The incandescence that had flared to produce this marvellous character had quite died down. The book had to be finished because the first chapters had been published and received with almost hysterical acclaim. He could not disappoint his publisher—and he needed the money, which was considerable. But already he was loathing the task, more than loathing it, despising it. What was he doing—spinning a yarn about an imaginary affair of an imaginary heroine, when the only thing that mattered was that life was intolerable because it ended in death and he did not know why? It was only his amazing, perhaps unparalleled mastery of the novelist's art that enabled him to finish what was to be his supreme masterpiece when his heart was no longer in it, was, indeed, barricaded. Even then, at the very end, he had to give Levin his head, blotting out with his own huge unappeasable question-mark the living world of color, joy, suffering, grief—and courage.

Like Levin, Tolstoy was near to killing himself. Like Levin, he hid the rope lest he hang himself, left his guns in the rack lest he shoot himself. Like Levin, he went on living.

Tolstoy's life from now on was public property. He insisted on making it as public as possible—which, with his great reputation, was very public indeed. This man who gave years of his life to demonstrating the absurdity of the pretensions of the Napoleons of this world to influence the course of history was to spend the next thirty years insisting that he alone saw the light and that the world must abandon its old ways and follow him. Tolstoy in his search for truth was farther from the contemplative than it is possible to imagine. He had no time for contemplation: the moment he glimpsed what he took to be a truth, he seized his pen to ram it down people's throats. One of the stranger aspects of *War and Peace* is the absence of any generalized awareness of the vanity of human pretensions, *all* pretensions: Tolstoy's disdain is reserved for specific categories of pretension, above all political pretensions. The trouble was that he did not really believe in the vanity of all pretensions: he was full of them himself. Just as he did not, even when writing about Napoleon, show any sense of the corruption of power as such—only political power. He himself was, not to put too fine a point on it, a man of power. That is to say, he sought not merely to offer his views to others as possible solutions, or contributions to solutions, of problems of interest to us all; he sought to impose them on others with all the weight of his personality. And he was unscrupulous about the methods he used to this end. He hectored and shouted down the opposition, he ridiculed it, he sought to crush it with that terrible gaze. And of course he shouted down himself as well.

As we have seen, he was an overbearing man, and selfish. He went on incessantly about sincerity and the lack of it in everyone he met, but he himself practised double standards. He was consciously and deliberately the master of his own material domain and every living creature in it, from Sonya downwards. Sonya must do as she was told, even though breast-feeding her first infant might kill her. As the children grew, he could be on occasion the gayest of fathers, brilliant and happy in inventing games for them and with them. But the children were the children of Count Tolstoy, and must never forget it. Tolstoy himself might pretend to be the quintessential muzhik in one breath and in another play the village schoolmaster, but the young Tolstoys were aristocrats. We read the sad little commentary of Ilya Tolstoy, the second son and the nicest of all the Tolstoy children:

"The world was divided into two parts: one composed of ourselves and the other of everyone else. We were special people, and the others were not our equals. . . . It was mostly *maman*, of course, who was guilty of entertaining such notions, but *papa*, too, jealously guarded us from association with the village children. He was responsible to a considerable degree for the groundless arrogance and self-esteem that such an upbringing inculcated into us, and from which I found it so hard to free myself."

At this time, too, unregenerate in his worldly attitudes but already, as we have seen, long convinced of the superiority of his own moral nature, he was still very much the landowner, driven by a positive hunger for accumulating property and rejoicing in the peasant slyness that enabled him to plan sharp deals. Even when that sort of operation was a thing of the past, and when he railed against Sonya and everyone round her for gluttony and luxury in a starving countryside, he still sought to exercise his power over his adult children. When two of his daughters, Tanya and Masha, hitherto submissive, apparently devotedly convinced of the truth of his teaching about the evils of the flesh, suddenly awoke, fell in love, and announced their intention of marrying, he was sick with rage.

The year is 1897. It is Tolstoy's seventieth year, and he has long been preaching the need for total renunciation of the world and the flesh. Tanya is thirty-three, and the man she wants to marry is a decent, respectable and hard-working liberal, a widower with six children. Here is the father's counsel to the daughter: "I can understand that a depraved man may find salvation in marriage. But why a pure girl should want to get mixed up in such a business is beyond me. If I were a girl I would not marry for anything in the world. And as far as being in love is concerned, for either men or women—since I know what it means; that is, that it is an ignoble and, above all, an unhealthy sentiment, not at all beautiful, lofty or poetical—I would not have opened my door to it. I would have taken as many precautions to avoid being contaminated by that disease as I would to protect myself against far less serious infections such as diphtheria, typhus or scarlet fever. . . ." *

He gloried in power, and nobody has ever given so clear a vision of this aspect of him than Gorky, who stood up to it, bent to it without giving way, but found it hard to struggle against. As a rule, however, like a good general he was careful not to put forward his power unless he knew he could win. When he tried and failed he was almost ill with humiliation. Hence his rage with Tanya and Masha: he thought his power over them was absolute and found he was in error. Hence his fury with Turgenev, whom he could not subdue for the simple reason that Turgenev was incapable of falsity to himself: he did not think much of himself, but what he was he unmovingly and unquestioningly was. With the much younger Chekhov, all diffidence and modesty and internal steel, Tolstoy was old enough to know what he was up against. But he could be fatuously silly about his power and influence until the end. In the last year of his life he was told by his young, naive, but clear-seeing disciple and secretary Bulgakov that as a direct result of his, Tolstoy's, "moral teaching," the percentage of male virgins among the students of Russia had risen from 20 to 27. "So there you see!" the master observed, "these things are never in vain."

Was this self-mockery, or did Tolstoy mean what he said? Each must decide for himself. Shestov was convinced that the terrible old man was not taken in by himself. Tolstoy, he wrote, would fix his friends with that beetling, unanswerable gaze, and *dare* them to question his sincerity—to say, in effect, you know very well that no matter how you may pretend that your only concern is with the life of the spirit, in fact you are rooted in animal life—and love it. I think this is too simplified, but it is touched by a

* Quoted in Troyat, *Tolstoy*, pp. 525–526.

254

Opposite: Leo Tolstoy. Painting by I. E. Repin, 1887.

Anton Chekhov and Maxim Gorky.

shadow of the truth. We know that Tolstoy in old age enjoyed embarrassing gentle souls with his earthiness. Gorky tells us how he teased Chekhov: " 'You whored a great deal when you were young?' "

Poor Chekhov, who had done nothing of the kind, could only look embarrassed and murmur something inaudible. "And Leo Nikolayevich, looking at the sea, confessed: 'I was an indefatigable ——.' He said this penitently, using at the end of the sentence a salty peasant word."

And there is the problem of the disciples. When he was a world figure Tolstoy was either visited by, or in correspondence with, many of the most distinguished, or potentially most distinguished, figures of the age—from Bernard Shaw to Gandhi. But he also allowed himself to be surrounded by a host of followers and admirers, at best absurd, often parasitic and corrupt. He became a living cult. He never seriously protested, although he must have regarded most of those who swarmed round Yasnaya with contempt. He grumbled, but drank their flattery down, content to be celebrated as the master, the guru, never saying: "Do not follow me. I am fallible— Think!"

His use of power was ugly. When he was writing *Anna Karenina*, he was driven to thoughts of killing himself because life was a lie, but it does not seem to have occurred to him that articulate spirits since the dawn of consciousness have been ridden by despair at the futility of life and the impossibility of discovering if it has a meaning, and, if so, what. Faced with this question there are two possible courses of action: to kill oneself, or to shut up and get on with living as decently as possible. Many have killed themselves; more have not. Tolstoy was far too vital to be content with killing himself, and the *Confession* is in effect largely an apology for continuing to live. Whom was he to apologize to for behaving as all humanity behaves? And even in that moment he managed to put himself far, far above common humanity, including his own family:

" 'Family' . . . , I said to myself. But my family—wife and children— are also human beings and find themselves in just the same situation as I: they must either live a lie, or else see the terrible truth. Why should they live? Why should I love them, guard them, bring them up, or watch over them? That they may come to the despair that I myself feel, or else live stupid lives? Loving them, I cannot hide the truth from them: each step in knowledge leads them to that truth. And the truth is death."

So, in the end, Tolstoy is driven to feel communion with the peasants, with the myriads of illiterates all over the world, who, he says (who was

The entrance to Yasnaya Polyana.

Opposite: Russian peasants. The man in the middle is playing a balalaika.

he to say?), ask no questions and are at one with destiny because they share this or that simple faith. "My position was terrible. I knew I could find nothing along the path of reason and knowledge except a denial of life; and in faith nothing but a denial of reason, still more impossible to me than a denial of life."

He was to go on working out the implications of this familiar dilemma for the rest of his life—and at the top of his voice—in the course of it throwing out the familiar life-denying panaceas about non-violence, vegetarianism, chastity, and universal love.

We must separate Tolstoy the artist and Tolstoy the man and prophet. It is a familiar argument that in contemplating a work of art any consideration of the artist's personal life is irrelevant or even deleterious. Be that as it may, the argument cannot apply to Tolstoy, whose personal life was less private than that of any artist in history. He blurted it all out as he lived, either in his novels or, in later life, in a continuous barrage of confessional revivalism. As much as anyone who has ever lived, Tolstoy set himself up to be a good man. He failed with almost awe-inspiring thoroughness. Far from reducing his stature as an artist, this failure as a man enriched his finest work, including a number of stories and plays, and the third major novel, *Resurrection,* written in his later years, in which he moved out of the world of aristocrats and peasants to take in the urban middle and lower classes, whose existence he had seemed so long to deny. But the causes of this failure do in fact help us to understand certain peculiarities in the great novels and stories. And when on occasion he uses all his marvellous skills to produce a piece of fiction that is manifestly evil, because deliberately rejecting life, as *The Kreutzer Sonata,* or (as it appears to me) falsifying it, as the incomparably brilliant *The Death of Ivan Ilych,* where the virtuosity, allied to the guilt feelings aroused in the reader, numbs the critical senses, it is useful to know the reason why. But his failure as a man does have the strictest possible bearing on his pretensions as a teacher and an "influence": it nullifies them.

Time and again, when one had made up one's own mind about the ugliness and loveliness of Tolstoy, one is brought face to face with the insurmountable fact that he was loved and revered not only by committed disciples, who were legion, but also by men of great shrewdness and penetration who rejected his teaching and yet found him irresistible. There is no need to elaborate this, for the examples are many, from Turgenev to Chekhov, one of the truly good men of our age, and Gorky.

260

Opposite: Leo Tolstoy with his family at Yasnaya Polyana, 1887.

Chekhov could write when Tolstoy was ill: "I dread Tolstoy's death. If he should die, there would be a big empty place in my life. To begin with, I have never loved any man as I love him. . . . As long as there is a Tolstoy in literature, then it is easy and agreeable to be a writer; even the realisation that one has done nothing and will do nothing is not so dreadful, since Tolstoy will do enough for all."

Gorky, who puzzled and puzzled, and fought to resist the spell, saw him finally as a god among men: "He is like a God, not a Saboath or Olympian, but the kind of Russian god who 'sits on a maple throne under a golden lime tree,' not majestic, but perhaps more cunning than all the other gods."

His name was legion, but he was not good. What did they love in him, these younger men who were not easily taken in? Obviously they were overwhelmed by the power of his intellect—by, to borrow from Isaiah Berlin, "his appalling capacity to penetrate any conventional disguise, that corrosive scepticism in virtue of which Prince Vyazemsky invented for him the queer Russian term 'netovshchik' ('negativist')." These qualities emerge in every word he spoke in maturity and come out as millennial wisdom in old age. But love? How did they love the detached and unloving? Here, I think, we touch, but must not dwell, on the wholly mysterious problem of personal magnetism, which has nothing to do with virtue (though a virtuous man may possess it). Why did men love Napoleon, a man without love? I have no idea. I have no idea why they loved Tolstoy either; but I feel that much the same sort of elemental magic was at work. It is magic of a kind to be regarded warily.

We, his readers, can never come under that spell. We cannot melt as he treats us, smiling but not radiant, as children to be chided and encouraged—and shown elementary truths, as by a man who knows all about truth and has lived with it for so long that he treats truth as a familiar—or as a younger brother. We can only see what he wrote and said and compare it with what he did. And one of the things he did, this man who preached universal love, was to destroy his own wife.

Heaven knows, Sonya became a tiresome woman, one of those women with a smattering of intelligence and culture who consider themselves qualified thereby to take their places at the high table. She was excited by her husband's work without having the least idea of its unsurpassed grandeur: he was a successful and venerated author, and she was proud to be the author's wife. It is a not unfamiliar story. There have been plenty of

Sonya Tolstoy's room at Yasnaya Polyana.

gifted men with tiresome wives who, for one reason or another, have preferred not to separate or divorce and have borne their cross quietly, without
fuss, and often with consistent kindness. Common sense would suggest a
number of solutions: there was, for example, nothing in the world to
prevent Tolstoy, at fifty, with his greatest work behind him, loaded with
fame and honours, financially more than secure, but increasingly obsessed
with his own spiritual salvation, from turning his back on the world and
secluding himself, giving himself to meditation while making over to Sonya
his worldly goods and the responsibility for the six surviving children. But
in fact one of the pillars of his newly emerging faith in its first manifestation was the sanctity of marriage, and it was not for another ten years, with
four more children born to Sonya, that he suddenly discovered—gaining
his authority from that somewhat arcane observation in Matthew 19:12,
about the three kinds of eunuch—that the ideal to be aimed for in marriage
was for husband and wife to live as brother and sister. It was this new
revelation that was pursued and elaborated with such a hysteria of violence
in *The Kreutzer Sonata*, on the face of it a tale of almost pathological
morbidity about a man who, driven insane by jealousy because of the at-
tentions paid her by a violinist, murders his wife—and actually a diatribe
against sexual love in general, the conventions of marriage in particular,
and an exposure of his own most secret and intimate relations with his own
wife.

It used to be wondered why Sonya, who had, as always, to copy out
this story, appealed personally to the Tsar, who had been shocked by it, to
reconsider his ban on publication. Shouldn't she have sunk back in relief
in the knowledge that this outrage would remain suppressed by the decree
of the All Highest? But, of course, it was not suppressed: it was circulating
in innumerable duplicated copies from hand to hand and discussed with
malicious delight. Sonya told herself that only by putting herself forward
publicly to champion it could she triumphantly prove that it referred in
no way to her own married life.

At forty-five she was already desperate, clinging to her husband by
the only power left to her: precisely, sexual attraction. Tolstoy demanded
that they should sleep in separate rooms in case he fell to temptation; Sonya
said no. So they went on sleeping in one bed and again and again Tolstoy
"fell." The diary, now re-activated, offers swift but searing glimpses of the
terrible reality of what was now a hidden domestic horror behind the public
life of the great teacher of chastity and universal love. Thus towards the

264

Vladimir Chertkov, Tolstoy's secretary, disciple,
and executor of his will. They first met in 1883.

end of that year, 1888, he was writing: "The devil fell upon me. . . . The next day, the morning of the 30th, I slept badly. It was so loathsome as after a crime." And later on that same day; "Still more powerfully possessed, I fell." * And nearly a year later, in August 1889, abject and pitiful beyond all measure, because now and for the first time he was lashing himself not purely because of his own weakness but (almost unbelievably) because he feared what others might think: "What if a child should be born? How shameful, especially before the children. They will reckon when it happened and will read what I write [The Kreutzer Sonata]. It has become shamefully sad. And I considered: not before people, but before God one must be afraid. I asked myself: In this relation how do I stand before God, and I at once grew calmer." †

There were in fact no more children; but he went on "falling." Ten years later, as he approached seventy, he confessed to his disciple, translator, and biographer, Aylmer Maude, "I was myself a husband last night, but that is no reason for abandoning the struggle. God may grant me not to be so again." God, in fact, did not so grant; and it was not until his eighty-second year that he announced, to Maude again, that he was no longer troubled by sexual drive. Long before then, the terrible quarrelling with Sonya had been public property. Not only about possessions and "respectability." We may take as an example the almost lunatic uproar over Sonya's pathetic infatuation with the composer and pianist Sergei Tanev. In 1895, shattered by the death of her last and most precious son, the seven-year-old Vanichka, Sonya was also driven nearly frantic by her husband's remoteness, except when he needed her in bed, and by his increasing submission to his baleful and sinister disciple, the wealthy ex-Guards officer Chertkov, who considered it his duty to destroy Sonya and hold Tolstoy to his most extreme and absurd positions, bullying him and accusing him of heresy and backsliding if he so far forgot himself as to behave with human decency or common sense in his family circle. In this situation Tanev's piano playing triggered off all her long-suppressed dreams of romantic love and soon she was making a public exhibition of herself—even though the little composer himself was the last to realize what was happening. Tolstoy was beside himself. He was sixty-seven. He had long before made it clear to Sonya that she meant nothing to him. He was preaching universal love. He was the wisest man in the world. But he was

* Quoted in Ernest J. Simmons, Leo Tolstoy (London and New York, 1948), p. 493.
† Ibid.

Opposite: Leo and Sonya Tolstoy, toward the end of his life.

seized with a terrifying passion of jealousy that was close to physical violence. How characteristic indeed that Sonya's sad aberration should have echoed in real life the theme of *The Kreutzer Sonata*. Entry after entry in his diary about "this degrading madness," this intolerable burden that had been put upon him, about "senile flirtation or still worse" was followed by a whole series of letters to Sonya and a growing determination to go away forever. Of the worst of these documents he was ashamed. One of the most horrible diary entries he tore out to destroy, but on second thought sent it to Chertkov to show what he was called upon to suffer—with instructions to destroy it after reading. Chertkov destroyed it—but not until he had had it photographed to use as ammunition against Sonya.

And so it went on until the last terrible quarrels about the will and the flight into the wilderness and the death at Astapovo station.

Tolstoy the novelist—none of this matters. It seems to me that it matters very much in Tolstoy the teacher. Sainthood cannot be achieved by precept. Splendid as some of his conceptions were, they were nullified by his behaviour. A man is as good as his actions, and Tolstoy's actions were too often simply bad.

Not always, of course. There were occasions when he harnessed his power to great causes, using the full weight of his immense reputation to alleviate human suffering and achieve a humane goal, himself labouring to the point of exhaustion and defying the authorities to do their worst. There can be no minimizing the grandeur of his efforts in the terrible famine of 1890, when he not only organized and presided over famine relief in the field but also braved the Emperor's displeasure by publicizing in every way open to him the extent and horror of the calamity which the Government of Russia sought to conceal, preferring to allow tens of thousands, hundreds of thousands to die of slow starvation than, by inviting help from outside, admit its failure. There were plenty of other instances of the great man bestirring himself to intervene on the side of the weak against the strong. The most spectacular, as the century drew to a close, was his very active and practical intervention in behalf of the unfortunate Doukhobors, a heavily persecuted sect of pacifist vegetarians who would have been rounded up and destroyed had Tolstoy not first raised an uproar, then, through his disciples, obtained permission for their mass immigration to Canada, and, by finishing his last major novel *Resurrection* and diverting the proceeds from Sonya, helping to pay for this migration. Indeed, for the last twenty-five years of his life Tolstoy was engaged in a determined running fight with the censorship and the administration as a whole, with the Tsar himself. They were years of constant challenge to the Tsar, inviting exile or imprisonment—a challenge the Tsar dared not meet because the whole world would have exploded in protest; it was the disciples who had to suffer exile, while the old man went on fulminating away at Yasnaya. These challenges, though magnificent, were also in essence assertions of power, presented in all too much the same spirit as that sad little episode at Lucerne, so long before, when the young Tolstoy had seized on the wretched street singer not out of love but to demonstrate his contempt for convention and his own virtue.

What was lacking, as always, was humility. For Tolstoy's partisanship of the underdog, of the weak and oppressed and fearful, had nothing in common with the quietly sacrificial, patiently heroic, unremitting labours of Chekhov, or of such a man as his own younger contemporary V. G. Korolenko, who—without fuss or publicity, without a great reputation to fortify and sustain him, with not the least thought for himself—went into the streets at the time of the pogroms to interpose himself between a raging mob and the Jews they were bent on killing. By all means he would move mountains to save the Doukhobors, Tolstoy's Doukhobors; but at the same time he would refuse to associate himself in any way with liberal fellow countrymen who, through political action and patient education of the masses, sought to change or ameliorate a system that let Cossack cavalry loose on gatherings of unarmed men, women, and children for protesting against war. This was politics. Politics were useless. Those who sought reform through politics were, if not invariably corrupt, absurd and impure.

The artist in him never died. One of the most puzzling aspects of an extremely puzzling man was the apparent ease with which Tolstoy could fall to writing fiction when the mood took him, as in *Resurrection,* or the great play of his last phase, *The Live Corpse,* or tales for both simple and sophisticated readers. In these spells of creativity he seems to have been unaware of any contradiction between his story-telling and his frequent condemnation of art as frivolity. As early as 1888 he declared in his famous letters to Romain Rolland that the meanest manual labour in the service of others, working a field for a sick peasant, rearing a calf, cleaning a well, was infinitely superior to "the dubious occupations which are proclaimed by our society to be man's highest and most noble callings." But contradict himself he did. And in the last years of his life he found himself once again touched with the sort of light—of peace, it is perhaps not too much to say—that had illuminated *Anna Karenina* thirty years earlier.

He was seventy-six when he finished the story of Hadji Murad, the legendary figure who, in Tolstoy's own Caucasian days, deserted his leader, Shamyl, and went over to the Russians. *Déraciné,* distrusted by the Russians, hated by his fellow tribesmen, he does not repine but bears the shame he has brought upon himself with dignity—until, overcome by a desire to see his son, who also has rejected him, he makes his way back into his old mountain fastness, is discovered, pursued, and killed. It is impossible to read this marvellously direct and perfectly constructed tale, classical in restraint, elegiac in tone, without a sense of overwhelming sadness. For here is Tolstoy the artist—the artist we saw being born in those magically fresh and translucent pages of *Childhood,* the artist we have seen tortured and torn to pieces by pride, by ambition, by the angry pretensions of the man who had to prove that he knew everything, that what he did not know was not knowledge—returning at last like Hadji Murad himself to the inheritance he had betrayed: "He remembered how his mother had shaved his head for the first time, and how the reflection of his round, bluish head in the shining brass vessel that hung on the wall had astonished him. He remembered a lean dog that had licked his face. He remembered the strange smell of the cake his mother had given him—a smell of smoke and sour milk."

As he wrote those lines Tolstoy was recalling his own earliest memories—of being bathed as an infant, of the mother who died when he was two. He was, too, it is impossible not to believe, looking back with doubt in his heart at the life-long struggle between the artist endowed with supreme perceptions and sensibilities and an agonized sense of the incompleteness of life, who fought and lost the battle with the stiff-necked puritan who, driven by "insane pride," set himself to lay down the law to God.

Opposite: Yasnaya Polyana, in autumn.

BIBLIOGRAPHY

In Russian the whole of Tolstoy's output, including letters and abandoned drafts, is contained in the great Centenary Edition in ninety volumes: *The Complete Collected Works of L. N. Tolstoy* (Moscow and Leningrad, 1928–53). A handier and more accessible collection of the novels, stories, plays, essays, together with a broad but incomplete collection of letters and an abridged version of the Diary, is *The Collected Works of L. N. Tolstoy* in twenty volumes (Moscow, 1960–63).

The standard collected edition in English is the Centenary Edition edited by Aylmer Maude (London, 1928–37).

The bibliography of books about Tolstoy is immense. I list here only those books quoted from or referred to in the text:

Biographies of Tolstoy in English
Maude, Aylmer. *The Life of Tolstoy*. London, 1929.
Simmons, Ernest J. *Leo Tolstoy*. London and New York, 1948.
Troyat, Henri. *Tolstoy*. Translated by Nancy Amphoux. New York, 1967.

Miscellaneous Works in English
Bayley, John. *Tolstoy and the Novel*. London, 1966; New York, 1967.
Bulgakov, V. F. *Leo Tolstoy in the Last Year of His Life*. Translated by Anne Dunnigan. London, 1972.
Berlin, Isaiah. *The Hedgehog and the Fox*. London and New York, 1953.
Forster, E. M. *Aspects of the Novel*. London, 1927; New York, 1956.

272

Gorky, Maxim. *Fragments from My Diary*. Translated by Moura Budberg. London, 1972.

———. *Reminiscences of Tolstoy, Chekhov, and Andreev*. Translated by Katherine Mansfield, S. S. Koteliansky, and Leonard Woolf. London, 1934.

Gunn, Elizabeth. *A Daring Coiffeur*. London, 1971.

Moore, George. *Avowals*. London, 1924.

Simmons, Ernest J. *Chekhov*. London, 1963.

Tolstoy, Ilya. *Tolstoy, My Father*. Translated by Anne Dunnigan. London, 1972.

Weinstock, Herbert. *Tchaikovsky*. London, 1946.

Wilson, Edmund. *A Window on Moscow*. London and New York, 1973.

BOOKS IN RUSSIAN

Turgenev's letters are in *The Complete Collected Works and Writings of I. S. Turgenev* (12 vols. Moscow/Leningrad, 1966–68). Botkin's letters to Turgenev are in *Botkin and Turgenev: Correspondence* (Leningrad, 1930). The main source for the details of Tolstoy's relations with Turgenev and Nekrasov is *My Recollections* by A. A. Fet (Moscow, 1890).

The correspondence between Tolstoy and Countess Alexandra Tolstoy (he wrote in Russian, she, as a rule, in French) is in *The Letters of Count L. N. Tolstoy and Countess A. A. Tolstoy* (London, 1909).

Although I have not referred to it directly, the best and most complete study of Tolstoy in Russian is B. Eykhenbaum, *Leo Tolstoy* (2 vols., Leningrad, 1928; Moscow, 1930).

INDEX

Italic numbers indicate pages on which illustrations appear.

Illustration Credits

The author and publishers wish to thank Mrs. Andra Nelki and Mr. Pierre Waleffe for their assistance in collecting the illustrations which appear in this book. They are also very grateful to the following for their permission to reproduce the illustrations on the pages noted after each source: *The Bettmann Archive, Inc., New York,* pages 42-43, 68, 110, 259. *Bibliothèque Nationale, Paris,* pages 156, 158-159; 16, 83, 85 (photos by Roger Viollet); 88, 88-89, 118, 177, 191 (photos by Françoise Foliot). *British Museum, London,* pages 12, 37, 55, 123, 229 (photos by John R. Freeman & Co.). *Historical Research Unit, Collection Mollo, London,* pages 69, 119, 120. *Institute of Slavic Studies, Paris,* pages 201, 251, 106, 109, 181, 208 (photos by Françoise Foliot). *Inge Morath,* pages 25, 70. *Novosti Press Agency, London,* pages 6, 115, 155, 231, 235, 241, 244, 256, 261, 267; 18, 24, 46-47, 57, 63, 99, 178, 200, 214 (photos by Geoff Goode); 30, 31, 263, 271 (photos by V. Malychev). *Photographie Bulloz, Paris,* pages 13, 77, 121, 138, 146-147, 167 (photos by John R. Freeman & Co.); 183 (photo by Geoff Goode). *Photographie Giraudon, Paris,* pages 242-243. *Society for Cultural Relations with the U.S.S.R., London,* pages 53, 92, 114, 124, 133, 193, 247; 15, 19, 21, 22, 38, 59 top and bottom, 75, 94, 95, 108, 129, 137, 161, 173, 224, 225, 265 (photos by Geoff Goode). *Tretyakov Gallery, Moscow/Royal Academy of Arts, London,* pages 61, 64-65, 215, 255. *Victoria and Albert Museum, London,* pages 26-27, 28 (photos by John R. Freeman & Co.).